Additional Praise for

Women's
Intuition

"*Women's Intuition* is a gift to any woman who is determined
to connect with her own feminine body."

—**Marion Woodman**, author of *Addicted to Perfection*

"This gracious book is for all who suspect that the body
knows things we do not know. We've yearned to free the
wisdom locked in the body's images, symptoms, and
movements; Reeves gives us a burnished key."

—**Jill Mellick, Ph.D.**, co-author of *Coming Home to Myself*,
author of *The Natural Artistry of Dreams*

"The 'wisdom of the body' is finally being rediscovered
in our generation. Paula Reeves has provided a book filled with
practical guidelines and insight for women—and men as well."

—**John Granrose, Ph.D.**, Jungian analyst and Professor
Emeritus of Philosophy, University of Georgia

Women's *Intuition*

Unlocking *the* Wisdom *of the* Body

Paula M. Reeves, Ph.D.

Foreword by Marion Woodman

Afterword by Belleruth Naparstek

CONARI PRESS
Berkeley, California

Excerpted from *Naked Song* by Lalla, translated by Coleman Barks, Ph.D. Translation copyright © 1992 by Coleman Barks, used by permission of Coleman Barks.

Cover Image: Images copyright © 1998 PhotoDisc, Inc.
Cover and Interior Design: Suzanne Albertson
Cover Art Direction: Ame Beanland

Conari Press books are distributed by Publishers Group West.

ISBN:1-57324-156-3

Library of Congress Cataloging-in-Data
Reeves, Paula M.
   Women's intuition : unlocking the wisdom of the body / Paula M. Reeves :
   foreword by Marion Woodman : afterword by Belleruth Naparstek.
        p.   cm.
   Includes bibliographical references and index.
   ISBN 1-57324-156-3 (pbk.)
   1. Intuition (Psychology)   2. Women—Psychology.   I. Title
BF315.5.R44   1999   99-22487
153.4'4'082—dc21   CIP

Printed in the United States of America on recycled paper
02   01   00   99   Data Repro   10 9 8 7 6 5 4 3 2 1

To My parents, Paul and Laura Mumma,

My husband, Don,

Laura, John, Donald, Diane, Kimberly, and Lee,

And Jennifer, Christina, and Christopher

Genetic threads in the eternal weaving of the ancestors.

Women's Intuition

List of Excercises

Foreword

WOMEN'S INTUITION IS A GIFT TO ANY WOMAN WHO IS DETERMINED to connect with her own feminine body. Its language is the poetic voice of a woman who, through years of concentration, has learned to relate to her own cells, her own illnesses, her own ecstasy. Through her adventuring into her own depths, through her focused attention on her clients' symptoms, through her research, Paula Reeves brings to her reader a depth of experience that has matured into conscious body wisdom. She honors the body, confident that it is the deepest link to Mother Earth and to the Great Mother who manifests within the Universe.

Paula Reeves and I met at a bodysoul women's workshop in Switzerland almost twenty years ago. The theme of that three-week intensive was the relationship between *psyche* (soul) and *soma* (body) based on the work of the Swiss psychiatrist, C. G. Jung. Many of the participants were there because they wanted to clear out redundant baggage—anger, fear, and grief—lodged since childhood in their musculature. They wanted to wake up their partially numbed bodies. They knew that their dreams and their symptoms were carrying essential messages that they could not decode. They wanted to explore the dream image as the bridge between psyche and soma. When we attended evensong at Einsiedeln, the sanctuary of one of the most famous Black Madonnas in the world, we knew from the shimmering in our viscera that this was an experience of the feminine that far exceeded our own personal experience. We knew that we were droplets of water in the great wave that was bringing Her into land.

Like so many other women, Paula and I have continued our exploration into the dark humus of our bodies. With Mary Hamilton (dance) and Ann Skinner (voice) and hundreds of women, we have prayerfully excavated the sacred soil that is our body. And we have glimpsed the luminous pearl that radiates Her light throughout our Being, transforming our experience of feminine/masculine relationship.

For those of us who have been forced to the edge when body can no longer be treated as a poor dumb animal or a high-tech machine, forced to that edge by addictions and illness, this book is a revelation! A common sense, mystical revelation! By relating to our instincts with the compassion we have for the dear animal that is our beloved body, we learn to value its wisdom and beauty. By relating to our dreams with the concentration we bring to our beloved friends, we are stunned by the multi-foliate metaphors and their messages that are so essential to our healing. We can be equally shocked by their bawdy humor and say-it-like-it-is honesty. Working with "embodied intuition" we step out of the cages that have locked us into the archaic institutions and patterns that falsify and deaden us. We learn to speak our own truth from the depths of our own matter.

The love that Paula has learned from her own sweet animal comes through in her language. Repeatedly readers will feel tinglings of recognition in their own cells as they feel that love. No longer will the perfect mother be outcast on a pedestal that is dangerously high; no longer will the sacred Earth be outcast as a "filthy prostitute" or a "fluffy plaything." Embodied intuition integrates the feminine into the sacred wholeness that is our birthright.

Marion Woodman is the author of several books on feminine consciousness, including *Addiction to Perfection, Leaving My Father's House,* and *The Pregnant Virgin.* Her most recent books are *Coming Home to Myself,* with Jill Mellick, and *The Maiden King,* with Robert Bly.

Marion Woodman, author of
Addiction to Perfection

Introduction

When we neglect what matters most to us
that then becomes the matter with us.

—*[pmr]*

MECHANICAL GREYHOUND RACES AND BETTING WERE FOREIGN TERRI-
TORY in my childhood. As I cut through the game salon of an ocean-
going pleasure liner bound for Hawaii I paused with youthful curiosity
to watch the metal dogs racing after their mechanical quarry. The adults
who surrounded the table were supplying energy enough to balance the
passive metallic canines as they repeatedly circled the course. One of my
mother's friends invited me to choose a winner. "For luck," he said. I
knew the outcome that lay ahead immediately and said so. Happy with
my "lucky guess," gamblers asked me to repeat this curious feat five or
six times, with success each time, until I, bored with the repetition,
begged to be excused and left. To this day I can recall both the spoils and
the eventual responsibility my experience brought me.

Elated with his winnings, Mother's friend gave me several beauti-
fully decorated chocolates from the tea tray that was passed around at
three o'clock. I had never seen such exquisite bits of sugar before—treasures beyond belief to my tender seven years. Three days later in the
excitement when we docked, I left my precious bounty behind in the
drawer of the dressing table. Gone but never forgotten.

This is not a story about chocolates, nor about the dangers of
youthful gambling. This is about the mystery that is intuition. I left the
salon that day puzzled and indelibly impressed by the mounting awe and

conversation that accompanied my "luck." To me, it wasn't luck at all, it was common sense. Didn't they all know which dog would win? And if they didn't, why bother with the game at all? I knew that the adults felt that there was a flavor of specialness about what I'd done, and I could neither ignore it nor feel comfortable with it. Intuition is rather like the number thirteen; there's a cultural superstition that surrounds it for no particular reason—just because it always has.

My next real foray with my intuition came two years later, as I lay confined to bed, unable to walk or put any pressure on my spine by standing because of a mysterious malady that had compressed three of my lumbar vertebrae. The adults were repetitiously adamant: Do not under any circumstance stand or apply any weight to my feet. I awakened one morning with the distinct impression that I was being told if I wanted to walk again I was to stretch my legs until I could touch the foot of the bed and then push against it as hard as I could. So I did. Daily, for weeks. During this time I began to realize I could trust myself in ways that were new and different. This was the second time in my first decade of life that I had been thrust into a lively relationship with the effects of following my intuition.

Decades later, after a flashing image of a woman in a large straw hat with a sunflower drooping over the edge of the brim appeared in my dreams nightly for several weeks, I went to Switzerland to study. As I was checking into the hotel, a woman entered wearing the hat, sunflower and all. But by then I was neither surprised or mystified by the actual appearance of an intuitive image. I was simply aware that we two were destined to be here together, if not to meet, and my task was to stay awake and note the occasion.

It wasn't until I began writing this book that I realized how strongly I regard my dreams as intuitive messages. I don't remember ever separating those images from the richly variegated tapestry of my waking life. I have always asked my dreaming psyche for assistance as I sort out the dilemmas of life. The first dream I can remember was of a witch and a clown. As I grew older, I told myself that Spirit sent me these images before the age of four to prepare me for a warm acceptance of what I now call "sacred witchcraft"—the intuitive wisdom of the body. And the clown? Well, the clown has taught me about the human side of the Holy—the irony that suffering is after all a sacred condition of our humanity. It is through the wounding, the illness, the life challenge that we are most often awakened to our deeper capacities, to our incarnate divinity.

When I began listening to the dreams brought by my clients, I always had an ear for the relationship between their dream images and their physical bodies. Over and again I found a kind of cross talk going on. If the client was physically ill, the dreams inevitably held some prescription for healing. So, I wondered, why not "ask" the body what wisdom it can offer when the psyche is ailing? How to do this had yet to reveal itself. Then I remembered my experience at age nine, when my intuitive sense led me to trust my body. So I began to explore the relationship between an image or a thought and the spontaneous body movements that arose when I quietly narrowed the focus of my attention to either the image or the thought. In less than a year I had roughly developed what I later called Spontaneous Contemplative Movement (SCM), a noninterpretative way to honor the integrity of the ongoing interactive relationship between consciousness and the unconscious in the body. This form of movement naturally evokes what I call embodied intuition—insights into the neglected, but ever-present, knowing that we all have. Unlike our cognitive functions, the body is simply and directly honest, never evasive or obscuring whether the problem is emotional, physical, or relational. Discovering embodied intuition is, as one woman said, "an introduction to the wisest and most loving aspects of my self."

My intuition has brought me humor, grief, wisdom, ridiculous slips of the tongue, and all manner of strange and wonderful relationships. Not given to impulse, I have gone to a restaurant, canceled a trip, quit a job, and taken a challenge because I simply knew I was supposed to. Not infrequently, even when speaking with strangers, my body will sense their physical or emotional state and a tumble of information will unfold. I don't know what, if anything, to do with these insights, just to observe and let them pass by me. It gives me profound pleasure when I hear about the respect that medical intuitives are receiving today. How good to have the "extraordinary" humanized once more.

On the practical side, intuition is grand when looking for misplaced items. Equally, I have learned to listen to my intuition and not speak, to hear and not know, to inquire and not reveal the reason. As I use SCM myself, I have learned what heals and what does not. I have found, as have numbers of other women and men with whom I have worked, that symptoms always have a lesson to teach, their own unique story to tell. I do not believe my personal experience has been unique. Many people have told me stories not unlike my own. Through experience and attention, intuition has become my primary language. It does not descend upon me intellectually but emerges from within my body. I have learned to appreciate the intuitive intentions of the body's metaphors and the dream's images. As it has been my delight to discover, so also do many, many women. And mostly, they keep this to themselves.

Much of the sadness and the confusion carried by women may spring from our inability to feel safe in expressing ourselves intuitively. It has been centuries since the oracular energies of the soul have been courted and treated with grace. We have learned our cultural lessons well. Accusations of witchcraft, craziness, or of being a "space cadet" have not fallen on deaf ears. Thus, intuition, one of the richest and most profoundly creative aspects of the soul, stays muffled, or worse, extinguished. This book is offered as an evocation for women everywhere to search out and tell their own stories about embodied wisdom. Listening to body's wisdom we find all manner of healing, personal and ancestral, lies waiting within range of intuition. More important, wholeness lies there also.

I have written this book as an invitation to the reader to seek the ever-present intuitive wisdom of the feminine in matter, to learn to love the body that contains and teaches you with a depth and breath of trust that no one and nothing can diminish. This book offers an invitation to be intentionally and cleanly honest with yourself about your relationship with this wisdom, to dare to identify and be taught by the rejected

Women's
Intuition

parts of the self that contain it. And, to refuse to settle for anything less. It's a call to learn to listen intuitively to and be taught by your symptoms, your dreams, your feelings. And most important, to allow your heart to break a thousand times over only to discover it has never broken at all, it has only expanded, revealing anew the intuitive truths of your heart's desire.

> She who knows little of her body knows less still of her soul.
>
> —*[pmr]*

Chapter One

RECONNECTING TO OUR BODY WISDOM

In 1988, HOLGAR KALWEIT WROTE: "Only human beings have come to a point where they no longer know why they exist. They don't use their brains and they have forgotten the secret knowledge of their bodies, their senses, or their dreams. They don't use the knowledge the spirit has put into every one of them; they are not even aware of this, and so they stumble blindly on the road to nowhere. . . ."

As these words were written, a group of ordinary women were meeting at the behest of Sharon, a mutual friend. Sharon's daughter, Lila, had prematurely delivered twin boys, both of whom were gravely ill. Sharon awakened one afternoon from a nap with the distinct impression that if she gathered together a circle of her closest female friends they would know how to heal the babies. She spoke to her daughter, asking Lila's permission to follow her inclination.

At her invitation the women met, listened to the grandmother, and decided to form a circle and let intuition be their guide. Before they parted that evening, they knew their contribution was to keep the boys' photos within a symbolic circle of healing energy. Solemnly pledging to do so, they sent for photographs, agreeing to meet again in a few days. After three weeks of meeting for several hours each week and sharing how their bodies felt as they thought about the boys, one of the women in the circle asked if she were the only one who had an intuition that the continuing deterioration of one of the twins was linked to the emotional health of the mother. Others agreed; they too had the same insight. One women said that when she first became aware of this feeling, she felt like she had a "band around my heart. I knew that something was causing Lila heartache and preventing her from being able to love both boys equally." With her permission, Lila's picture was added to the circle. On the eighth night, two of the women came in and said they had strong feelings that both boys were going to be fine. One reported she was taking a shower "when I thought of the boys and I wanted to laugh and sing." Six weeks later the pediatrician confirmed their "remarkable recovery" and the group turned their attention elsewhere.

I was part of this circle, and the experience only strengthened my conviction that women are often more far more effective and influential when they trust their intuition to guide them in situations when intellect is not enough. The twins were under the care of an excellent physician, yet the intuition of these women, myself included, led them to create a healing ritual that complemented what was being done.

Finding Our True Home

Each of us has the capacity for intuition—that sudden inexplicable insight that tells us we know something we had no idea we knew. By nature, we women are highly intuitive. By puberty we are learning how to direct our attention to the myriad of internal signals that are preparing us for menarche and childbirth. For each of us this heightened sensitivity introduces the strong true strain of intuitive wisdom that reposes within us and is expressed by our bodies as much, if not more, than by our minds. That's because intuition is a *gut* response—butterflies in the stomach, a twinge in the solar plexus, a sudden shiver, or a flutter of heartbeats. These are the signs that something is going on beneath the surface of things—that we are being alerted by signals from an embodied nonverbal wisdom—our intuition.

While it's true that everyone has intuition, not all of us have the same capacity to use it. There are many women who are highly intuitive and so practiced at using this function of the bodymind that they take it for granted. Others feel their intuition is a disposable gift, arriving unexpectedly and rather inexplicably, to be accepted, marveled over, and discarded when the novelty has worn thin. Others treat their intuition with suspicion, avoiding it as they would a threatening mystery. And there are those of us who seldom, if ever, recognize its presence, discounting the multiple ways we all access intuition daily as habit, lucky guesses, or even coincidence.

In actuality, intuition is a major part of all your decision making and every creative inspiration. The dictionary defines *intuition* as an immediate cognition; sharp insight; the act or faculty of knowing without the use of rational processes. In other words, knowing what, moments before, you didn't know you knew. Medical intuitive Mona Lisa Schulz, M.D. says, "If you have a brain and a body, if you have memories, if you sleep at night (or any other time), then by definition you have to be, you *are,* intuitive." When you are cooking and you creatively add an unexpected seasoning you just feel will be right, or you get up in the morning and have an inkling that you should change your plans and do so,

RECONNECTING
TO OUR
BODY WISDOM

or you follow a hunch about something, you are using your intuition.

Women have been trusting the wisdom of their bodies and listening to the insight of their dreams and intuitions for centuries, since long before recorded history. In the earliest inscribed tale of the feminine, the story of Inanna, Queen of Sumer, and her sister Eriskigel, Inanna's life is dependent upon her reception to an intense keening and wailing from the "Great Below," which she takes seriously. Inanna's intuition alerts her to respect the summons from her inner self and prepare to do the business of Soul. However, intuition is neither the gift of queens nor the folly of innocents. Intuition is the voice of embodied Soul.

Unfortunately, most of us have become so alienated from our bodies that it is difficult to access our bodies' wisdom. This is a grave handicap. For body wisdom contains the essential truths about what matters most to a woman and ultimately to the human race as a whole. Body wisdom especially amplifies the inherent sacred relationship between a woman and the deep feminine. If she doubts this, she has but to turn to the exquisitely sensitive cycles of her body that have been teaching her since puberty how intimately she is influenced by the innate intelligence of her biochemical bodymind.

This relationship is sacred because it has deep and abiding roots in the collective history of womankind. As the science of psychoneuroimmunology is beginning to demonstrate, body wisdom is transmitted through the instinctual biochemical language of tissue and bone, of movement and symptoms, through the ebb and flow of hormonal tides, neuropeptide cascades, and the flux and peaks of energy knit together by breath, by heartbeat, by touch. It is within this ongoing transmission that intuition is most active.

Unfortunately, we in industrial society have lost much of the understanding of how to tap into those signals and to read them. We lack the time and the energy needed to reflect upon the wisdom of our bodies. We have been taught to live our daily lives as if our body is a machine, designed to act, react, interact, as needed. Meanwhile, each and every cell of our body is profoundly affected by our environment, inner and outer, every moment of the day. Every dream, every physical symptom (headache, backache, irritable stomach), every mood, every addiction, is a message from our bodymind.

Ignorance or indifference toward the keen intelligence of the matter that houses soul leaves us buffeted by gale-force emotional winds stirred by our neglect. Carl Jung, the Swiss psychiatrist, warned that when a culture loses contact with the divine, the desire to relate to the Ineffable is carried by the body as disease. The last language left to the ignored body is the physical symptom, and the final act of defiance may be addiction. Deaf to the invitation to evoke embodied consciousness, we are more likely to proceed mechanically, ignoring our images, "curing" the symptoms while dismissing our intuitive messages. Inevitably when we ignore what *matters most to us* that then becomes *the matter with us.*

This, then, is a book about claiming a conscious soulful relationship with your body, the only true home you will ever have in this lifetime. Within these pages lies help in learning to listen to and trust the deep spiritual energies that manifest as wisdom in every cell of your matter. To do this is to discover your destiny and recover your authentic voice in order to speak your truth.

I have been a therapist for many years, helping people decipher the messages from their intuition. The material in this book began to be publicly articulated years ago, as a series of lectures. Much to my surprise I found that men and women alike, in Australia, Europe, and the United States, were deeply moved by the invitation to leave the realm of logic and rationality and descend into the intuitive realm of matter. In the body workshops, tears flowed and bellies churned as person after person fell back into love with their own matter. Through movement, not words, through sensations, not statements, the metaphoric realm of the feminine came alive as a physical experience. From this and many other experiences, I began to understand deeply how much intuition is body-based, and how unless we return to the wisdom of the body, we will never be fully able to access our inner knowing.

Our Beleaguered Heritage

Unfortunately, in general women have become disconnected from this wisdom, not only because of personal traumas such as sexual and emotional abuse that may have caused us to dissociate, but as inheritors of a centuries-old fear of women's power that is expressed through her intuitive knowing.

Prior to the advent of patriarchy, from conception and incubation to the delivery of every birth, through the care and nurturance of children, the cultivation, preparation, and the blessing of food, and the gathering and use of herbs for healing and worship, to the eventual bathing and preparation of the body for burial, the experiential, embodied knowledge of women was essential, basic to the ongoing stability of the community.

Before the legislation and licensing of medicine and psychotherapy, the care of the body rested in the hands of the medicine man or woman, the soothsayer, the midwife, and the herbalist, while the care of the soul rested in the hands of the shaman and the priest. Often interchangeable, the role of healer or spiritual guide as intermediary between the known and the unknowable was both a sacred duty and a practical necessity. Performing a soul retrieval, the shaman then might work ceremonially with the physical illness that such a loss engendered. The herbalist's prescription often included a potion for the relief of physical symptoms in combination with a bundle of herbs to ritualistically protect the wearer from future distress. This sanctified relationship between human nature and all of nature was an experiential given. Astrology, divination, ritual, herbology—all were treasured resources for wisdom and guidance. Synchronistic events, dreams, spirit animals, totems, even changes in the weather were well noted, reverentially acknowledged as guides, as teachers.

Women and the valued principles of the shamanic feminine were influential cornerstones in the foundation of the art, science, religion, and law of most preindustrial cultures. The culture's sacred rituals depended upon the endurance of these cornerstones for stability.

Earliest evidence of this history lay scattered in the Neolithic cave sites where female bear skulls and cave etchings leave us remnants of the artifacts prehistoric people may have chosen to represent the potency of the female spirit and the endurance of the feminine principle. The transmission of these principles was oral, the apprenticeship often not completed until midlife or later.

Informed by nature, those wise clan leaders of the past were, of necessity, steeped in an intimate knowledge of the Earth, of herbs, the mysteries of childbirth, and the ecological cycles of renewal. Drawing upon the rituals and laws of nature, they developed a profound understanding of the soulful relationship between the body and the emotional, imaginal realm of Spirit. Secure in this knowledge, they unhesitatingly related the evolution of a human life to the evolution of this planet—and beyond—to the heavens above.

As patriarchy took hold in civilization, this essential body-held wisdom began to be openly attacked. In the 1500s, untold numbers of women, labeled as witches, died because they freely offered to others the instinctual skills and intuitive knowledge that came naturally to them. The strength and commitment from this bond of sisterhood confused and threatened those who wished to see it eradicated. For the crime of an infinite love for nature, ordinary caring women were treated with utter contempt. Mercilessly they were burned at the stake, drowned slowly, horribly tortured, and mutilated in the cultural attempt to frighten the healing energies of the feminine, with its repository knowledge of ritual and the body, into extinction. Brutal though the method, invariably these attempts were futile. This energy can't be extinguished. It may retreat and go underground, yet it waits, to resurface over and again.

Those who have never lost touch with this energy offer powerful examples of intuitive knowing. I was once a member of a party of three men and four women who were making our way deep into the outback of Australia. The Pitjantjatjara tribe that we were staying with communicate telepathically—a kind of outback Internet. The messages are felt rather than thought. At the end of my stay I became quite ill.

In spite of the fact that all the men of the tribe were far away on walk-about, the shaman "knew" a European woman was ill and in need of healing. He appeared at the flying doctor station shortly after I arrived in a Land Rover. Since he was on foot, that meant he would have had to anticipate my destination and leave before we had even decided to break camp.

The opportunity to discuss this incident with our guide, Australian tracker and anthropologist Diana James, never presented itself. However, in his book, *Tracks in the Wilderness of Dreaming,* Robert Bosnak describes his experience with the communication style of the Pitjatjanjara: "This is the first time I have actually heard of a systemic, collective, physical grammar of extrasensory perception." Dr. Bosnak is referring to the ways in which the Pitjatjanjara interpret their percep-tions depending upon which part of the body is aroused, is twitching or itching, or tingling.

Listening to Our Body's Signals

From this and much other evidence, I am convinced that intuition func-tions through our often unconscious picking up of not only our own body sensations, but other people's sensations as well. These usually unrecognized sensations are as influential in determining how we feel about ourselves and other people and the choices we make as those we *are* aware of. One way or another we always respond to our gut feelings, making adjustments for what we assume they mean.

Try it yourself. The next time you are with someone and you become aware of a physical sensation that appears out of nowhere, check and see if you are sensing something going on in the person you are with. I remember a client who came to me because he had been down-sized in a company merger and felt depressed at his inability to find another job. He reported that he'd had several promising interviews, but when the suggestion was made that he was overqualified, he invariably lost his temper and the job. He wanted to solve the problem of his defensive response. During the second interview I begin to have distinct pain in the area of my heart. When I turned part of my attention toward my body, I realized my heart felt fine, I didn't have indigestion, or cramps. I asked my client, who said he felt fine also. The next week I had the same experience, so I told him and asked if any of the metaphors of heartache, such as "heavy heart", would describe his experience, but he said no. I only saw him once, briefly, after that. His temper was in check and he was still unemployed. Several years later I heard from his former employer that he had died "of a heart attack. His heart was never in his unemployment, it was more than he could take." If I'd been a Pitjatjanjara I might have said something like, "That fella, he heart just don't take it, this doin' nothing all the day, he break."

Sometimes the messages are more global—less specifically personal and more about a culture or a community or the underlying attitude of the group you're with. During that same visit to Australia I unexpectedly met a representative of their collective unconscious. Offered a painting by a Pitjatjanjara artist of Manu-Manu, a toothy underground member of the sisterhood of the repressed feminine, I declined. As our group walked away from this encounter, our demeanor shifted subtly. I later remembered that we made small joking references to the "potency" this mythological Aboriginal figure represented. We used our humor to shake the pervasive feeling that we had misstepped somehow—brushing aside a principle foreign to us but significant to our hosts. That night I was taught a lesson about the humility of acceptance. Within twenty-four hours Manu-Manu visited me in a series of dreams, each highlighting a specifically moving experience of the trip. At the end of each dream she said, "Now pack and go home!!" I lingered, trying to figure this mystery out, and fell violently ill. I was fortunate to get out, scathed but intact. One of the cardinal principles of embodied intuition is humility—the willingness to listen to, quietly observe, and learn from body wisdom *even when* the intellect can't figure things out.

Western humankind has forgotten the healing art of humility. We have lost our inner perspective; our intuitive guidance system is on the blink. Our shamans dead, our priests removed, seldom do we realize we are mourning for guidance into the sacred domain of our instinctually intuitive wisdom so we might balance the intellectual domain of logic and rationale. An intense yearning to awaken to this basic feminine reality plays around the edges of our dreams, plucks at our heartstrings, plunges us into malaise, excites us beyond bearing. Alienated from conscious embodiment, emotionally bereft, we have become spiritually parched, soulfully dried up—depressed.

To reclaim our true feminine power, it is time to remove the layers of superstition, with their origins in the distant past, that have been designed to frighten us away from our body's intuitive, expressive wisdom. Now, with the burgeoning renaissance of bodymind exploration, is the time to reawaken and reclaim humankind's ancient connection to the many innate gifts that this heritage represents. This body wisdom lies ready and waiting within our cellular memory. We can learn to explore and profess our body wisdom with no apology, rather with focused commitment, as we become once again stewards of conscious embodiment. We can learn anew how to recognize and articulate the unspoken, nonverbal soul-filled languages of the body with confident authority. Unless we do, we will never be as fully alive as we are capable of being, we will never regain access to the fullest depth and breadth of our intuition, no matter how many books we read or intuition training workshops we attend.

Disembodied intuition can send us into flights of boundless imagination and uncontained anxiety, but embodied intuition refocuses the natural nonverbal wisdom that courses through every cell in our bodymind. Pause a moment right now and remember the "craziest" thought or impulse you've ever had. Review it and note what part of your body, at this moment, seems most responsive to this memory. Now ask yourself, in the light of this particular feeling, what might your body's wisdom be telling you that the "crazy" thought or impulse might have been trying to bring to your attention? What was really going on? Be your own witness and take your inner wisdom seriously. Do you feel excited, anxious, happy? Couple the feeling with the impulse and observe if your attitude changes or there are further body messages. Now ask yourself how you know yourself more intimately now that you've allowed your body her due. Don't dismiss irrational thoughts as "crazy." Instead, listen, be curious, discover what they are telling you about yourself that you will benefit from knowing. These irrational thoughts and impulses are soul talk—messages from the deep feminine that will teach that you who you think you should be may be quite different from who you are capable of becoming.

The Two Types of Intuition

Intuition can present itself to consciousness from two slightly different directions. I say "slightly different" because the difference is really a matter of perception. The first are thoughts, guesses, hunches that seemingly come out of nowhere, almost as if someone or something is speaking to or through us. The second are sensations in the body that then become feelings or images, or even thoughts. I am familiar with both kinds of experience.

Frequently I will hear a "random" or "spontaneous" thought, even a full sentence, as if out of nowhere. I learned a long time ago that these sudden thoughts are always intimately informative. For example, I was talking to a neighbor who was full of high energy—laughing and teasingly challenging me to play hooky with her. I heard a voice say, "Then there's always Gary Cooper." Startled and curious I said to my friend, "Do you know anyone named Gary?" She looked shocked, her eyes filled, and she said, "How did you know? That's why I don't want to be alone. My brother's best friend, Gary, was just killed in a car accident. We three grew up together."

On the other hand, that same week, while with another friend, I kept feeling light-headed while she was talking about her vacation. I checked my breathing to see if I was holding my breath or if there were any clues to indicate that something in my body was in distress. All seemed OK. When I told her my experience, she said, "That's strange, my doctor is concerned about the mountains we're going to hike. He said he's afraid my oxygen will be compromised and I could have respiratory distress."

These examples describe my intuition in relationship to someone else. The intuitive voice I am inviting you to listen to will teach you, first and foremost, about yourself. Later you may find that your intuition is available in a variety of ways. However, the most common dilemma with personal exploration is that it is largely interpersonal (outer directed) not intrapersonal (inner directed). While intuition is useful both interpersonally and intrapersonally, this book encourages you to become inner directed, to focus on your life, your symptoms, your experience, and how these influence and affect your spiritual growth, your health, and your self-development. Evoking a trusting intrapersonal relationship with the deep feminine is an essential first step.

The Importance of Embodied Intuition

As women, being in touch with our body wisdom is crucial, particularly given all the challenges we face in modern life. As life becomes more and more fast-paced and full of change, we simply cannot navigate well unless we are in touch with our intuition. For relying solely on the linear mind in decision making in the unknown is limiting— you simply cannot anticipate the future based on the past, which is what analysis does. Instead you *must* rely on your intuition as well: Should you take this job or that? Buy this house or that one? Get involved with this person or not? After adding up the pros and cons, ultimately you must use your intuition, your best guess, as to what is right for you. But until you are in touch with the wisdom that your body already knows, the messages from your intuition will be unclear, indecipherable. It is only when we read our bodies well that we truly are able to use our "women's intuition."

Personally, accessing body wisdom will protect you against becoming divided against yourself. One of the psychological buzzwords is the word *neurotic*. We hear it often: "I'm so neurotic." "Oh, for heaven's sake stop being so neurotic." Actually a neurosis is the bodymind condition that occurs when we have two choices of equal weight and cannot choose between them: Do I date Jon or Paris? Should I spend this money or save it? Do I say Yes or No? Intellectually and emotionally we are pulled first this way and then that while getting nowhere at all. When you find yourself in this ambivalent state, it's time to turn inward and ask your body. Pause—note what each possibility *feels* like. Now ask yourself, What is this feeling trying to tell me?

Our body will register and mirror the conflict, but the body itself is never divided, never ambivalent. It is the nature of matter to move toward balance, toward wholeness always. Once you become practiced in trusting your body's responses you'll begin to relate intuitively to the constant gentle feedback you are receiving about every aspect of your life.

Another personal benefit will be a quiet increase in self-confidence and self-respect. When you begin to develop a freer access to your embodied wisdom, inevitably a quiet self-confidence develops between your capacity for logic and reason and how this is enhanced by your intuition. I call this learning to consult your inner self first. Many of us use the *MotherPeace* cards or the *I Ching* in this way. Unfortunately we give the cards some magical sort of spiritual power to predict an outcome, without realizing the cards are but a reflection of our inner state—a mirror for our emerging intuition. The cards or the *I Ching* provide us with the same kind of focus that noting a body sensation does. Intuition has to have focused containment so it can be savored, observed, listened to, and learned from, otherwise it appears mystical, fleeting, and unreliable. When we practice embodied intuition, we learn to rely on our body signals on a regular basis and so we receive messages on a daily basis.

There is yet another benefit, probably the more important one, to practicing embodied intuition. More important because it affects us not only in a significant personal way, but it affects and greatly improves our relationships as well. When we ignore our innermost life, our unconscious desires, fears, and yearnings, the only way we can recognize what is most pressing in us is by "recognizing" that quality or feeling or atti- tude in someone else. We take our own rejected and discarded desires and experiences and assign them to another. This is called "projecting." It's rather like the bodymind as a big movie house, randomly rolling film that it neither wants to take responsibility for having loaded into the projector nor is interested in watching the results. Meanwhile it is anx- iously looking for someone else to blame for the show. Projecting is an instinctual condition of human nature. What we can't bear to look at about ourselves we can easily see in another. There is a perverse and temporary relief in being able to convince ourselves that we are blame- less because the other is more at fault.

When we ignore our women's intuition about our own wants and needs, fears and desires, we recognize them in other people and ignore them in ourselves. Often this results in them ultimately manifesting as symptoms—a bad back, a disease, chronic headaches. Let me give you a way to take the pulse of when you are doing this.

Take a moment and make a list of the five things you most dislike about someone you are intimately related to (best friend, lover, spouse, relative). As you make this list, compose a brief sentence including a feeling about each dislike. For example: When B. doesn't listen, I get so angry. Now, erase B's name and add your own. Your list will begin to look like this. *I* don't listen, and then I feel angry when it's pointed out to me or I discover I've missed the point, or whatever. You'll want to protest that these don't fit, they aren't you. OK. Now read your list and observe what your body is telling you. Does one of these get you between your shoulder blades? Do you feel an uncomfortable feeling or even a spontaneous guffaw or does your stomach rumble?

Trust the feeling and make up your mind to edit the film. Yes, it's true—the other person does do these things. However, the intensity of your bodymind is telling you that you must clean your own house first. Then, miraculously you'll find yourself putting less and less energy into your concerns about someone else's behavior and that energy will be yours to use more creatively. You'll appreciate yourself more and even may find that you view the other person differently. It is infinitely easier to change yourself than to change someone else. Each time you edit your own behavior you'll find your relationships improving and your capacity to love and appreciate yourself deepening. The positive benefits are an enhanced immune system and a happier life.

Grounding in the Body

Awakening the intuitive energies of the embodied feminine in order to come to terms with your essential self requires differentiating between social and spiritual realities. At first, sorting out the differences will pitch you into a confrontation with the previously ignored realm of your inner life. This process of differentiation, of conscious exploration, is an earthy, nature-centered, embodied quest that puts us in touch with the "non-ordinary" reality of dreams, visions, personal knowings, interlaced with strong emotions and self-doubt—a reality the ego wishes to avoid.

Across the many stages of a woman's lifetime there is a steady pull to ground herself in the body. Puberty, ovulation, menstruation, menopause, each heighten a woman's sensitivity to her intuitive body. Each is a very real, immediate expression of embodiment that speaks to a woman monthly not through logic, nor theory, but through the *law* of her body. When her moon time (menstruation) arrives, every woman knows the divine She Who Must Be Obeyed. Her ability to recreate another within the primordial waters of her womb may leave her sorrowing over the narrow notion of a single creator, male, and disembodied. The sacred activities of her womb teach her the profanity of singularity. Her compassion may allow her to hold her silence and participate in the pretense, but sooner or later her truth has to be expressed or her body will voice its sorrow with reproductive and genealogical distress.

Personally, we face the ultimate necessity of discrimination between what is uniquely sacred or profane for each of us if we are to develop a voice of our own. We must choose. We can no longer allow others to choose for us. Without a capacity for discrimination a woman will hand herself over to striving for a life not her own. Ultimately she will be felled by the futility of the pursuit. There is no well-defined line between that which is sacred and feeds the soul and that which is profane and leads to spiritual starvation. Yet when we cross that line we simply know. Our heart races, our breathing pauses, tears tumble fourth—our matter is telling us, *this matters.*

People who live in their bodies, awake and aware of their emotions and how those emotions are affecting them, have a level of self-confidence and self-love that comes from an experience of absolute somatic reliability. No one teaches us that we live our lives through the interactions of emotions and movements. How vitally alive we would be if only we were able to develop as much confidence in what we feel and how that is moving us as we do upon what we think and what that means to us!

Learning to rely upon and trust the intuitive wisdom of your body as you've been depending upon and trusting your cognitive mind marks a homecoming. Tissue and bone, cell and fiber, our bodies carry an unbiased desire for a genuine conscious relationship with the soul. Spiritually conceived by the metaphysical union of Spirit and Soul in matter, we are physically manifest from the union of sperm and egg. Enlivened by our dual conception, every personal journey has a contemporary stake in our day-to-day existence and its own ancient nonverbal roots in the prehistory of Eternity, of All that Matters.

Body's Biological History Book

This prehistory is transcribed into human form and transformed into tissue and bone with each birth. We each carry this legacy unconsciously. A conscious recovery of our ancient connections to the wisdom of the body, our feminine heritage, requires the disciplined commitment of a spiritual apprentice. We must be willing to come before the Sacred Feminine and be taught about the legacy of mattering, as children at her knee. We neither get to choose this ancestry nor do we profit by denying it. Bidden or not, the entire history of humankind is always unfolding within each individual as a cellular principle of our spiritual nature. This history is indelibly and quite literally inscribed, only in the female's mitochondrial DNA, generationally transmitted through each successive birth.

Mitochondrial DNA differs from nuclear DNA in as much as its genetic material is inherited from the mother alone. Researchers following the mutation patterns of this microscopic bit of genetic evidence as it appears and reappears in various Native American groups have been able to trace the migratory routes of the multiple generations that preceded the present one. These mitochondrial threads generationally link the ancestors by maternity until we find ourselves at the site of first woman. Mitochondrial DNA, claims scientist Karon Schindler, is "separate from nuclear DNA, and only transmitted through the mother, making it a virtual biological history book of women. . . ."

Women's Intuition is a guide to reclaiming the wisdom of our motherline through conscious embodiment. It is my deep desire that through it, you will learn to trust your body's signals and learn to read them before they become symptoms of illness or distress. Highly personal, ultimately authentic embodiment is every woman's journey, one in which each woman will recognize the déjà vu from childhood, when she was unafraid of her own intuition, when she was delightfully attuned to her own body wisdom. A precious time, childhood, when impulse becomes the action that evolves into an exploration of play and possibility. A time when all things symbolic have a vitality to be recognized, appreciated, shared. A time when the energies of the heart are a guiding force, a sustaining mentor. From earliest childhood we have the building blocks for an unshakable relationship with our body and the intuitive knowledge that this relationship contains our spiritual birthright waiting to be claimed.

Too soon we forget that the body is our finest instrument. Spirit is the musician, while Soul inspires the melody. This being human is a great work. Never cut and dried, it is a symphony always in process. The conscious woman lives in a body that is her guardian, teacher, and playmate. She can drop inward and find herself held within the sanctuary of her soul. She can pause and listen with an inner ear and discern the mystery lessons of generations past, present, and yet to come. She can trust that what seems irrational, illogical, or ill-conceived will make sense when she turns to her body, her tissue and blood matter, and asks for an intuitive insight about what truly matters.

Chapter Two

FINDING A MAP TO
THE BODYMIND

The unrelated being lacks wholeness, for he can
achieve wholeness only through the soul, and soul
cannot exist without its other side, which is always
found in a "You."

—Carl Jung

A FRIEND OF MINE, GAIL, WAS DIAGNOSED with a debilitating case
of eczema. I asked her what image came to mind when she
thought of her dis-ease. She intuitively replied, "An encrusted old turtle." She decided to allow herself to "become" that encrusted turtle for
a few moments and realized she longed to slow down to a turtle's pace.
Her profession has her flying all over the world, changing time zones
and continents more rapidly than most of us could tolerate changing
clothes. Taking her discovery seriously took her months of going into

her hotel room whenever she was able to garner some quiet time, and moving, dialoguing, and listening to what her turtle energies had to teach her.

Moving like the turtle, Gail found her choices in food changed. She was eating more consciously. Her desire for quiet introversion deepened. She was surprised that instead of feeling lonely, she began to be excited by the aspect of time to and for herself. When I told her that eczema often indicates that our environment is getting under our skin, she was pensive, reflective. Gail listened, slowly adjusted her lifestyle, and when I last saw her she laughingly said that her eczema was gone. It only reappears any time she starts forgetting how much she thrives on a slower and more natural pace. She is convinced that her symptoms of eczema were a spiritual initiation, an invitation from her body wisdom to stop and take seriously what her unconscious treatment of her body was enacting about her relationship to her soul.

As Gail's story shows, the language of the body, of intuition, is metaphor, and the metaphors have to be interpreted. Your body doesn't just send a straightforward "Slow down." Rather, a metaphor is a message that is disguised: it is de facto not straightforward. A metaphor veils the piercing glare of an inner truth without disguising its potency. For this reason metaphors are transformative. They simultaneously interest the mind while energizing the body and igniting the imagination. In a flash they link mind, body, and soul. But when we don't get the message, our body turns up the heat, getting more and more graphic until we pay attention.

In Gail's case, for instance, she had probably been receiving subtle clues from her body that she was overtaxing it before the eczema occurred, but she ignored the signals. So the message had to get even louder. But again, she would not have benefited from the warning unless she had taken the time to ask what the symbolic meaning of eczema was to her. From there she got an image, and the image was the metaphoric message her body was trying to convey: Turtle up—slow down!

Because the language of intuition is nonverbal and nonlinear, many people tend to ignore such messages or claim they don't receive them. However, every human being is receiving such messages all the time and has some capacity for intuitive language—an ear for the melody of the non-ordinary dimension. Even in despair, there is always a fleeting image or a subtle movement that affords an untrammeled intuitive glimpse. Those who say that they never remember dreams (which is one place that our intuition speaks to us all the time) still have slips of the tongue that reveal amazing attitudes or insights of which the ego is totally unaware. Those who claim no connection to a transpersonal power still take time for an occasional superstition—brief genuflection to an influential presence that is out there—in here—somewhere. Those who find themselves attracted to certain images or totems may overlook this clue that the deeper symbolism of a personal metaphor is at work.

Sharna, a professional dancer, remarked that she couldn't resist bits of string: "I've bits all over the place, in my pockets, on my dresser, in my car. I never do anything with them, they just get all tangled together, eventually discarded for another new bit or more." A chance remark turned the bits of string into soul work when her best friend said that those bits were a lot like Sharna's talents: "You pick up new techniques and skills faster than the rest of us but you never develop and use them. Instead you just discard them for a newer bit or something more current." Sharna's talents were lying all around her in tangled bits and pieces. Her intuition to pick up those bits of string was fueled by her soul's desire to bring something deeply significant to her attention. Sharna was treating the gifts of spirit like discards, never fully and consciously embodying what was hers for the taking. She was skimming along on the surface of her life, and her intuition was calling her to deepen and take her life seriously.

If you are not "intuitive," who's speaking when your tongue "slips" or a dream emerges that tells you what you've been struggling to figure out, or when a physical symptom describes your psychic dilemma perfectly? Who leads you toward the fragrance that soothes you and away from the one that depresses you? And if these other languages are something more than nervous system accidents, more than physiological impulses gone awry, how might you explore their intent? Consciously recognizing that there is an intimate relationship between the instinctual responses of your body and the intuitive responses of your psyche is the place to start.

The Body Mind Connection

To begin to tune into the wisdom of the body, it is helpful to understand what this wisdom is comprised of and how it works. The wonderful thing about intuition is that its signals can be felt concretely—if we learn to tune in. That's because there is a natural feedback loop between the body and the mind; indeed the two cannot really be considered separate, even though we've been trained to think of them as separate.

Mind and body react sympathetically to each other. Actually the notion of two separate entities—mind and body—is artificial, contrived. One of the simplest everyday examples of this relationship happens when we think we see something we are afraid of and we react to it with a flood of adrenaline, prepared to fight or flee, only to find we have misperceived what we're reacting to. In reality there is no danger at all. Thoughts translate into feelings that turn into symptoms with the speed of light. We are all familiar with the placebo effect—when we are given a substance with no medicinal value and told that it has healing properties. Believing in the healing property, we get better. What we think is never separate from what we feel nor how the body responds.

A further example of this connection is found in the growing body of literature about how the emotions of expectation, hope, and trust affect the outcome of illness and disease. We know, for instance, that the emotions, which respond instantaneously to thoughts, are in constant communication with the immune system. The immune system is the mechanism by which the bodymind manages health and disease. In *Molecules of Emotion*, Candace Pert reminds us that death rates peak on the days after Christmas for Christians and after the Chinese New Year for the Chinese. "Since these are all days with high emotional valence, one way or another, it seems clear that the emotions in some way correlate with the state of people's hearts."

We are also rapidly relearning what was a given for the healers of old—that touch and chanting or toning soothes the mind and heals the body. That what we believe can help to heal or sicken us. Moods are altered, anxiety alleviated, and disease reduced through touch. The pioneering work of the Simontons, who used imagery and verbal affirmations to affect healing during cancer treatment, is well documented in such books as their own *Getting Well Again,* and Jeanne Achterberg's *Imagery and Healing: Shamanism and Modern Medicine.* Today there is an entire field of medicine, psychoneuroimmunology, developed to respond specifically to the complex and irrefutable interactively dependent nature of mind and body, heart and soul.

Bodymind intelligence is comprised of three distinct methods of response—instinct, emotion, and intuition—which are mediated through three developmental levels of brain biochemistry. The first and earliest level is the brain stem, which is connected to your spine and receives all the incoming stimuli from your contact with the environment. This is the part of your bodymind that mediates your *survival.* The responses from here are *instinctual,* unmediated by cognitive decisions. Instinctually you will withdraw your hand from excessive heat or recoil from a noxious odor. You don't orchestrate instinct. Instinct happens to you. Your entire autonomic nervous system is influenced by this part of your brain. Breath, heartbeat, swallowing, the basic rhythms of your body are activated here.

Without any conscious intention on your part, your brain stem receives, sorts, and passes on to the limbic, midbrain, and neocortex over one million environmental informational impulses per second. This begins long before birth and, according to *The Three Faces of Mind,* by birth the brain stem is beginning to form patterns of sensory information based upon your preferences that will eventually influence the instinctual rhythmic responses of your body to play, ritual, mating, and attraction to social groups. A human being can survive as long as her brain stem is intact, even if her emotional and cognitive agencies are badly compromised. Her quality of life is virtually nonexistent; in fact we insensitively refer to this as a "vegetative" state. But the autonomic functions of the bodymind continue to instinctually support life.

As we grow and mature in understanding the complexities of our bodymind, we can begin to recognize the difference between an automatic, instinctual response and one that is mediated by the next level of biochemistry—emotion. The instinct to eradicate the part of the person that is angering you, even it means that person's death, is real—primitive but real nonetheless. The emotion that accompanies the instinct is equally as real, but unlike the instinct that has only two response choices, Yes or No, an emotion has a wide range of possibilities that counterbalance the narrow range of the instinctual response. Instead of mayhem you choose a more "civilized" response.

Emotions are generally believed to be controlled by the limbic system; indeed the limbic system is often referred to as "the emotional brain." Resting on top of the brain stem, it comprises six structures (thalamus, septal region, olfactory bulbs, amygdala, hypothalamic nuclei, and the hippocampus) that respond to stimuli and express as emotions. The limbic system's chemical emotions affect the entire bodymind by sending cascades of neuropeptides throughout your physical body. These chemical messengers are capable of turning your immune system on, in order to promote healing, and off, to impede healing, when the cells are flooded with hormones and other neuropeptides. Your feelings, and even more important, what you believe about those feelings, strongly influence the health of your bodymind.

A prime example of this is evidence that the majority of heart attacks begin on Monday morning around 9:00 A.M. People who feel they have no choice in influencing the outcome of the unpredictable and uncontrollable demands in their lives lose their desire to thrive. The bodymind responds to feelings of anger, resentment, and despair, and the accompanying levels of stress taxes respiration and blood pressure, wreaking havoc with the heart. Equally, those who love what they are doing, even if the work appears menial and demoralizing to others, thrive. Our emotions are a rich source of expression, especially when we learn that we have influence over them. Emotions are the interface between the intellect and the instinctual bodymind, contributing depth and variety of expression to every cellular response. While autonomic body responses are basic and direct, emotional body responses are multifaceted and complex. Most people are surprised to learn, for example, that the basic emotion of anger is always a secondary response. Some other emotion always precedes anger. It may be vulnerability or sadness or fright. Whatever the underlying feeling is, when you contain your anger and turn your attention to that preceding emotion, the intimacy of your relationship to yourself deepens.

If we can conceptualize the brain stem's primary function as an effort to survive, we can conceptualize the limbic system's function as a desire to thrive. Your bodymind is chemically danced, moved emotionally, by the neuropeptide responses of your limbic system. As children, our emotions express themselves spontaneously as affect (feelings) and through movements. A two-year-old learning to assert her individuality acts out what she feels. She will roll on the floor with delight, howl with anger, and curl up in a ball with sadness. But as we get older, we learn to "control" our feelings, limit our body movements, and as a consequence, often aren't even aware when we are feeling something. Without our even realizing it, an inordinate amount of energy goes toward keeping our instinctual urges in check while ignoring our emotional repertoire.

Intuition is the bridge that connects instinct and all its survival responses with our emotions and their elegant instructions on how to thrive. Intuition is a higher order of embodied response than either instinct or emotion. Intuition combines the best of each of the other two and expresses what instinct is too basic to examine and emotion too unfocused to describe. Our intuitions seem to emerge from the fertile ferment of an unfocused nonverbal interaction between our senses and our experience. It is as if in a flash of communication what we feel and what we know come together, creating an inner vision, an insight, that goes beyond our immediate awareness. It has been my experience that intuition precedes instinct—that our intuitive knowing "triggers" our gut response, not vice versa. As we learn to pay attention to our intuition the third level of the brain, the cerebral cortex, comes into play. Here imagination (right hemisphere) and logic (left hemisphere) join in making creative use and sense out of our intuitive information.

In *Your Sixth Sense,* Belleruth Naparstek describes intuition as a combination of mental logic and heart wisdom. The actual process is subliminal, just beneath our usual range of consciousness. Intuition is all manner of sensory information that comes to us from far more than our bounded personal reality. As Naparstek points out, "It's as though our personal boundaries were extended over more territory than just our own skins, so we pick up data from the environment as if it were about us."

How Intuition Works

How does intuition work? No one really knows. It is not necessary that you understand physiology in order to tap into the wisdom of your body. However I offer you some of the current research so you can appreciate that what we are talking about is a real, a tissue-and-bone experience.

Science is beginning to recognize and appreciate that there are principles of intelligence that govern our wisdom, our healing, and our creativity (to name just a few) that simply won't fit any of the models of "reality" we have heretofore relied upon. For example, we think of our body as bounded and concrete. However, even though it appears to be a solidly composed structure, it is in fact made up of energy and movement. The body is primarily water, water and minerals in constant motion. The rhythms of the entire organism we call the body vibrate in and out, up and down, at a rate of approximately seven times a second. These pulsing vibrations are much too rapid for the naked eye to catch, so we ignore the movement and fasten on what appears to be a static form.

Now there's a remarkable thing about any pulse or vibration. In order to establish a rhythm, there have to be pauses at the end and the beginning of each pulse. In the heart, we call this "the diastolic rhythm"—the resting cycle of the pulse or vibration. As the molecular vibrations that compose the body rest at the beginning and end of every seven times a second oscillation, these pauses create "gaps" where non-ordinary perceptions can insert themselves.

Deepak Chopra calls this "the realm of the Riishi"—the inner healer—whose wisdom can be perceived in the silences, "in the gaps between our thoughts." Itzhak Bentov in *Stalking the Wild Pendulum: On the Mechanics of Consciousness* convincingly describes this phenomenon as a body whose coherency (solidity) constantly pulses on and off. In all likelihood this cycling on and off is the basis for the electric patterns that govern our cardiology. Energy cardiology, a relatively new field that is testing and measuring all the ways in which the energy and intelligence of the heart affects the total system, has also uncovered some remarkable observations about the heart and its orchestration of the bodymind. Prayer, contemplation, spontaneous movement, meditation, placebos, chanting, touch, and absentee healing each appear to create an internal coherence that allows us access to the body wisdom that is most available during these vibrational pauses or gaps. Naparstek makes the point that the opportunity for accessing intuitive wisdom is vast when one realizes that if each second contains seven pulses, it contains fourteen resting periods (or gaps in Chopra's words) as well.

There is an ongoing search for clues to the origins and identification of this intelligence as it becomes increasingly evident that twentieth-century concepts leave much to be explained. Today it is generally understood by researchers that cells have memory (Candace Pert, in *Molecules of Emotion,* delineates the research very well) and therefore, since such cells comprise organs, organs have memory too. Memory by its very nature implies that there is a form of intelligence, a capacity to utilize experience that extends beyond the narrow concepts of dumb matter.

In *Advances: The Journal of Mind-Body Health,* Linda Russek and Gary Schwartz tell about a professional dancer who always maintained a careful watch over her diet, yet was taken with an urge to eat Kentucky Fried Chicken nuggets after a heart transplant. She later learned it was a favorite food of her donor, an eighteen-year-old "whose heart and lungs now lived inside her body." In the same article, an energy healer maintains that cardiac patients "seem to be carrying the energy of their mother's hearts inside their own hearts" and the influence of that energy affects the course of recovery.

None of us is a closed system. The heart is an "energetic communicator," as is every other part of the bodymind. Today much research is being done to provide clarity and a deeper respect for the relationship between thoughts, emotions, and the heart. In Boulder Creek, California, the Institute of HeartMath is responding to the growing interest in the relationship between psychic ability such as intuition and the health of the body. Meditation has already been shown to improve the interactions of the heart, brain, and body, slowing any discordant rhythms until there is a greater mutuality of coherence. As these primary systems of the bodymind pulse together, there is an increase in receptivity to non-ordinary, or what is becoming known as nonlocal, input. In other words, there is a kind of intuitive knowing that is by its very existence healing.

When we experience such knowing, we often also experience a sense of bafflement, because this sort of event comes unbidden and evades scientific inquiry or physical explanations. Yet the telephone rings and we know who it is, or we have a dream that redirects our present perspective, introducing a parallel reality that is somehow more real than the one we once held sacrosanct. Insights and intuitions flash quietly in and out, respiration slows, heart rhythms smooth out, health is improved, and life decisions are made based upon the influence of these events. Based on such evidence, it would seem that the body's natural rhythms are, in and of themselves, a complex organizing principle whose innate intelligence is both local (cellular) and nonlocal (intuitive).

Women's Natural Advantage

A woman has a unique advantage when it comes to the intelligence that is accessible via the rhythms of her body, because her external life is constantly affected by her interior relationship with the innate limbic rituals of her body. Until midlife, the cycles of her menses pull her inward, consciously or not, more than half of every twenty-eight days of her cycle. Her hormonal shifts urge her to introvert, to be mindful of her own matter, to listen for the signals of an age-old weaving that shortly may begin within her.

During this time, her interior rhythms are notably less receptive to the distractions and the stresses of the exterior domain. There is a biochemical summons to slow down, to eat differently, and to avoid stress. This is not pathological; it is natural. Her energy is spiraling inward and downward. A woman is always herself. However, during this time, she is not able to be *who others wish her to be* without great focus and a sacrifice of her innate desire to withdraw, to incubate if only briefly. For it is from within these pauses she has the space and time to listen deeply to her intuition. Thus, when a woman is in her moon (menstrual) time, the pull of external demands upon her time and energy are met at no small cost, not only to her but to the entire tribe, community, village, town, or culture.

Unfortunately, Western society has no place, no space, literally or psychologically, for the healing wisdom of the reflective nature of introversion. Modern medicine has labeled the internal shifts of menstruation *PMS,* and with the logic and reasoning of a male-oriented medical profession this complex and deeply sensate experience of fertility has been pathologized as an emotional disorder, and subjected to a variety of cures. Centuries ago this self-same premenstrual cycle signaled every woman, not just those who could not cope, that it was time to prepare for conception as her blood richly lined her womb in anticipation of a new life. If there was to be no pregnancy, so be it. Women gathered together not as ailing or inadequate, not because they were "bundles of nerves," but as keepers of the mystery, as celebrants of an embodied potency too powerful to be indiscriminately thrown about.

Women's intuitive powers are so strong at this time that my friend and teacher, the Lakota pipe carrier Pansy Hawkwing, warns that a woman in her moon time is " too much medicine" for the sweat lodge.

During her menstrual cycle she is intensely aligned with the lunar spirits of fertility and must not, except at the expense of her call to introversion, enter a lodge during her menses. Her presence will unintentionally disrupt the entire ceremony. During sweat lodge ceremonies a separate lodge is constructed for these women, who gather and talk women talk, earth mystery and moon wisdom, thus keeping the entire community harmoniously balanced. Younger women are free to enter the moon lodge and listen to the wisdom that abounds.

Science is verifying Pansy's knowing. In a recent study done by the University of Texas and reviewed in *Intuition,* a team of researchers noted that PMS sufferers not only show a heightened mental awareness but also a more acute sensitivity to the environment, possibly leading to their superior memory performance during this time. It is hypothesized that this may be due to an increase in serotonin and the *advantage* of a fluctuation in hormonal levels.

After a moon lodge ceremony in the mountains of North Carolina, a woman in her seventies mused on how our lives might have been changed and our communities served if we had been taught as girls to value and cultivate our embodied sensitivity during the sacred period of menstruation. Every one of us would have had an opportunity to develop a trust in our intuition and a delight in the mystery that is our embodiment.

Pregnancy, like menstruation, also belongs to the realm of feminine mystery, where its articulation can only be described through ritual. No other explanation suffices. Conception and childbearing happen to women only; the creation of a child remains a vast mystery to men. Even today, in spite of all our contemporary sophistication about the body, a complete understanding of the extraordinary complexity of pregnancy eludes us. You cannot be anything less than awed by the realization that *her* womb accepts *his* seeds, and from them, within the moist darkness of her body, makes another complete, ensouled human being. Touching the eternal pulse of this process with her pen, Nor Hall writes in *The Moon and the Virgin,* "Woman's timeworn work is the weaving of tissue to bone and the knitting together of the genetic threads of the ancestors." Surely this somatic handicraft ranks as the ultimate mystery, the ultimate in body wisdom.

Giving Birth to Ourselves

Conception and birth do not begin and end with the knitting together of DNA. For many women, particularly as they get older, their "births" become immaculate conceptions, penetrated by spirit, fertilized by the ferment of their creativity, nurtured by their disciplined sacrifice to the muse, midwifed by Soul. Art, music, weaving, potting—every creation adds to the iconography of birth. The potter at her wheel forming a vessel from earth and water, firing it in the heat of the kiln, offers the world a fragment of mystery, a pottery womb pregnant with receptive emptiness, waiting to be filled as the recipient chooses.

Creativity and intuition go hand in hand. The more we access the wisdom of the body, the more we long to express our unique individuality creatively; the more we express ourselves creatively, the more our creations become messages from our intuition, telling us who we are and what matters to us.

Julia Cameron, best known for her book *The Artist's Way,* speaks of her psychospiritual birth in *The Vein of Gold: Journey to Your Creative Spirit.* She wrote this book as a response to the personal experience of discovering, in adulthood, her own musical talent as a singer and a composer. Julia believes that we all need a way to see clearly who we truly are. We are all creative, she says, in ways we aren't even aware of. When you are "sourced internally," she writes, "if you are really grounded in your own worth as an interesting, authentic, powerful being, then you don't need quite as much from other people in a desperate fashion." When you turn to your Virgin, that aspect of yourself that is owned by no one but yourself, she will tell you what you most yearn for is within your reach. Reach for it and you will thrive—as long as you never measure the worth of this "birth" by comparison with another's or by how much money it will bring. Bring your soul child to fruition and then give it away, and it will return to you in multiple ways. You can tap into the vitality of your Virgin whenever you care to with this focused heart exercise.

FOCUSED HEART

The next time you find yourself yearning for something, take a large piece of moist clay and several sheets of newsprint. Focus on your breath and allow yourself to move your attention to your heart. Without anything to lead you but your connection to your heart and its desire, begin to form the clay into any shape that emerges, breaking it down and reforming it at least nine times. Don't look at it or interpret what you are doing until you have made and remade the form at least nine times. On the tenth time, allow the clay to rest on the newsprint while you move to your body and allow the energy of your yearning to form itself in you. If you want to play a piece of music, I suggest Mozart. Don Campbell's Volume #3, *Music for the Mozart Effect* is a fine start. When your movements have come to a close, go back to the clay and reshape it one last time as a promise to yourself that you will accept this yearning as an invitation. Now go and live the fruits of your yearning. Every time you doubt yourself, write your doubt on a slip of paper and leave it in or under your clay piece. The doubts must not be carried by you any longer if you are to nurture this virginal birth of your heart's desire.

When you are confident that you are committed to nurturing your heart's desire, choose an anniversary date—maybe the solstice or your birthday—and create a ritual of letting go as you burn or release those slips of paper. Take time to review and savor your disciplined commitment. Celebrate this new birth as you mature and embrace what you are teaching yourself. Honor your intuition by asking for an image, a symbol to carry you through the next stage of this growth. You'll know when it is time to release the clay piece. When you have fully integrated your heart's desire, return the clay to earth by dissolving it in water and returning it to nature.

Angels and Archangels

We live in an era where "seeing" is occurring in many totally new forms. The keen scientific eye of quantum physics has turned its gaze upon the grosser realm of physical matter, introducing us to a whole range of embodied physical activity that is hidden from the human eye, yet takes place within the body at a subatomic level. Miraculously, the human body can now be conceptualized as the result of a myriad of invisible interactive processes that are indeterminate (they can't be pointed out, pinned down, or cataloged for their cause and effect). In spite of their obscured and indeterminate nature, they are complementary, each acting both for itself and the benefit of other processes as well—a realm of "angels and archangels." If you have ever looked at an Escher drawing where the outer boundary of one figure defines the shape and form of the next figure ad infinitum, you have a sense of the natural complexity that is always present when there are layers of possibilities within any single image or event.

To add to the complexity, whenever any one of these interactive processes is observed, a curious thing happens. Because the focus of the observation—which singles out a particular piece of the phenomenon, thus artificially separating it by human sight—so narrows the breadth of the interactions that "trade-offs" have to be made. In other words, when one specific factor is brought into focused consciousness, the other complementary ones remain but fall into the background. Since everything that is involved in the interaction can't be taken in simultaneously, what is observed and how it is observed has a crucial influence on the outcome. The trade-off occurs in selecting one interaction in the hope of somehow learning more about the total event. It's rather like listening to a solo voice singing while backed up by an entire chorus of equally talented voices. Every voice is needed to create the effect: it is the observer-listener's selective memory and attention that attaches primary significance to the soloist. In any event, individually observed or not, the chorus continues.

We may think that we are focusing on some specific feature or event through a process of logic; however, we are also being directed by our intuition. When asked about their discoveries, innumerable scientists admit that they uncovered the thing that was crucial to the success of the experiment based upon a "hunch" or, in some cases, a dream. Intuition undergirds logic in innumerable largely undetected ways. We all know far more about what is going on in and around us at all times, but we have been taught to tune it out, change the channel, edit the information. Meanwhile intuition continues to fill our logic and our lives with its unspoken possibilities.

Why we choose one "voice" over another is unique and specific to each individual. Twenty-one years ago, my life was saved when my physician Dan had a hunch that my right kidney just didn't seem quite right. He apologized for "troubling" me with an uncomfortable and expensive test, but was adamant that I have it done immediately. I did, and the radiologist marveled that anyone could have diagnosed my cancer "before the chemical tests even registered it." When I asked Dan how he knew, he said he didn't; He just used his instinct and God guided his intuition.

Months before his diagnosis, I was on our boat at the lake when I felt this curious sensation in my right kidney as if someone or something prodded me firmly. When I turned my attention inward, I felt a sense of heaviness and dis-ease that I dismissed as too much physical activity. Surely when I walked into Dan's office that day his instinct and my intuition met and together the cancer was uncovered. What we select to focus upon may be less significant than what in us is inspiring our particular selection. Coincidences, choices, hunches, lucky events, windfalls, spontaneous thoughts are intimately related evocations to explore our intuition and take it seriously.

When a culture trivializes the intrinsic life-sustaining power of intuition, the body's energetic intelligence is depotentiated and its energies are driven underground. Once repressed, all our unexpressed emotions about this loss will be projected onto others to be acted out in some corrupt form.

Fortunately, intuition is once again gaining the recognition it deserves. Medical intuitives Caroline Myss and Mona Lisa Schulz are but two of a new genre of healers who combine an in-depth knowledge of traditional medicine with a natural capacity to diagnose intuitively. Once, in a telephone interview with Dr. Schulz, who does not know me personally, she asked me if my body was disproportionately shaped—much heavier in the lower half. It is not. She remarked that her impression was that it is. She then suggested that I had been living under the energetic influence of a particular archetype and my body was going through deep psychosomatic changes as I moved out of that energy and into a different one. When she described the attributes of the energy field I was integrating, I knew it intimately. I had given her no personal or symptomatic information. Her intuitions were as astute as if she had asked me in-depth questions about my lifestyle and my physical discomforts. Later, at end of the interview, I was able to tell her that one of the more troubling symptoms of a bout of chronic fatigue I was ending was a sensation of "sandbag legs," where my legs felt too heavy to move except with great effort. Metaphorically, the lower half of my body was exponentially heavier.

The Energetic Body

It is one of life's unfolding miracles that we live within a human body that has an electrical field of energy that both *permeates* the material body and *extends* beyond the obvious boundaries of skin and form. The edge where these two energies meet is the site where intuitive change occurs. We cannot predict what our body will or won't do. What we can do is become a participant in the innate energetic interaction that the radiant (electric, sensate, kinesthetic) body is having with the material body and discover what this matter that contains us is capable of teaching us. The apparent duality of dense matter and the lightness of being is, in the fullest sense, God in the moment, the gestalt of the interactive embodied soul.

Nature's influence is infinite, her wisdom eternal. The creativity of the imagination can activate the natural pharmacy of the immune system, arrest a disease in mid-progress, erase tumors, reduce blood flow from an open wound, and eradicate all manner of concrete evidence of illness. Embodied knowledge comes not from the intellectual friction of ideas and concepts, but from the alchemical broth of instinct (body knowledge) and intuition (insight), seasoned with practice. Awakening this capacity comes with a debt of responsibility. We must learn anew to become fully vested conscious children of this Earth. *Gaia,* Earth, is our mother. We, in turn, are children of her realm. Our body reflects the multiple ways we are inextricably aligned with the body of this planet.

The energetic interactive field of bodymind does not end at the skin. Each of us radiates a sphere of kinesthetic energy (called *ki* or *chi*) that is constantly interacting with the energy fields of the environment. One of the principles of the martial arts depends upon the effect that the thrusts and kicks have upon the "fabric" of a body's kinesphere. Sharp penetration into this energy field affects the total energy field of the recipient, weakening his focus, depotentiating his *chi*. Potently influential, when ignored these kinesthetic interactions remain darkly troublesome. Obscured by a lack of focus, suffering from the inaccessibility of the light of consciousness, the effect on us is not unlike a pebble in our shoe. Our emotional gait shifts to accommodate the hidden intruder: our sense of balance is inexplicably diminished.

Repressed, ignored, left to operate as they will, these uninvited changes affect us strongly as emotional and physical dis-ease without our being aware of the origins or its source. Under these conditions, our intuition is silenced, our body wisdom is mute. Even the roving eyes of another can pierce the kinesphere unexpectedly, doing subtle damage to body security. Have you ever felt vulnerable, uneasily aggressed against, and then realized a stranger was intently looking you over? When this happens it is healing—cleansing—to shake the energy off intentionally. To evict it from your energy field. Our senses receive the energy directed toward us even when the ego does not.

I once had a very lonely client whose only contact with community was to ride public buses. She would sit behind another passenger and stare at him until she made that person uncomfortable enough to change his seat. Aside from the obvious implications of this woman's behavior, she remained fascinated with how quickly the body language of her "target" would register the effect of her stare. I can't emphasize enough the good news that we do not begin nor end at our skin. If you'd like a broader example of this as a daily phenomenon, read Larry Dossey's books about the pros and cons of the affect (penetration) of prayer.

We are part and parcel integrally influenced by our external environment, intimately governed by our internal one. Consciously or unconsciously, we are forced to feel the impact of what truly matters. And when we are bereft of any true consciousness about how our body guides us toward our destiny, we suffer these communiqués as jolts. It is common knowledge that over 80 percent of all emergency-room complaints are stress-related. Body symptoms, like their psychic companion, the dream, provide a living interaction with the distress of the soul. Stress doesn't develop overnight unless it is caused by sudden and unexpected trauma. Stress is the effect of an accumulation of bodymind responses that attempt to get our attention about the state we are in. Stress is the bodymind's ultimate response to a depleted kinesphere. Just as a nightmare serves us with notice that we have to get serious about something we are ignoring, so also does a symptom signal us to wake up, take notice, and get serious about what is *mattering* us.

We cannot thrive until our interiority is in synch with our exteriority. It will not work to profess a spiritual life while abusing your body, or to go to workshops on healing and wholeness while continuing to live with rage, fear, and self-hatred. *Chi* is as easily compromised by what we do not do as it is by what is done to us. Compliance is never a soulful option if you wish to strengthen your relationship with body wisdom. The ego has to be taught that when the bodymind registers being chilled to the core, surging with heat, bones turned to water, or hair standing on end, this is not a cause for alarm, this is the language of embodied soul. These are the descriptive metaphors of a loss of *chi,* a shift of consciousness, an intuitive instruction for change. Body metaphors, unlike survival instincts, are a summons to thrive.

The Skin's Intelligence

If you desire to thrive, then you'll want to know that your limbic system's contact with the environment begins with the pores on your skin. Pores, says Elaine De Beauport in *The Three Faces of Mind,* are the eyes of the emotional brain, taking in the environment and conveying those sensations to the bodymind. We breathe in all sorts of mixed messages about what is toxic and what is healing. Internally and externally we are touched by the conditions of what passes through and gets under our skin. Allergens are real. Those we are most familiar with have shape and form and content. Others—thoughts, ambiance, images, fragrances—do not, yet they too "get under our skin," cause our flesh to crawl and break out in a rash. We are touched by love and toxins simultaneously, day after day after day.

Any loving touch, even our own, cleanses us and is healing. If pain and loving touch were imagined as two competing messages racing through the body together, we could say that the sensation of pain moves through the body at a ramble (of less than four miles per hour) whereas the sensation of loving touch flashes ahead at several hundred. Loving touch will outdistance pain, emotional or physical, every time.

Touch is a body language. Years ago, after the diagnosis of a kidney tumor, I spent hours each day resting my left hand over my right kidney and focusing on the sensation. Sometimes my hand would feel hot enough to burn, and other times I could feel intense cold radiating from my hand into my body. More often than not my hand would vibrate the entire time, continuing for several minutes after I had removed it from my side. I had no scientific explanation for why I knew to do what I was doing. I just knew. I had always used my touch to alleviate a child or an animal's physical pain, mostly because my grandmother taught me to trust my intuition and allow that to be a guide. Later I learned that those who practice hands-on healing utilize the same intuitive principles when they use touch to interact with the energy field of another for healing.

After my operation, my surgeon reported that the tumor was completely encapsulated in a fibrous sheath so all he had to do was lift it, along with my kidney, out. Even though the tumor was malignant, no further post-operative treatment was required. I will probably never know how or how much touch contributed to this outcome. Of one thing I am certain. I entered the most serious and life-threatening surgery of my life filled with a sense of deep calm, confident that I was neither alone nor was the experience without purpose. Touch awakened a deep personal respect for the body's, my body's, capacity to soothe and help itself even as my psyche was reeling with fright.

Guiding Imagery

If you care about reclaiming your intuitive wisdom, you have to become more conscious about the source of your imagery, for image is another of intuition's more powerful voices. Our truest nature beckons through the images of our dreams, the vitality of our symptoms, and the piercing poignancy of our desires.

Unequivocally, for many of us today, we run the risk of our prayerbook becoming the *TV Guide,* our demons and our angels simply images on a movie screen, our temple the video store, our primary ritual eating in front of the television. We move through life as bored onlookers. We speak of "the environment" as if the planet were created especially to provide first and foremost a cornucopia of human delights. In this wasteland, our soul hungers for the images that will sustain it, that will reconnect it to Earth. No wonder, then, that we are visited by symptoms and yearnings that beg more than an occasional audience. Our imaginal life is clouded by shoddy metaphors, shabby iconography, used-up story. The images of the TV or the movie of the week dance across our interior screen, evoking the discord and shallow associations of these manipulative electronic devices. We have lost the rich imagery of our deep unconscious and are filled instead with images of super-models, hyper-seductive commercials, and the latest sitcoms. How can we see our own intuitive imagery when our minds are cluttered with such pictures?

Unlike the empty prattle of a sitcom, a fairy tale's authenticity is worth its every line. The images and metaphors it evokes resonate within the unconscious, describing the rhythms and affect of our emotions as this relationship moves us body and soul. These timeless stories have much to teach about getting in touch with our intuition.

All our intimate beliefs about our personal self have roots in the nonverbal truths of our life. In childhood, the rich variety of characters and experiences offered by fairy tales helps us understand life's ups and downs. As children we are relieved to read about characters who feel as we do—unjustly treated, murderously angry, or lost and afraid. We listen to their dilemmas, suffer their mistreatment, and savor their solutions, relieved that we have found an ally. It is to our mutual delight and horror when the wolf eats Red Riding Hood. We are already bored to tears with having to be good all the time. We know something of our own toothiness, and for a moment it feels so good for the "wolf" to win. Somatically we feel easier, understood, and reconnected to ourselves.

Whether you realize it or not, your early childhood identification with a storybook character has shaped your embodiment in some significant way. Instead of rejecting your insight, delight in what you might have been recognizing about yourself when you related to this character. Can you own the attributes and appreciate them? Can you allow yourself to draw upon this energy consciously when and where it is needed?

WHAT'S YOUR FAVORITE FAIRY TALE?

Find a quiet moment and go back in time to your childhood. What was your favorite fairy tale? If it's handy, take a moment and reread it before you proceed. Which character did you like best? List the character's attributes or attitudes and then scan your present life. In what way has this character influenced you? How and when does it show up in your life today? If you can't find any evidence of its presence walk around with softly unfocused eyes and invite the character to inhabit your body. How do you feel? Which attribute came into your body first? How does the memory of this energy walk you? What can this energy teach you about yourself today? Can you relate this energy to feelings or symptoms from the past? Try drawing upon this energy for an entire day and note what you learn about yourself.

If our symbolic lexicon is filled with the abrasive clutter of unrefined commercialized imagery, we may find that anxiety, not relief, is a frequent result. Dr. Andrew Weil, author of *Eight Weeks to Optimum Health,* encourages us to eat well and then chides us for our abusive "diet" of news the first thing in the morning and the last at night. "Paying attention to the news commonly results in anxiety, rage, and other emotional states that probably impede the healing system." He goes on to say that we must choose more consciously just how much is correct for our own psychosomatic health.

I would go on to say that if we want to trust our intuition, we need to stop feeding on stories that cannot provide substantial direction or relief. Until we do, we cannot trust our intuition because we can't separate it from the cultural hype and commercialism.

Returning to the universally archetypal images (art, poetry, mythology, fairy tales, good books) helps us define and refocus our restlessness, our impatience to get on with who we yearn to become. They take us down deep within ourselves, to an eternally abiding source where we remember our connections to matter, to Soul, to the deep feminine. We go to the well of eternal wisdom and drink with no sense of time or place. When we close the book, turn off the Mozart, leave the museum, the images linger—playing in and out of our consciousness, dropping us into and bringing us back from the imaginal realm of soul where our dreams reside and our yearning rests well fed, reinspired.

The soul feeds herself with images. The soul relishes metaphor. For you, your Snow White or Carmen may be wounded birds attempting to fly. So your soul grows with this particular metaphor. Your soul talk will be an exploration of your wounded birdness, your fluttering attempts. For another person the same two images may represent strength or abandonment or indifference. Each of us must have the courage to find her own way, her own unique meaning *regardless* of whether it makes sense to or matches someone else's. What matters in matters of intuition is what a particular image means to you—not what a dream dictionary or your best friend says. Disposable shallow iconography provokes, requiring us to think or feel a certain way. Archetypal images evoke, inspiring us to seek meaning in our own way.

We may grow impatient with the journey until we realize that even this impatience is an embodied message that we are filled with anticipation, that we are on our way. Questioning the unlived life, the disappointments, the yearnings, we must come to terms with all the impatiences that envelop us before we can settle into the patience needed to wait for answers about what is true for us alone. Counterfeit stories, those whose metaphors are parched and without juice, will feed us the spiritual equivalent of a junk food diet. This fare leaves our spirit weary, our soul empty, restless, depleted, and depressed—just as a nutrient-poor diet leaves the body agitated and depleted. Too often we are weary or lonely for the nearness of the Ineffable—for Spirit—for soul talk, and we turn to the soaps or a magazine, a telephone call, or the mall. Junk food—no one has to tell us what that does to us. We know. Go to your journal instead and write as long as you need to: "I am starving." "I am lonely." "I am . . . ." Draw your feeling and wait. Your imagination holds the key to your relief—it will not let you down.

Be Still and Wait

As we learn to tap into our intuition for guidance, we need to develop patience. Asking a question requires a sincere desire to *wait* for the answer. Intuition cannot be forced, and waiting is not a sterling value in this culture. Rigorous dedication may become necessary in order to cultivate enough time to sit with the question until the answer pushes its tender shoots upward. The fragile tendrils of response have to make their way through layers of emotional strategies designed to thwart listening with an inner ear. Like the molecular biologists who patiently follow the clues of mitochondrial DNA, we must learn to trust that our exploration into the deepening of conscious will contain guidelines and clues aplenty about what matters most.

One of the best ways to do this is to keep a journal. Journaling is not keeping a diary, a dutiful recording of known events: we went to dinner with the Scotts, the weather was balmy. The kind of journaling I am describing is a profound and *private* conversation with yourself in which you engage your intuition, record your dreams, draw your images, and pour out your heart's story.

This deserves some thoughtful preparation. Take your time and choose a notebook or purchase a journal that you intend to use only for dreams and self-exploration. If you have the urge, decorate the cover. A dear friend of mine, Jeremy Taylor, the author of *When Animals Fly and Water Runs Uphill* and other splendid books on dream work, cuts out images from magazines, and collects postcards and cards people send him. He creates a collage on the front of a thick spiral note book (one like kids buy for school). When it's finished he has a personalized piece of art. Another woman I know makes her own covers from fabric, while her friend used two squares of thin but interesting wood, laced with leather, to bind her stationary pages. If you are daunted by the thought of *having* to be especially creative, put that aside. I have used plain hard-back law journals for years for several reasons. They are durable and they contain enough pages to each last me at least a year apiece. The beauty of your journal lies *within* the pages. You'll see.

Many women find it is inspirational to have a box of crayons or a handful of colored pens or pencils that are only used for journaling, so they are always available. Include an inexpensive sharpener; you'll find it comes in handy. Allow yourself to begin creatively feeding your soul as you chose these basic bits and pieces. Chose an appealing container for your colors and your pen. I found an inexpensive blue tooled leather pouch that I enjoy. Don't just grab any old thing. That would be more of what you yearn to be freed from. This process is a ritual of reclamation—of gifting your soul, awaking your imagination, coming home to your Self. The soul loves beauty, but even more importantly the soul thrives on authenticity. Be true to yourself. If you find you are disappointed, uninspired with your choices, trust your body's lethargy. Chose again and notice how you feel. Your body will register relaxation and pleasure when you are being true to yourself.

So how to begin? Maybe by having a conversation with that figure from the fairy tale, or the impulse that you keep ignoring or a feeling that will not loose its grip. Draw the images from a dream, have dialogues with inner figures, pour out your soul's pain and joy and then—wait.

Read what you are drawn to, not because you are seeking to be given answers by another, but because you wish to deepen your capacity to discern what teaches you, to discriminate between the popular, or the fashionable, and what you believe is correct in your life. Go back to your journal and tell yourself what you are discovering. Feed your soul's hunger by getting down to the true substrate of your authentic voice. Resist the urge to share your journal with others—a single remark, a well-intentioned interpretation, can turn your precious work to ashes. This is between you and your Self—no other. If you have no safe place for your journal, away from curious and prying eyes, lock it in the trunk of your car. Your journal is an altar in which you can lay out your most sacred treasures. You come as an apprentice, to explore your soul's purposes.

This exploration is led by a rhythm that doesn't give a damn for clocks, talents, education, or economics. This apprenticeship is led by unseen hands that guide yours; by unknown voices that know you better then you know yourself and spontaneous movements that express your feelings far better than words ever have. This is not a possession by an alien force that wishes you harm (even though your ego may yelp with frightened dismay and your friends may be skeptical). This apprenticeship is a reawakening of a precious vitality that is always as close as your conscious receptivity to its presence.

There are many who have preceded you, whose words can reassure, teach, and encourage you when you yearn for a community of like-minded explorers. For example, Jill Mellick's book, *The Natural Artistry of Dreams,* describes a myriad of ways for the novice to approach a dream, which is one of the first places women who are seeking to cultivate their intuition should turn, as dreams are nightly messages from the unconscious. Using any of her suggestions the dreamer cannot go away empty-handed. Robert Johnson unlocks the door to the inner world with his volumes on inner work that are mini-courses in spiritual development. And who among us can not find riches beyond imagination from the images of Meinrad Craighead and the books by Marion Woodman and Jean Bolen. This journey need not be a solitary one. The community dream work done by Jeremy Taylor provides us with a way to invite others to join us, if we care to.

Intuitional Help

Several years ago, in the midst of trying to understand a profound change that was taking place in my life, I received a gift of the carcass of a Red Cardinal. The person who gave it to me said he was driving on a mountain road, thinking about my concern, and decided to use his intuition to see if he could be of some help. Deep in thought, Joe noticed the red bird's dead body on the roadside. He retrieved it, feeling that it was an answer to my dilemma, preserved it and passed on to me, ceremoniously wrapped in linen and tied with a bit of red suede. Meditating upon the gift, I had the distinct impression that the issue I was struggling with had to be faced and worked through before the bird's body turned to dust.

Intuition is not a closed circuit. Rather it joins the energies of any who are open to it in a spiral helix, moving us up into consciousness one moment and down into the unconscious the next. I accepted the gift of this animal's death and meditated upon it. Much to my surprise, I learned I had to let go of an old fear before the carcass completely disintegrated or the fear would influence me, restricting my choices for the rest of my life. Totally illogical! Dead birds, even those who suffer as road kill, don't "talk." OK. Not sane! Nonsense.

Two years later, after diligent and deep work with my dreams and other techniques, I realized one day that I was no longer influenced by those concerns I had been struggling to understand. I went to my altar and checked the bird. When I touched the linen shroud I knew that there was nothing there but feathers and bone. The bird had, like my problem, turned into nothing more than dust. Both bird and problem are now transformed, but the insights that have come from the work are alive and richly inform my daily living. How could Joe have known what his gift—or his prayer—would mean in my life? How did Red Cardinal know to die in just that place at just that time? How? Spirit doesn't leave explanations, only invitations. I thank Spirit for all the Joes in my life and pray that my intuition will allow me to be a Joe for others.

Physical objects can carry a great deal of symbolic meaning. On the table next to the chair where I sit many hours each day is a collection of stones from all around the globe, arrange as a miniature dry streambed. Knowing the origin of each one, I can pick up a fragment and be kinesthetically in touch with India or Africa or my grandmother's front yard. Each fragment is a witness to a time I've had a woman tell me how she quietly used her relationship with a special object to help her make a choice. Invariably these stories begin with, "This is going to sound really strange, but...." Many of us use Runes or *MotherPeace* cards, not realizing we are actually intuitively consulting with our own embodied wisdom.

A beloved totem or a trusted image serves as an unbiased witness that can hold the energy of the quality or the action we are seeking to consciously develop until we are ready to claim it for ourselves. Honoring spirit animals, stones, inner guides, or goddess metaphors brings us into a livelier alignment with the presence of what is just

beyond our conscious reach. These icons, manifestations of our imma-
nent spirituality, ground us in our psychic explorations. Totems and personified images (such as the crone, the witch, the trickster, Snow White)
help us to deal with the foreign nature of the unconscious as we strive
for a deepening of spiritual identity by plumbing the depths of the
unknown.

Our Inalienable Legacy

As the wonders of science continue to reveal the multiple dimensions of
spirit in matter, we also have the potential to become revitalized by the
vast repository of spiritual, cultural, and genetic heritage we contain. We
have only to be willing to be as a novice, to ask all the questions we dare:
What can this dream tell me? What does this symptom want me to
know? Why is it I am so deeply and particularly moved by the ocean, or
Bach, or the sound of falling rain? We have only to risk asking with an
open mind, an open heart, and an open invitation, then the unbidden can
become a living dynamic Other. The Mystery awaits in the energetic
imagistic guise of metaphor and movement as teacher, guide, ally.

We must lay claim to our inalienable legacy—the right to be consciously fluent in the many languages spoken by our bodymind. But
how do we begin to tune into the delicate languages of feelings and
images before they become the voices of symptoms and attitudes? The
best way, I believe, is to listen to the wisdom of the body as expressed
through what I call Spontaneous Contemplative Movement (SCM).

Spontaneous Contemplative Movement is a method I have developed and used for the past fifteen years to allow the body's nonverbal
spontaneous movements to begin to make deeply *intuitive* intrapersonal
sense to the individual who is having them. This is not what we would
ordinarily think of as dance, however. The contemplative attitude of the
mover toward the movements allows the spontaneous energy to move
(or dance) the body—quietly and with symbolic significance for the
mover alone. The movement is done without interpretation or design.

By following the body's impulse to move, the mover allows the energy to spontaneously rise, diminish and rise again, while *intuitively* contemplating the deeply personal meaning that emerges. Using this method, a symptom or a dream's image, for example, becomes an embodied metaphor whose movements describe the body wisdom that is trying to express itself through the symptom or the dream.

Chapter Three

SPONTANEOUS CONTEMPLATIVE MOVEMENT

My teacher told me one thing,
Live in the soul.

When that was so,
I used to go naked,
and dance.

—Naked Song, Lalla

FROM THE AGE OF ELEVEN, LOUISE HAD known she "was quick with numbers and money." Entering my suite each week at her appointed hour, her first stop was to hand her prepared check to my administrator. Keeping her account straight was as easy for her as breathing. Curiously, it was her ledger of relationships that kept getting unbalanced, out of synch and beyond her careful management. Her elderly, divorced mother begged for her daughter's financial support, then thoughtlessly gave the allowance she received to her less-endowed bridge club partners. Louise's teenaged son borrowed money and couldn't seem ever to earn enough to pay her back. A recent love affair ended with the loss of a jointly owned summer home because her lover failed to pay his portion of the upkeep. Each review of these financial disappointments is punctuated with anger and a lecture about the way relatives think they have the right to spend "my money and cause me to lose sleep."

Unmarried and close to fifty, Louise has begun to have insomnia. Her dreams are harbingers of poverty, old age, and destitution. Lately she reports leg cramps and digestive problems. Worried about her health and her finances, she fears losing her job because she can't stay mentally sharp enough to trust her work with the corporate treasure trove of millions of dollars her decisions influence.

Sitting across from me on an October evening, Louise is detached from the autumnal beauty just outside the window. She is shivering and reports that she can't seem to get warm. She is convinced that her chill is in response to the memory of a song that she can't quite bring into consciousness. An unaccountable wave of shaking drifts through her body as she remembers. It's a show tune about a woman who had everything and then lost it gambling for "high stakes." Louise says she feels "an eerie feeling" because she had a dream about a gambler and a riverboat several nights ago.

Devoid of any conscious connection to the Gambler in her psyche, her body is physically signaling Louise with chills and shivers in an effort to awaken her from her indifference. Her memory and her temperature force her into another perspective, more authentic to what is going on. Her spontaneous and inexplicable chill is metaphorically speaking to her via a symptom. Since a metaphor is an indirect way to get to a direct truth, this is an invitation for Louise to use her intuition—to allow the meaning to present itself—nonverbally, spontaneously. Her dream maker has added to the process by stirring up her intuitive energies with the introduction of yet another metaphor—the Gambler. All of this is reinforced by the song which won't let her forget.

Louise's body is sending her an intuitive message about how she feels about her situation, jarring her into an awakening from the bewitchment of her denial about how she truly feels. She can literally feel the temperature drop in the presence of this energy. Since she has nothing concrete, nothing she can identify as "the problem," she is left with whatever she can learn from her dream, her symptom, and the song's lyrics. Entertaining the possibility that there are other clues to the identity of who or what turned down the temperature in her body-mind, Louise turns first to the song and its theme. I invite her to allow her body to move as it wants, without the censoring we adults have learned in "sitting still."

Louise's body is overtaken with shivering when she remembers the image of this high-stakes part of herself. This Gambler's imagistic presence has altered Louise's body temperature and darkened her day.

Body energy is an intuitive language in and of itself. When Louise was asked to intensify her chilled feelings as she described the Gambler, her body rocked spontaneously with uncoordinated movements. "What is your body saying to you?" I asked. "That this gamble I am taking scares me to death," she replies. "I'm foolishly giving away my money and there's no way to get it back. My money is all that I have to take care of my old age."

So who is this Gambler? The one who gives away the money? The one who plays for high stakes? The one whose presence chills Louise and shakes her about? There is no way to know until the Gambler "speaks" and Louise listens without any judgment or interpretation. Up until now the Gambler's energy has been emerging as moods or dreams or feelings. Without a voice that can be heard, the bits of soul held hostage by this part of Louise's inner life can neither free themselves nor thrive.

Louise accepts my invitation to stand quietly while she turns her attention to her breath. Slowly she allows her body to move spontaneously. She resists forcing herself to shiver or *do* anything specific. For a long while the room's silence is undisturbed except for Louise's quiet, even breathing. Then her left knee begins to tremble. Louise stays with the trembling until her body becomes quiet on its own and she observes, contemplating the experience, forcing no new movement until the next spontaneous movement asserts its presence.

Step by step, for almost forty minutes her body communicates with her first by one movement then another. During the pauses between movements, Louise is listening contemplatively to what her inner wisdom is making of all of this. At several points her movements come so rhythmically and rapidly that Louise appears to be danced *by* her Gambler, as her body's responses describe and begin to help Louise intuitively understand what is going on within her deepest bodymind. Using the physical chill and the symbolic meaning of the Gambler for inspiration (*inspire,* "to breathe or take in spirit"), Louise's essential self—her soul—is transmitting what is best and what is harmful about this powerful dilemma via the spontaneously authentic movements of her total bodymind.

As her energy slows, Louise turns to her journal and writes a letter to herself about what she's learned through her body's intuitive movements.

Following Your Body's Lead

Beneath every mood, each symptom, dream image, or feeling lies some unclaimed remnant of the true self, the original and as yet undiscovered, soul-filled Self. No matter how ignored or neglected, your dear body shelters and protects the embodied truths of your soul, despite the physical or emotional cost of keeping them deeply buried, out of sight, out of mind.

Many of us imagine that we give a good share of attention to our body. We feed and clothe it, paint and perfume it, we diet and exercise and memorize every lump, bump, curve, and wrinkle. And we criticize it—blaming ourselves for being housed in such an inadequate and stubborn wrapping. We are attending the machine or the dumb animal maybe, but not the complex, elegant, sensitive, wise, wild creature that is our body. Most of us would not treat a favorite piece of clothing with the indifference and neglect with which we attend the body. We ignore our body's messages to us even when to do so is folly. Consequently most of us don't even realize that, when given the slightest bit of attention, consciousness enters the body and enlivens it, and deepens our relationship to ourselves.

We need to consciously learn to pay attention to and take seriously the messages our bodies are sending all the time. This takes some getting used to. Often at the beginning stages of therapy or movement work, I'll note that someone's belly growled or her foot spontaneously kicked outward during the story she is telling. I note the movement or sound and ask, "What do you feel your belly or foot or whatever would say about this if you allowed yourself to use that voice?" More often than not I am told that's nonsense or pop psychology or "ridiculous," until the client learns to listen to such movements, and then a deeply intuitive inner wisdom leads her straight to her real truth. Therefore, when we wish to understand our intuition, we need to get out of our heads and into our bodies. Our dream maker knows, our bodymind experiences, and our limbic system (emotional intelligence) emotes.

I liken bringing consciousness into the cells of the body to an archeological dig. Bit by bit the debris must be sifted and cast aside—the true gems separated from the fakes—the mapping of the descent carefully cataloged and recorded, the boundaries defined. Bit by bit through the dialogue of movement and the language of metaphor, the wisdom held hostage under layers of neglect emerges. The best way I know how to do this is through the form I call Spontaneous Contemplative Movement (SCM).

The Essentials of Spontaneous Contemplative Movement

As I mentioned at the end of chapter 2, SCM is very simple. All you do is turn your attention to the rhythm of your breath and allow your body to move as it wants to (as Louise did), and then contemplate what such movements have to teach you. As you learn to identify and follow the spontaneous movements that seem to erupt unbidden when you allow yourself to move without censoring and trust the sensations that will teach you how your body expresses itself, it quickly becomes apparent that your body is an instrument of truth, an artist of emotions. Bit by bit you will discover that conscious matter is a medium through which the unconscious expresses itself.

Every spontaneous movement is an authentic movement, a symbolic voice describing the condition of your Self—of soul in matter. You will sense a movement arising long before it emerges. As you proceed, your entire being becomes a vessel that is being filled, moved, and emptied. Softening your eyes by blurring their focus, so you can see just enough to move as you are being led to move, you step into *kairos* time—sacred time—where five minutes can be a day and a day can seem like five minutes; where intuitions become insights (develop meaning) and images form and dissolve only to reform again. The process becomes oracular, a visit with a wise inner self.

On finding the correct way to address the oracle when using *The Book of Runes,* Ralph Blum writes, "No rules exist for consulting the Runes, beyond an attitude of seriousness and respect, for you are in effect consulting the Higher Self." Spontaneous Contemplative Movement is the same. It has no rules, only several principles. First, *Seriousness.* Because the soul will not be mocked or dallied with, you will want to keep this work fairly private. Next, *Respect* for whatever arises, without criticism or interpretation. And *Trust* in the benevolence of this process, that your bodymind wishes you to thrive—to be as fully alive and complete as you are able to be.

When you come before an oracle, clock time (*chronos*) is replaced by sacred time (*kairos*) and the unspoken becomes deeply meaningful. Oracular time has its own rituals, its own language, and its own ebb and flow. You will find the vibrational energies of your body will slow and begin to synchronize themselves with your spontaneous movements. The rhythm has no rules, no beat, no design or steps to be learned—it is uniquely yours and yours only. The pauses between the movements are where Kairos and Chronos meet, evoking a sense of *your timing*. Listening with an inner ear you will discover that these are not silent, empty pauses. They are filled with the voice of soul—the voice of your embodied intuition. As you teach yourself to quietly observe, to contemplate these pauses, you begin to sense a radiant inner voice that speaks to you through the many languages of your tissue, muscle, and bone. When you're willing to simply "hang loose," breathe deeply into those pregnant pauses, you discover that yet another vibrational movement is coaxing you to follow its lead. Now you are intimately in communication with your embodied intuition. Soul is moving and teaching you. Every lesson is tailor-made for you and you alone.

The embodied soul thrives on movement. Spontaneous Contemplative Movement describes the soul's cellular script, uncovering the blocks and the possibilities lodged in matter and imagination. Committed to exploring a more conscious relationship with your inner wisdom through Spontaneous Contemplative Movement, you will find your body image and your health shifting as you become filled with a new level of self-confidence, a clearer sense of self-containment and self-respect. A wonderful by-product is the slow, steady growth of protectiveness and love for the bodysoul. The word *atonement*—to be at one with yourself—is appropriate here. You'll begin to feel more peacefully centered, anchored in a clearer sense of inner purpose and direction.

Spontaneous Contemplative Movement can be done by anyone, because it is a natural response to the three levels of bodymind intelligence I described in chapter 2—instinct, emotion, and imagination. As you move, all three levels are activated.

At the instinctual level, your body responds spontaneously, automatically. If you've ever had your breath cut off, you've experienced how your bodymind signals a variety of immediate responses without thought or emotion. It's called the knee-jerk response. Hit a certain part of the body, interrupt a primary function, do anything to interfere with the survival of the organism, and there is an instantaneous response.

Additionally, in response to the emotions, the instinctual intelligence of your bodymind ceaselessly moves toward a basic, no frills, somatic (*soma,* Greek for "body") solution. Fear: the body gears up to fight or flee. Pain: the body curls up, the mouth opens, and sounds come out. Sorrow: the eyes fill, and tears roll down the cheeks. These are basic somatic responses to the sensations that affect the bodymind. When we are little, before we become coerced into not crying or making body noises or belly laughing, the instinctual intelligence combines with the emotional intelligence of the bodymind and we *express,* not hold back or *depress* what matters and consequently is affecting our matter. As children, if we feel something we respond expressively.

Together these two—instinct and emotion—make up the resourceful and variegated palette that colors the third intelligence, the imagination. When the instinctual and the emotional are openly interactive, feelings, impulses, images, sounds, movements—the extraordinary treasure box of the nonverbal imaginal bodymind—tumbles forth. Each of these is richly rewarding in and of itself. However, to go deeper, to listen to the intuitive wisdom expressed by these various languages of bodymind, we must be able to observe and quietly, nonjudgmentally, take the experience to a newer and more meaningful level of consciousness. Contemplation allows us to do so.

Contemplation is a state of *non-attachment,* a quietly observant state of nonevaluative conscious observation. It is not a state of *detachment,* where the ego loses interest and everything falls into the unconscious. Contemplation affords distance without defensiveness. Contemplation provides conscious containment, so you can uncover and integrate what your body has to teach you about the negative influence of an old attitude without becoming captured by the feeling and succumbing to the familiar responses. Contemplation evokes soul; it opens the door to the essential self. Metaphorically you are held in the outstretched hands of Spirit, nestled on Sophia's lap. SCM is not a state where you go wild or get silly; this is a state where you become bone honest—you get real.

Your preconceived notions about what you should *do* when you feel chilled, for example, are not going to be helpful. Allowing your bodymind to show you how you feel with this particular chill will. You'll discover you have no generic chill. Each new chill will carry its own specific and unique messages, its own metaphoric meaning. Contemplation will allow you to discern the differences and appreciate each subtle nuance.

Without some sort of containment, the entire experience of spontaneous movement can seem irrational, undisciplined, and wanton— simply a bunch of movements without much rhyme or direction. Intuitive meaning can get blurred or distorted by the intensity and jumble of so much. Here is where contemplation becomes the container that holds each expression gently and respectfully so that the inner oracle's voice can be discerned. When you allow yourself to pause periodically and contemplate the sensations and movements as they spontaneously arise, in an observant yet non-attached manner, you will begin to fall in love with your body wisdom as you were intended to.

Hatred is not an instinctual response, it is learned. Self-hatred is the cruelest of its lessons. Revulsion, disgust, and hatred of the body are forms of soul abuse. Contemplation introduces us to the gentle strength of the bodymind. Metaphoric movement will diffuse the most frightening of symptoms, uncover the most obscured clues, amplify the correct resolution. Meanwhile your respiration is being slowed, your endocrinal equilibrium rebalanced, your immune system enhanced, your disgust relieved.

Why Move?

Your body responds to emotions in a little recognized yet vitally significant way. I learned years ago in my work with Dr. Jackie Damgaard in Integrative Psychotherapy and Mr. Al Pesso in Pesso–Boynton System Psychomotor work that when you feel an emotion, your nervous system responds automatically by innervating your body to move. Innately, any energetic impulse causes the body to move into action and seek some kind of interaction to balance the process. We constantly move from instinct to emotion to desire. This happens billions of times daily, just beyond conscious intention, unless something brings it to your ego's attention—like pain or any disruptive emotion. Consciousness changes the possibilities for interaction and resolve.

The influence of your ego is central here. Nothing can be brought to consciousness in a meaningful way and worked with without your ego's nondefensive cooperation. If you freeze, flail about, or go unconscious and "space out," the emotional energy that the intelligence of the bodymind was attempting to transform into a healing response becomes lodged in tissue and bone as a symptom, a knot of emotion, a skeletal change, or as psychic distress, and the experience lies there waiting to be addressed in another way at a later date. The second time is harder because you have covered over the natural instinct with a limiting experience that is less natural, less in keeping with the bodymind's instinctual desire for balance.

The most conscious part of your bodymind intelligence is called "the ego." It's the *me* of the personality. Your ego doesn't like any threat to its sense of control, of its being in charge. Spontaneous emotions catch the ego unaware and can be frightening. Hence the expressions, "I'm *not myself,*" or "I don't know what got hold of me, I felt *possessed.*" Or, "I feel out of control, swamped, stampeded." That's the ego's version of the nervous system taking over and urging the body to "move past the resistance, express this energy now." If you fly to your head, your ego will "talk" you out of change, back into the old attitude or dilemma. The subtle healing intentions of your bodymind's metaphor language will be overridden—ruled out as irrational—unless you intentionally turn your conscious attention to the nonverbal realm of the metaphor—to the images and spontaneous movements that are your body's way of signaling you. For example, your ego's defensive function will disdain the value of becoming the Gambler as "absurd, silly, embarrassing." "When threatened, just avoid" is the threatened ego's initial response.

Your body, on the other hand, cannot lie. Your body's instincts and sensations are pure responses to the unsophisticated reality of how you are literally experiencing yourself, moment by moment, however your ego may ignore or misinterpret these messages. Body wisdom, like the message of a dream, is cryptic until it is respected as an intuitive language separate from that of the waking ego. Initially, when faced with a threat or an insoluble dilemma, the ego first responds to instinctual signals.

Your bodymind knows instinctually what excites excessively and what soothes the excitation. Even so, our instinctual responses remain less differentiated than our intuitive ones. Instinct responds to gross signals. It can and does override intuition. Instinct signals us that *all* fear is fearful—to leave it be. Intuition, on the other hand, signals us that fear is also a metaphor—a way of getting to something precious and healing. Intuition experiences fear as a message that there is something interesting wanting to come into consciousness. Intuition is less literal than instinct, allowing multiple gradients of tolerance between what we cannot bear and what is bearable. For example, as we prepare for surgery we instinctively recoil with a visceral fear of dismemberment while we simultaneously are able to hold any exaggeration of the fear in check, trusting intuitively from the heart that everything will work out OK.

These two, instinct and intuition, have to interact if the body is to develop any trust in the external environment at all. It is hard to trust our intuition when in our unfamiliarity we exaggerate its "mysterious" origins and treat it like some sort of vagrant magic. While the intuition of the bodymind uses images or symptoms for protection until a threatening experience can be brought to consciousness, instinct responds viscerally by immediately coiling up for protection. The ensuing gap between somatic fright and spiritual trust fills with undifferentiated intense emotions. If the fear goes unmentored, with no witness to bridge the gap between the instinctual body wisdom and the intuitive spiritual response, a phobia may take its place. Phobias erupt when the bond between instinct and intuition is breached by unmediated emotion.

The key to maintaining the distinction between instinct and intuition in the body is movement. Movement, bodymind's nonverbal voice, is an exquisitely transpersonal multilingual cellular translator. Movement constantly discriminates between instinct and intuition. Repressed memories and the disruptive instinctual energy that accompanies them when they rise into consciousness have a way of rattling the ego and mediating against change. Contemplative movement disrupts nothing. It cooperates with the bodymind's natural balance all the while bringing an intuitive soul-filled sense of composition and order to the chaotic babble of undifferentiated emotion and memory. Composition and order feed body, mind, and soul.

One of the more extraordinary accomplishments in life is to awaken to the realization that your cellular wisdom is the sweetest, truest, and most requiring mentor you will ever have. The spontaneous movements of your body will take the perceptions of a frightened ego and turn them upside down, all the while honoring ego's position by turning the threat into the very clue that transforms the experience into wisdom.

Surely Louise would have preferred to ignore her misery until it went away or she came down with the flu or anything that avoided the chill of the Gambler. Yet, by allowing herself to move spontaneously and contemplatively, her ego was reassured and strengthened, her body warmed and relieved, and her consciousness deepened and enriched. A strong, observant, nonthreatened ego is essential to growing up—emotionally, spiritually, independently. It is essential to finding your own ground—and essential in doing SCM.

In our groups, participants first learn how to create a protective sphere of personal energy (called a *container*) by mobilizing their egos through the use of a simple ego-breath-body contract. This gives them the reassurance that they can feel more in charge of their emotions while under emotional stress. Emotional strength is rooted in the confidence that you have a choice to continue or not—that the feeling does not own you totally, your willingly participating ego has a vote also. I'd like you to have this experience yourself. I urge you to make the following contract with yourself and rely upon it any time you feel your ego is at risk of being overwhelmed.

CLAIMING YOUR OWN GROUND

Stand comfortably with your feet about shoulder width apart and your knees slightly flexed, so they are not locked. Turn your attention to your breath as you image a consciously accessible and well-contained ego persona (identity). Sometimes in the beginning it is helpful to remember your professional or work persona, the one you find most reliable and well-ordered. (Do not use your parenting persona; you are more vulnerable here than you may be aware of.) Savor this fully, and then make a contract with yourself that anytime you feel overwhelmed or too frightened to continue your movement, you will get to your feet, intentionally breathe deeply then, literally and consciously, take one step to the right, into the ego persona you have identified as reliable and well-organized.

I imagine all of us have our own version of a ritual for reorganizing our emotional state. Counting to ten comes to mind right away.

This conscious choice to remobilize your ego becomes a stabilizing contract you can access after a particularly intense experience and *before* you go out and get behind the wheel of a car or attempt to carry on an important conversation. Many report that this contract evolves into a deeply reliant relationship with their good witnessing ego; the open nonjudgmental observer who can watch a process and remain benevolently non-attached to the outcome.

Once the nonjudgmental ego-observer alliance is consciously agreed upon, your work with the unexplored dimensions of your interiority can proceed without the paralyzing fear of becoming too vulnerable to protect yourself. Mobilizing and honoring the valued influence of the ego is essential, since the ego is the only carrier of a conscious identity link to the body. The fear of a loss of this identity is real and must be recognized as wisdom, not resistance.

A Feminine Form

Spontaneous Contemplative Movement differs from intentional movement. You wait, allowing bodymind's sensations to transform into their own instinctual movement while you are "moved" by the evocative liaison of psychic energy to sensation to movement to meaning. I think of this process as uniquely feminine because it is spiral and fluid by nature. Intentional movement, on the other hand, is thought out and has a pre-designed goal. If Louise had decided that simply shaking would help her understand her dream and her chill, she may or may not have moved past that point because her ego, not the wisdom of her bodymind, would be in charge.

In spontaneous movement a woman has only to tap into her body's natural receptivity to get in touch with her Self. For a woman, this is native to her way of taking in and being in the world. A sixth sense, eyes in the back of our head, anticipating what a child is doing whether the child is present or not, are certainly not exclusive to females but they are an intrinsic part of our feminine capacity to nonverbally relate to ourselves and others receptively to create family and community bonds. Allowing the body sensations as they arise to lead you, the movements that emerge will express your unconscious emotional energy in ways that you alone will understand. You do not employ cognitive (interpretative, left-hemisphere) consciousness. Your consciousness is nonverbally informed by your trust in your own instinctual movements. You don't think about the sequence of movements, you are moved *by them* as you allow yourself to attend to (contemplate) the images, sensations, and feelings the movements evoke. The work is slow and profoundly personal. You learn immediately to observe your own movements in a non-attached way. With soft or closed eyes, you allow them to pass through you while they leave the impressions that are teaching you about your unconscious and your embodied intuitive wisdom. As your energy ebbs, pauses, and then flows once more, the innate rhythms of your bodymind will be more authentic for you than any other prior experience you have ever had with these energies.

Nonjudgmental witnessing, the capacity to observe without interference or interpretation, *is* a higher order of bodymind functioning. Detached benevolent observation is primarily a function of the left hemisphere, of the neocortex. When the movement work is done in the presence of another who also is quietly observing without judgment or preconceived notions, the mover reports she feels deeply affirmed, deeply accepted *just as she is.* She feels seen but not exposed, contained but not restricted, protected but not impeded.

Gradually, a deeper sense of embodied confidence will develop. With contemplation, not interpretation, the undeniable evidence of how lovingly your body ceaselessly provides direction for you unfolds. Invite your bodymind to dance you, and spontaneous movements, physical symptoms, and dream images begin to take on a new depth of meaning. For, *whatever your psyche cannot bear, whatever your psychology cannot accommodate, the intuitive intelligence of your bodymind will express.* In a variety of unique and subtle ways, your body will describe your psychic, physical, or spiritual dilemma in an attempt to carry you through to the health and wholeness that is your soul's desire.

At first the language may be foreign, and it will require disciplined commitment to fall in love with the non-ordinary and seemingly paradoxical intentions of your own soulfulness. Eventually the spiritual meaning expressed by your movements, physical symptoms, or addictions will become clearer. If you wish to become as fully expressive of your destiny (your own unique spiritual journey) as it is possible for you to be, you must risk listening to and trusting in the confusion brought by change, without promise of any specific outcome.

Spontaneous Contemplative Movement evokes the embodiment of metaphoric language. Quietly following your body's impulses as a feeling or a symptom becomes an image that evokes yet another feeling, leading to deeper and deeper insight about the unique emotional and physical language you are being moved by, is truly a sacred and often joyful experience. I am confident you'll find yourself willing, eager even, to explore the most threatening emotions or the most baffling dream symbols as your ego begins to be drawn into an alliance with the healing function of the metaphoric language of bodymind. Resistance softens with the reassurance that the contemplation of what the metaphor expresses truly is a state of being, not a state of doing.

As you attend to your movements and bring them into the non-judgmental focus of contemplative consciousness, shifts begin to happen. You are no longer the captive of an inexplicable mood or the victim of a nagging symptom. Contemplatively you become a benevolent observer of *what is moving you*. Your Gambler becomes an ally, a voice from within urging you to wake up, to grow in consciousness, to clean up your excesses, to claim your wisdom, to speak your truth.

When an image is expressed by the body, the purest meaning of that image unfolds because your body does not know how to disguise the truth—*your body cannot lie.* Emotions are the diffuse means by which our experiences are incarnated; movement is the focus with which we are able to plumb the depth of an emotion as we relate only to our essential Self. When you follow your body's lead, you'll discover that the movements expressed by your particular emotion or symptom are quite different than the movements engendered by a similar emotion or symptom in another. Emotion moves the bodymind in intrapersonally specific ways. The meaning attached to any emotion is unique to each individual, its message soulfully conveyed.

Movement is the metaphoric weaver of the instinctual, the emotional, and the imaginal. Your bodymind relies upon three levels of movement. At the instinctual level the movement is pointedly reflexive; it spontaneously occurs. At the emotional level the movement is affective, more diffuse, and therefore more complex. You feel anger; the reflexive energy specifically curls your fists into balls; the emotional energy is less specifically colored by hurt or fright or sadness as well as anger. At the imaginal level, your movements become more organized; they begin to express themselves intuitively, symbolically weaving together instinct and emotion. A spontaneous picture or image of relieving action forms. Instinct awakens emotion which in its turn evokes the imagination. Movement allows the entire bodymind to intuitively express itself authentically and cohesively. Coherence, or clarity, follows.

Every cell of your being has a right to exist, to be respected, honored, and cared for. Al Pesso says that the soul is the totality of "all that I am." "Healing is the ability to be full of one's Self," to be fully and consciously ensouled. If soul is the incarnate essential Self, then embodied intuition is her voice, and Spontaneous Contemplative Movement is surely one of embodied soul's most accessible languages.

In chapter 4, I teach you several ways to use and make SCM your own. As I offer you certain exercises, feel free to record them for your own use so you can set this book aside and drop into your body without any interruptions.

Chapter Four

SOUL TALK

*Learning the Language
of Spontaneous Contemplative Movement*

You cannot travel on the path before you have
become the Path itself.

—*Gautama Buddha*

AFTER OUR SESSION, LOUISE SAT SHIVERING, attending inwardly
for a length of time. She then reached for an afghan and draped
it around her shoulders. Sliding down onto her belly, she slowly rolled
over and over, pausing periodically to shake all over. Then she appeared
to be immobilized, her breath shallow and barely discernible as she went
deeper into her own embodiment. After a period of time she began to

breathe audibly, and with each breath she appeared to be peeling off the afghan and slowly getting to her feet, where she began to unfold and then retwine her arms around her torso. She ended her movement session by spreading her fingers widely and clenching and unclenching her hands, and then shaking them vigorously until the movements subsided.

After movement sessions, many people make comments in their journals for later reflection. It is a curious fact that the ego is always striving for a diligent maintenance of the status quo. As new perceptions emerge, the ego can and will override the new information in an attempt to alleviate any anxiety created by the new perception. Writing your experience down, including feelings, images, and any inexplicable occurrences, will contain and record the emotional shifts that may be too threatening for the ego to allow. Later you can use this material to help you recover the full depth and breadth of the experience in a non-threatening way. This is also why a dream journal is so invaluable. When a dream is not written down, the ego conveniently "forgets" the feelings and the images of the dream. Eventually the dream's message is eroded away, reabsorbed into the unconscious.

Louise took time to write in her journal and then we talked. She described her reflective responses to her chill using the metaphoric language of her dream. "I recognized the chill as an old and repetitive pattern of internal shaking whenever I was afraid I was in trouble. As I sat absorbed by what that pattern felt like, my body moved and became the pair of dice. I wrapped myself in the 'cup-afghan' and sat waiting to experience the impulse that would move me into a gamble. Then the movement took precedence and I felt myself unwind from the old familiar tautness of the fright." Her clenching and shaking of her hands was, Louise felt, a way of consciously taking hold of the energy. Through SCM, Louise's subtle body knowledge is helping to sort out and integrate the wisdom of her dream.

Eventually, if we are to grow psychically and spiritually, each of us has to challenge the entrenched emotional position of an old set of unconscious beliefs that were designed to keep us "safely" stuck in a psychological wasteland without tipping our ego into distress. Making this change can feel scary—our stomachs roil, our knees feel weak, and we want to flee or cry, or both. Holding steady, at first you will not be able to recognize yourself in this new psychic posture. The old familiar emotions that you used to identify with as "me" and the new emotional position that has not yet come into the foreground of your consciousness are in the process of shifting, each tugging at you in a struggle for supremacy. Both are present in your consciousness for the first time, and each are just beyond your reach. You are neither whom you once were, nor are you able to claim a new identity.

This foreign nexus is where transformation and integration touch but do not yet blend. This is what the anthropologists call the *liminal* space: a condition of in-betweenness where the old attitude or response won't work any longer and you have no reliable replacement to count upon. A sobering reality slowly overtakes you, and you find that you are more solidly grounded in this liminality than you ever were in the rigid superficiality of your defensiveness. Because you have allowed this shift in consciousness to slowly emerge in a contained and nondefensive manner, your ego is less threatened, less resistant to the change. You in turn will be less likely to feel depressed or anxious.

Louise said that if anyone had told her previously to face up to the feelings behind her generosity and then to allow herself to openly express whatever she found there, she would have dismissed the suggestion as capricious. However, after allowing her body to lead her in a realization of what the Gambler represents, she solemnly affirmed that now she can't imagine continuing to live so inauthentically. Louise is individuating—consciously developing an authentic ego while deepening spiritually through her relationship to her subtle body as a result of listening to her intuition and allowing her body to teach her.

Trace Memories

There is virtually nothing in this industrial culture that encourages a woman to evoke a conscious relationship with her subtle body.

Contemporary woman has no context in which to express her intuitive knowledge without it being perceived as irrational or frivolous. Every woman builds her own inner world of images and then must deal with the feelings and the impulses that accompany them. The trace memory of the spiritual communities of ancient Greece or Aboriginal Africa or Arthurian England reside within each of us, even today. The age-old universal patterns (archetypes) of the feminine speak to us across the vast reaches of time and geography. We simply can't recognize their variations until the distance between those images and the potent healing energy that they carry becomes more than the bodymind can ignore or disguise. Then the body and the psyche are pulled into the interior realm of the Great Mother (*Mater, matter*) to show us what really matters, what is sorely needed to be brought to consciousness to set things right.

The mystery of the collective wisdom of the feminine is always available to the bodymind as long as we provide a protected context for its expression. Once we are able to nonjudgmentally open our consciousness to the language of the kinesthetic body, especially in concert with the images of a dream, the plans of the Great Mother Who Matters Us unfolds. Conscious embodiment is as crucial as mindful consciousness.

Marion Woodman's entire body of work has been directed to keeping women conscious about their emergent archetypal patterns. "Without them," she underscores, "the imagination dies." Our imaginations must have something greater than the ego's view of the world to live by—some sense of the eternal ever unfolding in each of us. For Louise, her Gambler led her straight back to a self-sacrificing version of the maternal who will nurture others in spite of the cost to the soul. Louise has to look at her own nature, not her mother's, to discover the faulty relationship she has with the Great Mother of All Nature.

As her body consciousness proceeds, Louise is facing into what matters most. She has been pinned to the sticking point of a blind commitment that kept her ignorant of the terrible price it exacted by its presence. Far better to pay the price of authenticity exacted by the chills and fright than continue to be bewitched by the lie that the cold wind blowing through her originated somewhere "out there." The lies perpetrated by our refusal to consciously embody both spirit and soul concretize into rigid muscles, warped skeletons, nerves that fray, neuroses that paralyze, and worst of all, a half-lived life. We trade the deep compassion of Spirit and the profound love of Soul for the bittersweet sop of denial. Through our willingness to pay attention to the signals we are receiving from our bodies and to move them through us, we can reclaim ourselves and live more authentically.

I believe there is a realm of nonverbal energy, a terrain within us that is omnipresent and steadfast in our behalf alone. I call this place *Soul*. It emanates from a level of energetic activity just outside of the threshold of awareness that most of us have been taught to allow into our consciousness. And I have come to know that without a deep personal awareness of our relationship to Soul, no one can ever become as fully human as she is intended to become. This energy is never more present or accessible than it is through our intuitions and our dreams. If you have ever worked with your dreams in depth, you soon realize that they are imagistic intuitions, full of the possibilities of what is and can be. Intuition, like the dream's image, shows us fleeting glimpses or flashes of feeling that reflect a tantalizing sample of the untapped vitality that seems to lie just beyond our reach, embedded as silica in the opalescent stoniness of our disembodied matter. Each time the veil thins, the reflection that reveals itself is, in that moment, indelibly etched upon our memory, calling us to come home, come home. Inevitably, when we have ignored our intuitive urges too long, a body symptom, a persistent thought, or a debilitating feeling will help us out.

Spirit in Matter

Carl Jung, the Swiss psychiatrist, risked his sanity and his reputation when he committed himself to the exploration of the unspoken and unconscious affects of the soul in his personal life. He first laid claim to his own scientific inquiry when he developed a way to record the subtle electrical interaction between the unconscious mind and the body. He witnessed and took seriously that there are brief moments in time when both mind and body are held hostage by the unmentionable. He was able to show through the use of a galvanic skin measure that the electrical activity of the body changed in rhythm with the inability to respond. It appeared that at the mention of certain words, the emotional associations to those words, specific to the psychological organization of the listener, was so powerfully influential that mind and body together fell, as it were, into a *lacuna,* a black hole, from which no energy could escape. The words were simple everyday language, *father, church, mother,* and so on, carrying symbolic meanings whose emotional charge was rendering the recipient speechless. Respiration changed and the palms begin to sweat. He found that certain words, because of the individual's deeply personal associations to them, have the capacity to both heal and kill the individual who is unconsciously governed by them. In the most rudimentary sense, Jung was uncovering the basic mystery of spirit entering matter and the "word becoming flesh."

Like many mystics before him, Jung struggled with the question of how spirit enters matter. He persisted with an interdisciplinary inquiry to examine even the field of subtle energy that permeates and surrounds every human body. This, Jung says, has its source in the Universal or World Soul (the *Anima Mundi*) always seeking to enter matter through Spirit, the energetic vehicle of penetration. Soul, that personal experience of the Ineffable, of the Self, has many forms of expression by which we can recognize its presence in our life. When it emanates from the psyche, it comes to us in dreams, in imagination, or in intuitive flashes. When it speaks to us through the body, it expresses through spontaneous movement, symptoms, and feelings. Together, conscious mind and body vivify and are enlivened by soul. Each needs the other to complete the fullness of human life. Soul needs a strong and conscious container in which to grow and differentiate into the articulated Self, and intuition is the way we build bridges to the soul.

SCM, like Jung's word association test, is yet another way to identify the symbolic impact of an event or an emotion upon the total being—the mind, body, heart, and soul. By moving and observing our movements, we learn who we are at the deepest level and how we feel.

It's so simple. We forget that the strongest influences upon our lives are always symbolic. Contrary to common belief, we do not respond to the actual or the concrete—we respond to what each event, relationship, or feeling means to us symbolically. While Jung measured a specific physiologic response (sweat on the palm) to demonstrate how the body carries the impact of a psychological dilemma, SCM allows the body to uncover this connection through spontaneous movements that are evoked by focusing upon a specific symptom or image. If we were to measure the levels of cortisol (a stress hormone) or some other variable pre- and post-movement, I am confident we too would find some concrete physiologic markers to indicate an intimate bodymind interaction to the symbolic meaning of the symptom or the image. However, SCM is not a scientific cause-and-effect experiment—rather, it evokes the innate relationship between the bodymind's instinctual responses and its intuitive solutions to the symbolic meaning. The insight that develops is so intimately unique to the mover that it can best be described as soul talk—an embodied conversation with the Self.

A Collaborative Experience

Spontaneous Contemplative Movement is not done to you, it *is* you; it is a collaborative body-mind-heart-soul experience of your deepest Self. Let me give you a personal example:

For days I had a nagging pain down the length of my right leg, beginning at the hipbone and extending to my right foot. This pain was joined by indigestion that radiated from beneath my left rib cage up and under my left shoulder blade. Symptomatically, I sensed I wasn't seriously ill. Yet I was distracted and fatigued. Then a dream told me, "You are being stretched on the bias; from the left shoulder blade, up and out: from the right hip joint, down and across. You are being tested on your bias." OK. Stretched on the bias—what bias—how might I learn from these symptoms?

Lying prone on the floor, I allow my breath to move me into the symptoms as they evolve into the dream time image. Turning my attention to the "bias" pull of the two pains, I breathe and intentionally follow the spontaneous movements that emerge. When I say *intentionally,* I mean I do not drop into a diffuse state of meaningless response, in reaction to the symptoms. Rather I maintain a quiet, nonevaluative curiosity as I contemplate the direction they are now leading me into. The energy pulls me first one way and then another. Spontaneously, my left arm stretches outward as my right leg curls and then moves to a full extension. The image of my entire physical body needing to be stretched and straightened out is alive within my nervous system. I can feel the muscles being innervated and pulled in a dance of bias. My active involvement with the dream's metaphor begins to transform into a different image. I feel an urge to "straighten my selvages." Slowly, only as the urge to move arises on the breath, I square my body as a cellular urge to open up begins to lead me into a full body stretch. Afterward I write in my journal: Lying on my back, my body is teaching me my need to consciously look at my biases and how they are stretching me out of shape, affecting my digestion and my balance. I feel a cellular need to get squared away, and as I spread my arms and legs out my inner spaces open—open as each cell becomes as a starpoint in the innermost galactic expanses of tissue and bone. I have an image of new energy twinkling and sparking as stars do on a clear night. A single synapse flashes—faster than light—igniting each starpoint it touches, relieving the pain. My body is the world body, the universe, arching over the Earth. I breathe and move, breathe and move into the fluid vastness of all that this body has to teach me through the beauty of these symptoms. I have a clear image of the necessity to let the biases go. I have a responsibility to uncover whatever is giving me indigestion, leaving me psychosomatically uneven.

After this work, my symptoms moderated and I learned in a very practical way of at least two behaviors that were stretching my physical body out of shape while diminishing my psychic life. This part is easy. Next, I made a commitment to change those behaviors as an act of self-respect and conscious embodiment.

The Seamless BodyMind

At first it is almost impossible to discern whether the movements create images that develop into insights or images evoke movements that express emotions that lead to insight. Soon it becomes clear that the sequence is varied and of no importance. The intelligence of the body-mind is seamless and extends far beyond the boundaries of the skin. We do not have to pinpoint when an emotion becomes a physical symptom or when a thought influences psychological distress. The bodymind is pure energy, and when we turn our soft eyes toward any single feeling, symptom, or movement we capture a synopsis of the entire story that is being cellularly enacted.

During the process of consciously attending to the spontaneous movements that arise from the body when it is intentionally quieted, non-ordinary reality (imagination) and gross reality (the corporeal body) meet on the threshold of conscious embodiment. This meeting contains a broader and deeper expression of the psychic or physical distress than the rational mind alone can either discern or comprehend. Because the movements are unique to you, the images and metaphors that accompany them are specific in their originality and personal meaning. It is a remarkable and humbling process to observe a chronic symptom, once it is focused upon and given the full range of its capacity for spontaneous expression, evolve into a deeply embedded personal metaphor about the individual's resistance to some central part of her life. As one woman said, "I never ever suspected these terrible leg spasms were my body's prayer for me to live."

Movement is the human body's first and most rudimentary form of expression. Withheld or blocked expression creates depressed energy, emotion, vitality, and purpose. When you allow your body to bend and move with the breath, *as it wants to,* while focusing on your tears or your anger or your depression, it will tell you what you need to know. The honesty of the body is so pure in its directness. In spite of how a faulty belief system reshapes muscle, tissue, and bone, movement releases the emotional integrity that your bodymind continues on some level to maintain.

Conscious Breathing

Often the first step toward an embodied authenticity is a conscious attendance upon the rise and fall of the breath. The simplicity of attending to the breath helps prepare one to turn her attention to the body's first impulse to move. Breath is one of body's purest expressions. Since earliest time, *Pneuma,* the wind of Spirit or Soul that breathes the universe into life, has been recognized and revered. Breath brings vitality, enlivenment, and ensoulment into matter. Conscious breathing awakens the unconscious body. Without consciousness your body remains as trapped and formless as a lump of clay before the potter's touch. Breath touches matter and awakens all the hidden potentialities. Without its presence we are dead. As you quietly observe the rhythmical rise and fall of your breath you begin to contemplatively respond to your body's spontaneous energies. As a beginning, contemplative breathing is a natural and quite unaffected introduction to one of the instinctual body's basic spontaneous movements.

BREATHING THE BREATH
OF CONSCIOUSNESS

Find a comfortable place to sit or lie down. Turn your attention to your breathing, and as you breathe in through your nostrils imagine that there is a tiny elastic cord between your navel and your spine. Breathing out *through your nostrils,* your mouth relaxed, and your lips lightly closed, tighten your navel back against your spine. Do this so easily that you sense rather than feel a slight pelvic tilt as you exhale. Continue to breathe this way until the rhythm feels easy, your body relaxed. Now soften your lips further and begin to breathe on one of your hands, observing your hand in detail as you brush each finger with your breath. Breathe along the length of each finger, then between each one. Do this contemplatively, really observing your hand closely, and with open curiosity. Pause as you notice each nuance, breathing consciously and contemplatively. This is one of the hands with which you reach out into your environment, shaping it with your touch.

As you continue to breathe on your hand, stretch your fingers as much as you care to, flexing them and watching the range of motion of which they are capable. Taste them and note the sensation, the taste. Smell your flesh and savor the intimacy. Now with soft eyes allow your hand to move only as the movements spontaneously arise, while you observe and get to know this dear old friend better. When you have had enough, compare this hand with the other. Is there any difference? Is one hand larger or smaller, more sensitive, lovelier, less appealing, whatever, than the other? Touch several different textures with your eyes closed, first with the unconscious hand and then with the hand you have breathed consciousness into. What can you notice? Have you had any insights, any images or sensations associated with this experience? When you have fully explored the differences, rub both hands together and shake off the energy. If there is a basin nearby, go and consciously wash your hands. Dry them and if you have lotion or oil use a bit on each one. After you have learned all you can about your "handiness," do the same thing with your other hand to maintain balance and for the pleasure of it.

I have been describing to you how, through the use of Spontaneous Contemplative Movement, you can "embody" emotions and deepen your understanding through the body's metaphoric language. Any spontaneous movement from a part of the body, or an organ or a body symptom both amplifies and deciphers the symbolic complexity of the experience when you consciously attend to what the experience means to you.

In the previous exercise, you have consciously awakened your relationship to your hands by using both breath and movement. Now I'd like you to chose a symptom you have or an image from a dream you want to learn more about.

SYMPTOM AS METAPHOR

Place a piece of music on your stereo to contain (give boundary) to your experience. When you are working alone music is helpful, vital really, to avoid falling into an addictive relationship with SCM by believing more is better. Often the individuals I work with will say, "Couldn't we do this all day or for a week, please?" The answer is Yes, as long as there is an agreed-upon beginning and an end. Soul will escape you if you fall into unconsciousness or chaos. Endpoints are healing in themselves. Knowing that you will work until a certain piece of music ends alleviates your ego's fear of *or* reliance upon an addiction to emotion. I suggest the CD *Secret Garden* as a lovely way to be contained.

Turn the music on and begin by dropping inward with your breath. As you do so allow your attention to move to the image or the symptom and wait for it to move one or both of your hands. This is not a dance to the rhythms of the music. This is an attendance upon what comes forth slowly and without regard for the beat or the cadence. As each urge to move arises, follow what it will teach your imagination about the symptom or the image. Observe and quietly contemplate how your hands move you. When the music ends after one or two pieces, discover by going to your journal or your art work what you know now that you didn't know before about the symptom or the image.

Soul comes to meet us at the altar woven by the body's tissue and fiber, resonant with much to teach us through the body's spontaneous desire to move. Move any part of your body to the inner rhythms only you can hear, only your body can feel, and your soul's bodymind wisdom will express itself. Stand, sit. Quietly wait for Soul's choreographer to coax you into the movement that will open the gateway to your inner sanctum.

Spontaneous Contemplative Movement stirs us as an alchemical broth. Pause and wait for the body to speak. Contemplate your instincts as they wordlessly ripple here, tug there. Allow these spontaneous summons to coax you into the postures the body seeks, moving from one to the next, being moved by an interior dancer. The energies blend, the thoughts, hopes, griefs, aspirations, flow through you and you are moved into an intimate relationship with how any of this *matters*—to you.

Here's another example of how it can work. My friend Mona muses, "I wish I could be like that hawk that flies so freely in your backyard." "So, be your own hawk, Mona, for your soul's sake find out what is lodged in you that the hawk represents," I reply. "Move with your hawk energy-imagery-fantasy-knowing and allow your body to do its own alchemical healing—to deepen and change you. Whatever is holding your 'hawk' hostage must be confronted. Your hawk is calling you to set yourself free." The movement is the easy part. The tough part is trusting in your experience enough that you *believe* what you find happening in your imagination, your affect, your soul. When a metaphor "dances" the body, the metaphoric meaning is incarnated, it is embodied. Every cell is touched, affected in some way. I watched as my friend listened to the urging of her body.

Turning her attention inward she becomes as one with the rise and fall of her breath. With soft eyes she raises her arms and then slowly lowers them, one at a time, while spontaneously making small whispered whistling noises. Her face is closed, her eyes narrowed against my gaze. I too soften my eyes so as not to intrude. She dips and glides, calling softly to her winged companion. Her movements are graceful, sometimes expansive, sometimes barely discernible. Periodically she appears motionless as she contemplates the story unfolding before her inner eye. After about thirty minutes she sinks into a chair and laughingly says,

"Even I don't know quite what to make of what I heard me teach myself!"

Curious, isn't it? Embodied wisdom teaches us what we know but don't realize that we know. Mona says what I have just introduced her to is magical. I remind us both that what we have witnessed is the dance of embodied intuition; it is not magic—it is *mattering.* As Mona ends her contemplation I don't pry—inquiry is out of order. As a witness it is my privilege to nonjudgmentally observe. That and nothing more. When I am able to sit quietly and accept Mona *as she is,* Mona is empowered to be far more accepting of herself.

In Our Bones

The images, energies, and metaphors of Spontaneous Contemplative Movement are often a woman's first introduction to who she truly is, authentically, in her bones. Body's metaphors are ruthless, in as much as there is a refusal to express anything less than authenticity, even if it brings the recipient to her knees in abject obedience. Mona tells me later that in a thoughtless moment she mocked her experience and started to demonstrate her "hawk dance" for her roommate. At first she was having fun, then she began to feel lightheaded and queasy. Nausea is the bodymind's signal that we cannot stomach what is happening. This is particularly potent if we are doing something to ourself. She was left with a sadness, "Like I have mocked myself, destroying a precious moment, a precious connection. Have I irreparably ruined that moment?" she asked. "I don't know, Mona," I respond, "you'll have to summon the hawk and inquire. It's more likely that you've uncovered a familiar way you diminish yourself with mockery." How often do we ridicule ourselves rather than risk the rejection of others who can't accept us as we change?

How many times have you attended a workshop or a retreat and gotten in touch with a totem or a spirit animal or a potent symbol? Maybe you did as Mona did and danced it or you drew it or even talked about yourself as Hawk Woman or some version of naming that related you to the experience. Then you returned home and found the experience ceased to awaken the depth of feeling it did originally. You felt the loss and grief as something precious slipped just beyond your grasp once more. Remember that the ego is always waiting to make everything fit a particular conscious format. So the ego rules, your Hawk woman is pushed aside, and the soul sorrows.

If you'll go back to any meaningful part of your experience, remember it and then drop into your body with your breath. SCM will teach you the why and how come of that first experience. Mona did this by remembering her nausea. She imaged a nauseous hawk and then allowed her body to move her into the depth of meaning that her social demonstration had "mocked." Mona found an old admonishment to "keep everything light and fun" had been influencing her desire to become serious about an intuition that she needed to learn to meditate. She had been taught to make fun of her spirituality as a child because her orthodox upbringing was an embarrassment to her. Her hawk, Mona said, was her strong desire to "rise up above my fears and get a bird's-eye view." For Mona it couldn't be any bird—she needs the strength and stamina of the Hawk. She found this truth when her body repeatedly undulated with the wrenching of her imaginary nausea. These undulations evolved into the rise and fall of the Hawk's great wings. Mona has always been afraid of heights. She feels that if she is to integrate fully the symbolic metaphor of "Hawk" she must look more closely at this fear. She is quick to point out that she already feels quite different—more in charge of her life, more anticipatory of new experiences.

Awakened from the languor of our unconsciousness by the non-verbal meaning that the contemplative repetition of a single movement can convey, we wonder why something taken for granted yesterday has the impact of a summons today. We begin to realize that we are enlivened viscerally by our spiritual connection to the transpersonal feminine each time we feel a dimension of relatedness that is within the realm of our domain. All the common physical metaphors—a breaking

heart, stomach turned wrong side out, heart stood still, breathless inde-
cision, tickled pink—are evidence that even your more rational attempts
to separate mind from body, emotions from matter, is a ruse. Each
metaphoric assessment is succinctly descriptive of what is truly affecting
you, urging you to awaken and commit yourself to thrive.

The Steadiness of Movement

If evoking body consciousness shakes you to the depths of your being,
it also steadies you in ways you can only imagine. During SCM, the
three seemingly disparate perspectives—psyche, matter, spirit—reveal
themselves as a trinity, each a representation of the other. Any portion
of work with one will reveal itself as inseparable from the whole. Delve
into the dark environs of soul, and spirit is made lighter, brighter. Raise
or deepen your focused spirituality, and soul is enriched. Attend to the
spontaneous languages of your body speechlessly flooding your consciousness, and you will be introduced to dimensions of yourself that
will surprise you by the depth of their maturity and wisdom, their
capacity for practicality and play. The point—to dance with the
Ineffable. The endpoint—transformation. Mona's experience is a good
example of this.

As we get in touch with our intuitive energies, the question moves
to: How do we encompass these energies daily in a meaningful yet practical manner? We wish to know when, and how, and what, to speak from
the heart, the breath and the belly. These are questions we will explore
as we move onward.

But first we need to look more deeply at some of the issues that
keep women from their body wisdom. No one yet knows when exactly
the spark of divinity that allows a human being self-consciousness enters
the mass of tissue and bone that comprises the body. Therein is the
source ground for our exploration of consciousness, of Soul, in matter.
Nor do we yet understand how a feeling such as anger or sadness can
become the embodied chemistry of an ulcer or a psychological disor-

der, or when a dream or a habitual thought or a memory manifests as a cancer. What we do know from mindbody research, personal experience, and intuition is that there is a vast repository of benevolent wisdom, just beyond the range of our cognitive perceptions, that is waiting to be uncovered.

83

Chapter Five

TENUOUS
BEGINNINGS

*Soul's First Relationships
with Matter*

I went everywhere with longing
in my eyes, until here
in my own house

I felt truth
Filling my sight.

                                    —*Naked Song,* Lalla

NAOMI SAYS SHE HAS NEVER BEEN ABLE TO TOLERATE the wail of
a siren. Never. When she was little she used to feel short of
breath and "sticky" each time she heard one. Recently on a trip to visit
her mother's sister she mentioned her "affliction," and her aunt said,
"Guess that's a reaction to your birth. You were born in an ambulance,
racing toward the hospital, sirens blaring, for over twenty miles." Naomi

was shocked. No one had ever told her she was born in an ambulance. Her family never thought it was important. Sirens have been an intimate birth memory for Naomi, maybe her very first as she pushed her way into consciousness. Naomi also loves strawberry ice cream. As far back as she can remember her mother has kidded her that she developed her taste for the cold treat in utero—it was mother's biggest craving during Naomi's gestation.

Every life event leaves a body memory, some more influential than others. One of the reasons it is so hard for us to come back into our bodies is that they have been the sites of much trauma. Traumatic events leave more potent traces than the majority of daily experiences because of the tension the trauma evokes. Consequently, far more has been written about the obvious trauma of birth, for example, and the psychosomatic imprint of accidents, injuries, illnesses, surgery, sexual abuse, or rape than the insidious affect suffered by the unwanted fetus or the unloved infant or the child whose physical or mental deficits prevent her from giving or receiving love. Equally, the persistence of the seemingly mundane events of pre-birth and early childhood leave just as indelible a mark, shaping the way we feel about being fully present in the world and our capacity to be fully conscious of our place in the daily events we call life. As our sense of self is forming, each trauma, each message that this is not a safe environment or there is no safety here for me, or even the often, more subtle message that somehow we are just not good enough, causes us to shrink emotionally and spiritually from a full claim to our embodiment.

Many of us come into the world unwilling to face even the rudiments of embodied consciousness because the journey has already been too painful. Our soul seems tucked away in some far corner of our matter, unwilling or unable to claim the vitality needed to fulfill the destiny of conscious incarnation. Equally, many of us arrive with a body alive and filled with the experience of being welcomed and celebrated, and we are eager to taste life and all of its flavors. It may be that the first intuitive message we receive at birth is the soul's sensate assessment of whether it is safe to be fully conscious in this body, as it is received by this family.

Joy is easier to receive than pain. Joy is radiant, warming, and sensately expansive. Pain or fear, on the other hand, is constricting. The body recoils—the breath becomes shallow and the viscera tighten in order to sustain the discomfort. The larger the pain, the smaller the body attempts to become. All pain constricts—physical and psychological. Even the tiniest breath or the slightest thought can be felt as risky, too expansive during a constrictive period. Fortunately the bodymind can learn to deal with the most excruciating trauma by "forgetting." Amnesia is the relief employed by the physical intelligence. Amnesia protects the bodymind and the ego's vulnerability, but the pain remains—our unconscious carries the psychological memory and our tissue and bone carry the body memory.

Tor Norretranders, the Danish science writer, in *The User Illusion: Cutting Consciousness Down to Size,* reminds us that the *I* by which we identify ourselves is not in control of our life experiences. The nervous system takes in and assesses over 11 million bits of information per second in order to form our perception of the world and our concept of *me* in the world. What we don't realize is that consciousness deals with fewer than twenty bits of this information per second. All the rest is being discarded and stored in our memory bank, most of which will remain inaccessible and irretrievable by the ego.

Think what this means. The majority of what we perceive is out of reach, filtered by the "me" that is picking and choosing what is most influential, least painful, as our perception of reality is formed. Your ego can register even confusion or ridicule or shame as traumatic, too painful to want to keep in consciousness. Meanwhile the illusion of what is real or not real governs the truth of our fuller range of experience (all those multimillions of bits and pieces stored away in the archives of the unconscious). It is this great repository that your intuition dips into and draws its wisdom from, because our intuition has free access to the unconscious.

Like the fairy tale's wise woman with second sight or the dwarf who holds the key to the jewel box, your intuition transits freely between the illusions of "the real world" and the deeper truth of your full range of perceptions. Only a very small part of our essence—of what we are capable of knowing and what we are capable of becoming—is ever fully in our consciousness. Benevolently that essence, the soul, speaks to us intuitively, symbolically and metaphorically inviting us to deepen—to wake *down,* not up.

Soul can't reach the ego through an image or an intuition until the senses are engaged. Sometimes the intuition is ahead of the ego's capacity to tolerate it—to keep up with the energy coming into consciousness. Frequently a dream will image an illness long before the body becomes symptomatic. If your body is unconscious, nothing will take, and the image will slide off as if your senses are Teflon-coated. Fortunately there are multiple sensate entry points where Soul can stir the imagination, arouse the senses, bring the forgotten into consciousness, and awaken us to our true self, because body memories are not locked into a linear timeframe. Like a dream's images and actions, they exist in a fluid state. Ready and waiting, the sensate visceral record of everything that is important to your somatic, psychological, and spiritual well-being is registered, recorded, and deposited in your somatic memory bank, just waiting to be tapped.

Last week I put on a jacket I hadn't worn for over a year and found a twenty-dollar bill tucked in the pocket. Such a nice surprise! Well, that's a lot like intuition. It brings us what we have tucked away and never really registered we had and when we "find" it, our bodymind is filled with a new energy, a new way of perceiving what we call reality or the facts.

Make no mistake, according to *Gray's Anatomy,* your dear body is an elegant and miraculously sensate instrument. Intricately and practically compact, it is orchestrated by no fewer than fifteen vital organs, supported and protected by 206 bones and 1,200 muscles, fed by 30 trillion blood cells and enervated by 10 billion nerve cells all bathed in exactly the right combination of nutrients by an untold measure of blood vessels and constellations of glands. Every cell knows what its own particular task is. Eleven endocrine glands regulate the rhythms, maintain the defense, and effect the repair of this miracle of embodiment.

Most of the human body is made up of water and a balanced chemistry of fluids that mystify exact replication. Yet, the body is more than tissue and blood, more than a shelter for the ego. Architecturally your body is a vessel of exquisite design in which, in the words of Nikos Kazantzakis, "two streams collide: the ascent towards immortality and the descent towards death." From these two flow the stream of consciousness.

A conscious sensate relationship between the languages of the bodymind and soulful wisdom is always mediated by the strengths and traumas that began with the nonverbal sensory experiences of sufficiency or lack within the womb. For it is here, at the earliest stage of human development, that your body begins to develop a cellular context for the guiding narratives of *trust in* or *fear of* your own embodiment. These two basic building blocks in the endowment of personality and health are fundamental to nearly all of our perceptions about what we are or are not capable of becoming. Here, in the womb, a most obscure and influential body codependency is spawned.

Bewitching Biology

"Our biology," says Christiane Northrup, "is our biography." From the moment of conception, the exquisitely complex matrices of the fetus' physical and emotional development are intimately influenced and shaped by the uterine environment. Whether the womb is a crucible or a chalice, our capacity to tolerate cellular consciousness is defined by our prenatal intrauterine gestalt. The unborn infant is affected as much by what is without as it is affected by what is within. The mother's physical, mental, and emotional state becomes an interactive blending of her internal and external experiences, and she has no choice but to pass that blend on to her fetus. This combination creates the only environmental choice the infant has. All that the mother experiences is translated to the prenate through the mother's endocrinal system. The level of emotional nurturance and stability that is available to or missing for the infant in the womb infuses the prenate with potently influential somatic responses at a nervous system level. We are born carrying a sensate trust in or a fear of the body experiences we have already had. Symbolically, we come into consciousness with a body that is soulfully relaxed and receptive or constricted and cautious.

Memory, dreaming, and REM sleep are already present during gestation. The first cells of the central nervous system appear at twenty-two days of gestation. Brain life is thought to begin between twenty-eight and thirty-two weeks of development; however the hormone connected to memory traces is in operation by the forty-ninth day after conception. The senses can function in utero before they are fully matured anatomically, according to Judith Orloff, M.D., in *Second Sight*. Remarkably, the ear is functional at fourteen weeks of gestation and what the prenate hears influences the quality of development. "Imagine," writes Don Campbell in *The Mozart Effect*, "what effects sounds can have on the delicate cells, tissues and organs. Vibrating sounds form patterns and create energy fields of resonance and movement in the surrounding space. We absorb these energies, and they subtly alter our breath, pulse, blood pressure, muscle tension, skin temperature and other internal rhythms." Our bodymind intelligences are being formed from earliest conception.

Dr. David Cheek, obstetrician and gynecologist, has spent the majority of his adult life researching the effects of the pre- and perinatal environment upon human development. Using a combination of well-researched and documented procedures, he has accumulated an impressive record of pre-birth memories. Regressing the adult back to meaningful in utero events, Cheek has uncovered the individual's capacity to recall accurate memories of pre-birth events. His research shows that as early as between six and eight weeks after gestation, a fetus can accurately sense the mother's reactions to her pregnancy. Favorable or unfavorable, the fetus' body has no choice but to feel and physiologically identify with the reaction. Remarkably, since the hearing mechanisms are not *fully* developed before the fifth month of gestation, these earliest reactions can only be telepathically transmitted to the unborn infant, emphasizing the profound impact and range of nonverbal communication between the developing child and the environment. I have listened to convincing accounts by sonogram specialists and midwives about the capacity of the infant to respond to the mother's touch and move over to one side of the womb so an amniocentesis can be more safely performed.

I suggest to expectant mothers that they regularly place their hands on their bellies and sing favorite childhood songs, camp tunes, or whatever gives them happy childhood memories to the prenate so that after birth, when their little one is crying, they can sing the same tune while holding the baby close to their body. Mothers report that this familiar ritual, begun during pregnancy, is soothing to the baby. The baby viscerally as well as aurally senses the vibration of Mother's voice and can feel at home in her infant body. Later these little ones indicate a special affinity for that song—that rhythm.

The umbilical cord has its own unique function in shaping body-mind perceptions. It becomes an unimpeded feedback mechanism directly infusing the rapidly developing fetal body with the hormonal results of the maternal emotions. According to Cheek and others, mixed signals of delight and distress are telepathically communicated, mother to fetus, from the moment of conception and irrefutably affect the fetal survival responses after birth. The difficulty with these intrauterine communiqués is that the fetus receives them in a nondiscriminatory context. The result—the prenate is unable to separate itself from the experience, so that "every intrauterine message becomes a personal one." As Mother witnesses a movie scene in which her body is flooded with hormones because the scene is frightening, her body telegraphs the experience to her unborn child not as a temporary entertainment but as an actual lived event. In utero the somatic-emotional field between mother and child is virtually unimpeded. Your relationship with your soul cannot be redeemed unless the sensate body is refined and brought into a fuller consciousness of the influence of body's memories. We cannot embrace what we refuse to feel.

To add to the complexity of the immediate susceptibility of the unborn child in its telepathic connection to the mother is the evidence that the mother's personal feelings of acceptance and love toward her fetus are *overridden* by her negative emotional reactions to her environment (i.e., an illness, the economy, world events, even the quality and rhythm of the images and activities she selects for recreation). Apparently no matter how secure the mother is with her pregnancy, or how happy about her conception, the cumulative ongoing emotional climate of the mother is received by the fetus with just as much, if not more, potency as the mother's love.

Fair or not, it is the nature of human gestation that the bodymind of the prenate is shaped and tempered by the maternal environment. Neither you nor your mother have control over this phenomenon. How complicated or fair it may be is not the issue. These are all romantic notions of how life should be. This sort of romantic or sentimental attitude toward life seduces the ego into a love affair with its most under-developed aspects. Pregnancy, gestation, and birth are an intricate matrix of influences far beyond the control of the mother, no matter how she feels about her pregnancy and a very real tempering in the development of the crucible from which each of us must refine our own personal sense of relationship to the Ineffable—to Spirit.

In many ways we can argue that these first telepathically transmitted communications form an influential rudimentary somatic consciousness preforming the first irresistible stage in the intuitive development of *every* human life. The neonate's in utero absorption of the mother's emotional matrix becomes the foundation for later psychological strength or vulnerability regarding somatic trust and fear in what the bodymind offers, including intuition.

When the mother is not able to be at ease, receptive to the new life she is carrying, the unborn child cannot bond with the maternal body rhythms in a secure and life-affirming way. Al Pesso in *Experience in Action* is another strong voice in the support of the responsible evidence that the initial building blocks of bodymind development begin in utero as the fetus somatically absorbs and mirrors the maternal relationship. He too has found that subtle body deficits, developed through the unavoidable emotional and physiologic codependency of the maternal-fetal environment, are later expressed by the bodymind in one or more significant pre-birth metaphors. Pesso defines the physical manifestation of these subtle body deficits as an emotional inability to feel nurtured, supported, protected, limited (well-contained), respected, to have a place, or to claim an inalienable sense of birthright—to feel at home, in matter. In his work with movement and psychotherapy, Pesso confirms that any of these deficits can become a governing physical, psychological, or spiritual symptom when an individual is confronted with a situation that requires more fortitude in one area or another than the original fetal-mother bond could provide a basis for. I have found that the intuitive body can be of immeasurable help in healing an unfulfilled basic need.

We experience the immediate affects of an unfulfilled basic need when as adults we become confused between the instinctual pull of "need" versus the more focused state of "want." When we are captured body and psyche by a sense of overwhelming need, the affectual result is usually instinctual. Because it is instinctual, it appears as a perceived threat to our survival. This threat is unmediated, bypassing any focused adult state that can sense a deep desire, determine what to do about it (including tolerating the limitations of doing anything just yet), and then make conscious choices about how to get the need met. Instead it stems from a preverbal dependent state where we only wish to be taken care of. Now! When a woman doesn't know how to tell the difference between *I need* and *I want* if her desire is unfulfilled, she will find herself filled either with rage from feeling ignored or abandoned, or despair at feeling unloved, unlovable. The preverbal bodymind needs what it needs and feels only desperation and abandonment when it is not forthcoming. In this state no intuitive information can get through. On the other hand, the adult bodymind has the ability to recognize the yearning of an inner unloved part of the self, to listen to the need, to respect and comfort the hunger or the ache, and then create a focused resolve, an "I want" that will meet the need. SCM is especially effective in bridging the gap between the instinctual need stemming from pre-birth and the more focused stage of "I want." Each time we recover a lost or abandoned part of our instinctual energy it is made available to us as creativity, sexuality, and play. Our embodied intuition can only benefit by nurturing and protecting the lost parts of the self as we grow them into fully expressive and creative aspects of the authentically embodied woman.

Basic Needs and Metaphoric Body Wisdom

Pesso, along with his wife, Diane, developed the Pesso-Boyden System Psychomotor Psychotherapy. Using a combination of psychodrama, movement, and rescripting, the individual tells her remembrance of an event while she enrolls other members of the group as symbolic figures (mother, father) or objects (like a favorite car or a location) in order to kinesthetically reproduce the original experience and recreate a more favorable outcome (rescripting).

Studying with Pesso for four years and his colleague Jackie Damgaard for ten, I found that the basic human needs they delineate as originating in utero are valuable for helping women regain their metaphoric body wisdom. For example: feeling weak in the lower half of the legs may translate into the metaphors "weak-kneed," or "not a leg to stand on." These metaphors emphasize a developmental lack of trust in support, since the legs actually support the entire body in our developmental movement to mobility and uprightness.

Such body metaphors create an image that nonverbally clarifies how the deficit is inhibiting the natural expression of full embodiment. Remember Louise's chills? When I asked if she was shaking like a leaf she replied, "No, like two pebbles in a rain barrel." My leaf image fell on deaf ears while her image of pebbles in a rain barrel resonated for her on every level. Leaf metaphors would lead us to a dead end. Louise's intuitive wisdom "knew" that "pebbles" would lead her to the die that her Gambler rattled in the spiritual game of chance that she was playing. As she shook like two pebbles, her knees trembled and Louise could literally feel her rubbery legs—her shaky underpinning—as long as she relied upon her faulty attitude. Her body intuition was clearly underscoring what Louise knew but was ignoring at the peril of her own psychological security. When Louise followed the intuitive suggestion of her symptom, to shake until she became conscious of what mattered, her movements expressed the subtle body message clearly. The Gambler metaphor became an instant ally rather than the enemy he had first appeared to be. Louise was not to gamble away her inner wisdom, her soul-filled resources, unless she was willing to live with shaky underpinning, chilled to the bone.

I am going to describe the Pessos' descriptions of intrauterine deficits because I feel they are well thought out, tested across many years, and very useful for anyone wanting to unblock their relationship to their body wisdom. Through personal experience, I have made additional contributions, relating to the pre-birth development of trust or lack thereof in embodiment. In many ways these basic needs describe the ideal universal relationship between the unborn child and the intrauterine environment. Ideals, however, are for the gods—humans are imperfect and no infant comes into the world without one or more of these needs somewhat, or a lot, unmet. An unmet intrauterine need creates a psycho- (psyche) somatic (body) vulnerability, a weakened link, either emotionally or physically, in the chain of relationship between the ego and the soul. Your wounded or tender places, these less sturdy intrapersonal vulnerabilities, are the doorways through which soul can reach out to the ego and your intuition can speak to you metaphorically about your Self.

Combining the Pessos' differentiation of "Basic Human Needs" with my understanding of the bodymind responses of trust in or fear of embodiment, I have created the following. For clarity the Pessos' contributions are in italics.

Basic Human Needs and Their Developmental Responses of Trust In or Fear Of Conscious Embodiment

1. **Nurturance** Represented by all the intrauterine qualities of *filling up and emptying out;* of feeling nourished. *During infancy, the breast and the provision of adequate and sufficient sucking reinforces the goodness of the nurturance experienced in the womb.*

> **Trust** Shows up in the body as the natural movement of digestion and elimination; takes place highlighting that this bodymind can trust the nutrients that are being received and let what is not necessary pass through; satisfaction is also evidenced by the *curling movement of the toes* as the infant feeds. When an infant feels satisfied emotionally or physically, her toes will reflexively stretch and curl.

> **Fear** Appears as *biting and chewing tendencies.* Later there can be self-mutilation such as nail biting, or hair or cuticle tearing when feeling emotionally stressed. A deficit in a good enough sense of nurturance can lead to *an inability to recognize your own needs and ask for them.*

2. **Support** Influenced by the *consistent cushioning effect of the total surround of the amniotic fluid, the body's first terra firma.*

> **Trust** *Confidence in the long bones and a flexible strong spine.* Even under stress there is limited fear of letting oneself down when an adequate sense of feeling well and safely supported has developed in utero. This later becomes the basis for the development of a psychological connection between a sense of self-worth, power, and a strong voice.

> **Fear** *Inability to stand upright; weak or locked knees and ankles and curvature of the spine. Fear of falling down.* A deficit in support can lead to difficulties with independence and risk taking—there is no bodymind connection between the feet and the center of gravity—the navel.

3. **Protection** *An invasion-free womb.*

> **Trust** *The world is a safe place. The body is a safe environment.*
>
> **Fear** *No safe place, expressed as body vulnerability especially front and upper torso and the back of the neck.* Protection deficits can lead to an inability to feel safe in new experiences, to speak out or be autonomous, or to stand fully upright.

4. **Limits** *The walls of the womb provide shape and containment. This is the first rudimentary body sense of mortality. The body that I am is all that I am; not all that Is.*

> **Trust** *Able to contain self; provide a well-contained ego.* An ability to acquire and value impulse control and a respect for boundaries between self and other. An ability to maintain an observing ego that is unthreatened by what it does not understand.
>
> **Fear** *That you will fly apart, are uncontainable, omnipotent, that your feelings will be too much for others to handle or contain. This deficit may leave you with a fear of your own power and the distortion that if you aren't careful you can overwhelm others with your strong emotions.* In an effort to compensate either an exaggeration of self-effacement or bullying can develop. *The entire boundary of the skin is affected* with metaphors such as "jumping out of my skin," "beside myself," and "all over the place" appropriate here.

5. **Place** *The development of a sense of unconditional acceptance physically affirmed by the bonding that occurs immediately after birth and through unimpeded eye contact and firm touch between mother and infant as she is fed.*

> **Trust** *A sense of belonging,* of tribal connection.
>
> **Fear** *A pervasive sense of abandonment, eviction, no inalienable right to be.* This deficit leads to shyness, insecurity, a pervasive sense of disconnection, and an inability to identify with and relate to others. Felt as a tissue-level mourning or yearning, a pervasive sense of orphanage.

6. **Respect** A unimpeded existence with the space and freedom to become uniquely yourself.

> **Trust** There is room for me to be uniquely myself. *My existence is welcomed, acceptable.*
>
> **Fear** Without this kind of intrauterine experience, an individual is born with a somatic sense of *a mortgaged existence, a sense that your existence carries a price.*

7. **Birthright** A culmination of all the basic needs being met. A sense of conscious incarnation, of having a right to be in your body, in the world, in this family, ensouled. (While I was studying with Pesso, he did not elaborate on this particular basic need. I have continued to use and develop the concept, and he too may have expanded upon it in later work.)

While the Pessos' focus is on the psychological impact of the developmental deficits in basic needs, my work has extended into the broader context of the relationship of the body-mind-heart and soul. For instance, when the psychosomatic issue of support appears in the body, psychologically the sufferer may respond to images such as "weak in the knees, spine like jelly, brought to my knees, bones turned to water," while the story the body tells may encompass a spiritual dilemma or a heart's desire that is unfulfilled even though the psychological intelligence of the bodymind is doing OK with issues of support. I believe Justine's experience helps make this clearer.

When Justine first came to see me I immediately sensed the gifts of her childhood. She grew up in a multigenerational home where children were loved, enjoyed, and expected to behave without their spirits being broken. By age nineteen, she had traveled widely with family, with friends, and on her own. She had a clear sense of purpose, a zest for life, a well-educated imagination, and a good marriage. By her report this is a woman whose life experiences belie any evidence of a notable deficit of basic needs. What then, I wondered, was the issue? Justine said she found herself in the midst of a mystery. While in Rome on vacation she began awakening with a melody playing "just beyond my consciousness" that stayed with her throughout the day, evading identification. She noticed that she felt a mix of "bittersweetness," a hint of indescribable joy, and a flavor of deep sorrow. The experience came to a peak one morning as Justine was walking across a plaza. "I stepped into a patch of bright sunlight and every detail of the pavement stood out in relief. I was flooded with the melody and the bittersweetness it brings. I could do nothing for a long while—seconds, minutes, who knows how long—I was arrested in mid-stride and transported elsewhere." Now Justine feels she has to solve this riddle. What matters so very much that her ears, her heart, her very being is engaged?

Justine symbolically recreated the plaza pavement on my office floor. She placed two chairs where the columned entry gate stood and laid out sheets of typing paper to represent the paving stones. Almost immediately she entered *kairos* time. Her inner sense of what she was doing responded as it had in Rome. Justine began to hum and feel the bittersweetness. Her body began to curl forward and then relax, curl and then relax. Justine begin to chant first "sweet" then "bittersweet" as she curled inward and then stretched upward. Soon her movements took precedence and she followed where she was led.

At the end of the hour Justine sat quietly with tears rolling freely down her cheeks: "It's the baby I never knew whether I was pregnant with or not. It's the baby come to tell me it's OK one way or the other—it's OK." In her early twenties Justine though she was pregnant for two months, but she was in Europe and decided to wait until she returned to her personal physician to find out. One morning she was "crossing a sunlit plaza in Spain" when she was filled with cramps and her period started, "heavier than ever before and painful." She went in to a public restroom in a nearby cathedral where she felt a clot pass, relieving her cramps. She philosophically went on with her life, since she had "formed no particular attachment yet to the idea of pregnancy." Justine would have said she had never felt impeded by any lack of the basic needs as Pesso describes them. However, when she followed her body movements she uncovered a deep inner longing to nurture someone the way she was nurtured. Justine's nurturance needs were so well met in utero and after that she feels the bittersweet loss of having no baby of her own with whom to continue the legacy.

I offer this example to keep in balance the fuller spectrum of the basic human needs as they affect us both in their fullness and in their absence. Either deficit or sufficiency affects the bodymind in some way. Your subtle body will offer one resolution to compensate for a deficit, your physical bodymind another, and your ego yet a third, each a variation of the same purpose—to find relief and become more fully conscious. When we remain unconscious in spite of our intuition, than the energy invariably becomes an illness to help uncover the truth behind the fiction we are living out.

Your ego compensates for these early deficits with its own intricate fiction especially designed for your psychological survival. I may ask you if you feel marginal, anxious, and like an outsider in a new situation. Your ego may tough it out, protesting that such a proposal is an exaggeration, you feel a little vulnerable, sure. But anxious, regressed, scared? No way! Now address the same question to the body and ask yourself to let your body express how you truly feel, and your body cannot and will not tough it out. Your belly will growl, your posture slump, your color change, your breathing become more rapid or shallow. Your body has no fiction. All it has is cellular integrity. What you are capable of as an adult is always wed to who you are at your most basic psychosomatic level.

Developmental Metaphors and the Chakra System

I believe that all human development, psychological, spiritual, and somatic, follows the developmental metaphors first begun in the womb. The degree to which each metaphor (Nurturance, Trust, Limits, Support, Protection, Place, and Birthright) becomes an unalienable life quality in our physical bodymind and a strength in our psychological

FETAL METAPHOR	ENERGY (CHAKRA) CENTER	EMOTIONAL CENTER	PERSONAL ATTRIBUTE	
Birthright *Conscious Embodiment Psyche vs. Soma Split	**Crown** (Top of the head)	**Spiritual** Self-commitment	Purpose Wisdom Altruism	Finitude Humility Joy
Place *Acceptance vs. Alienation	**3rd Eye** (Forehead) Sensory Centers, Brain, Imagination, Perception	**Self-confidence** Can make a place for self alone or in community	Focus Clarity Insight	Vision Morality Imagination
Respect *Worth vs. Worthlessness	**Throat** Thyroid, Esophagus, Neck, Stomach	**Self-expression** Ability to speak up and out	True Voice Truth	Integrity Naming
Nurturance *Love vs. Hate	**Heart** Breasts, Lungs	**Self-love** Able to nurture self and others	Creativity Compassion Receptivity	Thriving Relationship
Limits *Control vs. Chaos	**Solar Plexus** (Midpoint. bet. rib cage/navel) Liver, Spleen, Diaphragm, Sm. Intestine, Upper Spine	**Self-respect** Sense of boundary	Patience Authority Autonomy	Influence Competency
Support *Confidence vs. Lack of Self-esteem	**Sacral** (Pelvic Basin)	**Self-esteem** Personal grounding, personal identity	Generosity Security	Sexuality Sensuality
Protection *Security vs. Helplessness	**Base** (Coccyx/Sacrum) Sacrum, Tailbone, Legs, Feet	**Self-Awakening** Discrimination/choice	Standpoint Choices	Independence Curiosity

*Issues of vulnerability

bodymind determines the extent to which we are trusting of our embodied intuition and spiritual vitality. To paraphrase another—Soul without a birthright is a ghost, and body without an enlivened soul is a corpse.

Western psyches have not been taught to rely upon the Eastern concept of energy called *chakras,* but they have a lot to teach us as we attempt to understand our bodymind and our intuition. In particular, each chakra (energy center) corresponds to a particular fetal developmental metaphor, emotional center, and personal attribute associated with a fully embodied relationship with the deep feminine.

As you can see, the emotional centers of the bodymind are like stepping stones on the pathway of conscious embodiment. These stepping stones correlate with the stages of body consciousness in the development of the personal attributes of selfhood and their metaphoric descriptions. Now I offer some ways to work with each chakra to help balance and heal any old issues stored there.

The Base of Your Bodymind: Self-Awakening (The First Chakra)

Location At the base of your spine, often called your tailbone or coccyx, and including the anus and pelvic floor.

Movement Tightening and releasing your buttocks and your sphincter muscles as you use the affirmation below. Side B of Gabrielle Roth's *Totem* is useful to play while using SCM to work with the base chakra.

Affirmation I have deep roots in this body, and I can trust what matters to me.

As you begin to claim the energy of your coccyx, you have to come to terms with the emotional energies of waking up, claiming your family roots, putting down your own roots. This is the emotional center for making choices. These choices will awaken energy in your feet and legs as you begin to discriminate consciously between what you need and what you want.

As you integrate this work, the personal attribute of an intuitive *standpoint* emerges. You begin to know instinctively what you stand for, when to put your foot down, and when to move on. Each of these—the energy center of the coccyx and the emotional center of self-awakening—strengthen any deficit you felt in utero around cellular protection and vulnerability. A fetus cannot put her foot down, nor can her nervous system guarantee that her tenuous hold in the uterus will produce roots strong and unshakable enough to prevent eviction. If her endocrinal system is threatened by the uterine environment she enters the world tentatively, not able fully to trust her own body.

Developing the strength of a consciously embodied standpoint grounded in a reliable sense of intuitive wisdom rewrites your personal pre-birth history. Awakening the base chakra energies of your body will lead you to dealing with all sorts of family issues and your relationship with tribal affairs such as religion and social rules. As you intuitively work on your standpoint, you will be working on the skeletal strength of your bodymind and your emotional self-awakening. This is not consciousness raising; it is consciousness deepening.

Sacral Limits: Self-Esteem
(The Second Chakra)

Location The span of your lower back between the hip joints and down to the coccyx. If you place the backs of your hands across this area with your forefingers pointing down and meeting several inches above your anus, you can feel the energy center of the second chakra.

Movement Begin with Roth's *Initiation,* side B. Lying on your back, allow the spontaneous movement of your belly and hips to express this center's energy. Follow your impulses until they take you to your feet as you continue to move spontaneously; pause and contemplate the energy, absorb it and wait for your hips and belly to move again.

Affirmation The deep feminine is creatively alive within, midwifing the rebirth of my Self. I alone own my sexuality and my pelvic energies.

With a strengthened standpoint you can open yourself to the rich fertile darkness of your pelvic basin, untangling your pelvic energies from the historical shame that is projected onto female sexuality. The sacrum is the somatic point at which all that is seeding in you is deposited. This energy center affects the development of your self-esteem and rewrites your pre-birth history around boundary. As you seek what matters to your second chakra, a clearer, more definite sense of choice about where you begin and others end develops. As you embrace the affect of the rules, ideas, concepts, and commitments that you will or will not live by, a keen somatic sense of personal limits emerges, teaching you how far you will go and why. In the second chakra of the body we learn how to be creatively sexual, to give birth to our creativity, to deal with the issues of shame that we are flawed because of our femaleness. Omnipotence, the mistaken notion that if we express our full power we will be overwhelming or too much, must be dealt with as well.

The sacrum is often called the holy bone, the cradle of all that is fertile and fermenting as soul and body blend. I prefer to call it the *seed-bone*. Working with body intuition and your pelvic basin affects your inner strength about your reproductive organs, gynecological concerns, sexuality, your bowels, and your holding in, holding back, or holding on.

Once you have claimed your standpoint, your sacral energies will provide you with insight into your emotional ability to contain your energy as you wait for an idea or an instinct to come to maturity. This is the area of your creative mobility. Here you can learn much about your omnipotence, your fear that your sexual energies and your desires are too much for others to tolerate—that they will somehow be destructive or overwhelming. Here also you can learn much about your capacity for limits. For experimenting with how little or how much it takes to claim a deepened sense of self-esteem—of truly liking who you are and what you are becoming.

Midpoints: Self-Respect
(The Third Chakra)

Location Solar plexus, midway between the rib cage and your navel. Includes your upper spine, liver, spleen, diaphragm, and small intestine.

Movement Using Mike Rowland's *Fairy Ring* side A, focus on your breath, feeling the boundary created by your diaphragm, that internal band of tissue that encircles your body just below your rib cage and expands and contracts with the expansion and contraction of your lungs. Contemplate how the upper torso is joined to the lower torso at this chakra. The solar plexus energies of the bodymind affect the balancing and blending of the energies of the lower chakras with those of the upper chakras. As you move, allow yourself to experience unfolding from the more primal energies of the coccyx and the pelvic basin into the energies of uprightness, sturdiness, and flexible stability.

Affirmation I claim my identity as a fully spiritual woman, upright with a clear and evolving sense of self-respect.

The solar plexus carries the energy of emerging into a fuller consciousness of your intuitive individuality, a clearer self-image. Solar energy is the energy of focused self-respect. Here the embodied sense of uprightness, developing a spine, a backbone, is present. You are rewriting your prenatal history of issues around identity, individuality, and merger. Awakening your energetic relationship with your spine allows your intuition to traverse the endarkened regions of instinct, of pelvis, bowel, and belly, and the enlightened regions of expression, compassion, and empathy.

Just as your diaphragm encircles your body at this chakra point, so also does your increased sense of dignity and self-respect encircle and contain you. As you experience spontaneous movements in this area, you are deepening your insights about your anger and your capacity to integrate what you are able to stomach. Your ability to move, bend, be flexible, fluid, or "hang tough" are metaphoric companions for this exploration. You will discover as you tighten your navel against your spine on the exhale and release your belly as you inhale a visceral potency expressing through the undulations of your womanly body.

Heart: Self-Love
(The Fourth Chakra)

Location Center of the chest. Includes the breasts and the lungs.

Movement Using Paul Winter's *Wolf Eyes,* turn your inner eye toward the yearning of your heart. Moving contemplatively while listening to your heart's desires, pause periodically to bring them to consciousness. This is the energetic area of compassion and relationship. Love your sweet matter and bless the heart that rhythmically pulses you into being.

Affirmation I am able to love and be loved. I accept the nurturance of the deep feminine that radiates from within with each and every beat of my heart.

All of your intuitions about nurturance are located in this area. As you are able to nurture yourself intuitively, your capacity for self-love will grow, opening your heart to connections and companionship as easily as you once closed the door. This is the area of expansive receptivity with no fear of falling apart, losing your rhythm, or breaking in two. When your feet are grounded, your spine upright, and your creativity expressive, your heart can speak intuitively with no fear of rejection or lack of fulfillment. This area affects the breasts and the glands of the upper torso. This is the area where the heart, lungs, and thymus carry the emotional embodiment of the bodymind. Your ability to listen and respond to the heart's desires will increase your capacity for joy, quiet acceptance, and intense feelings.

Throat: Self-Expression
(The Fifth Chakra)

Location Between the chin and the shoulders. Includes the neck, esophagus, stomach, and thyroid.

Movement Speaking and sounding your name. Chanting in rhythm with your breath. Using any meditative chant, such as the *Benedictine Chants,* contemplatively follow the spontaneous movements of your body while expressing your own sound.

Affirmation My voice has strength and integrity. I am fully able to speak my own truth.

As your heart opens and your lungs breathe more deeply, you will find your own pitch, your own voice. The throat is the center of communication and the intaking of *Pneuma,* of vitality and spiritedness. Issues of trust and the tensions of safety of expression are rewritten here as you learn to voice your standpoint and speak your heart's desire. The throat is a channel for both ingesting and expelling energy. Personally this center expresses your intuitive truth. The throat can either separate or connect the head and the body, carrying energy for continuity and resistance. The desire to speak one's heart and one's mind relates this center to the base chakra and a strong or a weakened standpoint. Here you can deal with feelings of self-worth or worthlessness. Naming yourself will allow you to declare that you have rebirthed your self into an intentional consciousness of purpose and integrity.

Third Eye: Insight, Self-Confidence (The Sixth Chakra)

Location Center of the forehead. Includes the eyes, ears, nose, brain, imagination, and perception.

Movement Using Galway, *Song of the Seashore,* while focusing on your breath, begin at the chin and tighten and loosen your lips, your nostrils, wrinkle your nose, puff out and then suck in your cheeks, wrinkle your forehead, squeeze your eyes shut and then open them wide. Rub the palms of your hands together and then place them over your closed lids for a few seconds. Gently pull your ear lobes and insert your little fingers gently into your ears and shake them a bit. Massage your scalp from the base of your skull across the top of your head, ending with a gentle massage of your face. Using your tongue scrub your teeth and gums, the roof of your mouth, and the insides of your lips, ending by moistening your lips. Blow out and take a big breath. Stretch your lips in a wide smile while frowning hard. Allow yourself to laugh and laugh again until you are belly laughing. Hug yourself and move expansively all over, stretching and delighting in your third-eye energies.

Affirmation I welcome the insight and vision of my intuition that guides and leads me always.

This center links you with an interior spiritual community by uniting all the levels of self-development Providing inner vision, you are linked to the family of mankind grounded in your emotional development of self-confident wisdom and acuity. The fetal body metaphor of birthright is now fulfilled. This energetic center affects inner and outer vision—the eyes, the ears, and the head.

Because this is the mental center of the bodymind, your intuitive work in this area will deepen your insight while sharpening and clarifying your intellectual focus. Here you are claiming the energies of your natural birthright to self-confidently feel at home alone or in community. Closing your eyes and entering the cathedral of your imagination you will step into time outside of time: into the river of soul.

The Crown: Self-Commitment (The Seventh Chakra)

Location The crown, the top of the head. Includes your dreams, meditations, and intuitions.

Movement Use your favorite meditation tape or one such as *Miracles* by Rob Whitesides. Sit or stand quietly and empty your mind of any focus except that of your breathing. As your inner rhythms fill you, allow the spontaneous movements of your body to draw you into a contemplative relationship with the deep feminine. Release all sense of time or place and simply be.

Affirmation Give me the eyes to see and the ears to hear. Teach me and I will learn.

The crown chakra encompasses all the personal and emotional centers of the bodymind, balancing standpoint with compassion, creativity with waiting, power with humility, uprightness with flexibility, love with limits, and logic with intuition.

Awakening to a sense of self-commitment you open to the embodiment of the transcendent as it relates to the deep feminine. This chakra combines the energies of the masculine and the feminine, of Spirit and Soul. This vitality moves your focus from the external world to your spiritual interiority.

All reality is perceived with renewed energy. The stability of this energy is pervasively reassuring. Embodying the quiet yet undeniable relationship between your Self and a benevolently mentoring intuition you find you are never without a birthright. Life takes on a depth of new meaning. Contained by the Ineffable, if only for thirty minutes a day, you cannot deny the profound possibilities of consciously embodied intuition. Here you will lay claim to a cleanly honed acuity, a sense of nonjudgmental wisdom and of soul's purpose. Humility and service are present as well.

Coming to Body Consciousness

As we have been seeing in this chapter, the imprint of the maternal-fetal bond is, according to Joseph Pearce in *Magical Child,* "like a time bomb for which none of the parties to the crime has to pay for the explosion takes place in slow fusion over the years...." Further, "No matter how abstract our explorations of controlled thought and created reality, the mind draws its energy from the brain, which draws its energy from the body matrix, which draws its energy from the earth matrix." The fundamental life of every cell is basic to the fundamental life of the entire organism, and the state of consciousness in each cell is fundamental to the range of consciousness in the individual.

Fearing that body consciousness will awaken old wounds and events too painful to bare is erroneous. Consciousness in the body is always balanced by the entire bodymind as the body, mind, heart, and soul unite to share the experience and participate in the healing. What will not heal is to force consciousness in an interpretative or premature manner. What is always healing is to trust in the bodymind's intuitive sense of homeostasis—of what is needed now and just how much. Intuition helps to bridge the disparity between a limiting belief about ourself and the truth of what is possible.

That's because metaphors counterbalance the concretization of a belief. There is a world of difference between feeling like or as a dunce and believing that you are a dunce. The flexible *like* or *as* adds a fluidity of choice that the restrictive concretized belief *am* or *are* won't allow. To be born mortal is to suffer the natural order of imperfection—to suffer also the capacity for self-reflection that allows us to grow and change. Our capacity for a relationship with soul begins viscerally, not intellectually. It moves through the bodymind fluidly mitigating against stasis as a double helix, half of the spiral pointing us toward consciousness, the other toward instinct.

Stasis is anathema to growth and change. Static memory is a curse. Metaphoric memory is a muse. Metaphors weave silvery webbed bridges of spiritual steel across the divide between consciousness and instinct, providing psychospiritual footing between the imperfections of mortality and blessings of god-likeness. Invite the metaphor to ignite your imagination, enliven your body, and challenge the attitude of your ego consciousness just enough to shift your interior perspective when you are intellectually unable to see any possibility yourself.

METAPHORIC TRUTHS

Try taking any symptom, a headache, anything that is troubling you, and find the metaphor that describes it best. For example, a migraine can be imaged as something that is going against my (mi) grain. The metaphor will turn a concrete symptom into a fluid possibility.

Now sit quietly and ask yourself (for example), What part of my body is most affected by this headache? Don't assume it is your head. Follow your intuition and just listen and observe. When you feel you have an idea or a hunch, then ask your body what movement will fill the need your headache represents. Allow yourself to follow your body-mind no matter how silly or unrelated the impulse seems. When you are finished record what you have experienced. Now find a way to fill that need before you have another migraine. Will your migraines disappear? I can't say. What I can promise you is a deeper understanding of what is going against your grain and a richer possibility for living a more authentic life—with or without the migraines. An unexamined symptom awakens the fear of the victim. An examined symptom awakens the strength of the oracle.

It will not take you long to begin to see how an early belief about your ability to be fully conscious in the world and in your body is restricting you as a symptom. Germs, genes, and accidents absolutely create symptoms and illnesses. How we relate to and learn from these symptoms is pure gold.

In This Land Flow Feelings

The greatest difficulty when working from the body seems to come when translating the sensations of the bodymind into feelings. Until a woman can identify what she feels, she cannot utilize her body consciousness to accept and express the full range of her instincts. Lacking either the freedom or the capacity to identify and name a feeling, she is developmentally stuck in the regressive child state of "I *need*" rather than the individuated adult state of "I *want*." How often have you thought, I don't know what I feel, all I know is that I *need* "it" to go away. There is psychological freedom in being able to differentiate between feelings— to say, I feel sad, and further, I *want* to end this conversation, or relationship, or whatever is the source of the sadness.

At the beginning of each SCM group, we each check in somatically. Participants begin to detach from the external world by focusing on the breath, attending to the body, and observing what feeling s they find within. Many, at first, have such limited experience with identifying a feeling that they describe their feelings with emotionless detachment:

"My chest feels like a heavy weight is on it."

"What does that heavy weight *feel* like?"

"Oh, I don't know. Maybe like pressure."

"Try the words: *sad, mad, glad, bad*. Will one of these fit?"

Basic descriptions are the rudimentary foundation for what will soon become an elegantly specific vocabulary of sensations and emotions. Eventually the same person will check in with a report that she feels tender or determined or excited and vulnerable.

Each feeling can be accurately located in the body as a specific sensation or a temperature shift. As a participant becomes more acutely aware of how she feels and where that feeling seems to affect her the most, she begins to develop an increasing trust in her body language and its wisdom. Participants begin to appreciate and rely upon the complexities of a lexicon of feelings as they learn to identify the simultaneous presence of several different body "messages."

At this point, instinct and feelings may appear to compete with one another. It is not unusual for someone to remark, "I am feeling OK about how I was treated, yet I have a primitive urge to scream or to strike out—and—there's a funny pain in my left knee." (A note here: Intellectually the response might be to suggest that the individual "strike out" by punching something while "screaming," which may or may not be what the bodymind is suggesting at all. A knee pain may indicate that the striking out is an impulse to kick, to draw upon the focused energy in the lower half of the body—not punch or swing the arms. Kicking often leads to putting one's foot down, indicating that a stronger standpoint is emerging, since the foot is the part of the body that stands beneath us, carrying the full weight of the total body.)

In doing this work, it is important to not jump to an interpretative conclusion about what you are feeling. That's because, as I've learned by watching literally thousands of SCM sessions, the body's own choice of response will unerringly take you straight back to the basic need that lies obscured behind the feeling. The instinctual response is pure and unadulterated by should's or should not's. I've seen kicking out turn into a dance, a leaden remembrance of abandonment, a playful game, and a rage-filled expression of hatred toward genocide. That's why it's important to make no assumptions of meaning, but allow the movement to create the metaphor intuitively so you will know what it means for you at this moment.

Often, allowing one part of your body to "strike out" while another part of the body responds in a decidedly different way creates a graphic picture of an internal struggle between the ego and the Self. More often this inner conflict works itself out in more debilitating ways. There's an old saw that says neurosis is holding tightly to your own wrist while fretting that you can't get loose, and psychosis is turning to someone else and accusing them of holding you. Meanwhile you are blind to how you and you alone are holding yourself captive with your faulty perspective.

Stepping into the river of your bodymind and asking who, or what, is moving you in this elaborate intricate ballet of body and soul can uncover an intuitive marionette master choreographing the movements with hidden strings. A string to the heart and it races; to the gut and it loosens; to the genitals and the passion flees; to the mind and we are dizzied; and so on and so on. A body belief built around an early preverbal, pre-birth even, deficit will autonomously act like a magnet. Outside of reason, the belief is attracting all manner of evidence to reinforce its primal influence while manipulating your physical, emotional, and attitudinal strings.

Charlene was well-recognized and appreciated for the huge murals she created. Her medium was a blend of enamels and thinners. After seventeen years, she developed vertigo every time she remained on a scaffold for more than fifteen minutes. At first she was convinced she was anemic (as she had been in childhood), then allergic to the fumes from the paint (her mother has many allergies), then she had her eyes and ears checked (because no one in her family could take much height without succumbing to vertigo). Nothing. At the same time she developed a desire to braid her hair in the plaits she'd worn one summer while roaming around the coastline of New England.

When she came into the movement group she reported she felt "excited" about painting and yet she also felt mildly "itchy" every time she entered her studio. Was it possible that something was under her skin? "No, I don't think so. I love my painting and my work." So we turned to her body. Another group member intuitively offered to braid Charlene's hair. Then as Charlene imagined entering her studio, her body refused to climb the ladder to the scaffold, yet her feet were full of energy. Focusing on her feet she shuffled them rapidly while reflecting, "This energy," she said, "is causing me to itch. I can't go forward and I don't want to just stand still." Eventually Charlene connected her desire to plait her hair with a deeper desire to do landscape painting of the coastal scenery she loved that one wonderful summer. Charlene's body was refusing to allow her ego to overrule her deeper desire to make a change. Eventually she will have to resolve the desire for change that she is resisting if she doesn't want to sicken herself. I've found that desire is usually an intuitively rich expression of something the soul must have if you are to thrive.

Desire is an affair of the heart with a rhythm and a cadence that deeply affects our respiration. Ignored, a desire can govern the rhythms of the heart in all sorts of assertive ways. Mostly it can lend an under-current of generalized anxiety to life.

Transparent Melodies

Your body's heart center has its own primal counterpoint of seventy-two beats a minute. Raise the beat of a musical piece above this base-line and a somatic acceleration of energy will match the increase. John Philip Sousa capitalizes on this with the energetic upbeat of the march. The vigor of a march increases our excitation levels while raising our anxiety level as well. For the majority of us the experience is pleasur-able—we want more. Anxiety has its place in the energizing influx of rhythms that please and excite us. Taken to an extreme, anxiety can be harmful, causing us to feel as if we have quivering unstable cells. Hence the expressions, "I have the jitters" or "the heebie-jeebies."

In healing, certain musical compositions can be used in conjunction with movement to maximize the experience. A relatively new composition, anxiolytic music, is one such benefactor. Anxiolytic music is designed to closely replicate the natural orchestrations of the human body's own rhythms. Created by choosing only those instruments that will interrupt neither the cadence nor the syncopation of breath and pulse, the harmony of woodwind, strings, and xylophone join the piano in creating a musical chalice of nondirective yet distinctly soothing sound. Designed to reduce anxiety, anxiolytic music avoids programming the listener with the seductiveness of a distinctive melody. The entire nervous system responds to the composition of soft sounds that intentionally evoke a relieving compatible musical background to the body's own natural anxiety free ebb and flow.

Anxiolytic music has been used successfully to reduce one of the least recognized areas of unconscious angst: the prolonged effect of post-surgical anxiety. The innate human fear of dismemberment is fraught with anxiety. Surgery is a literal dismemberment. The terror of handing oneself over to unconsciousness and a team of others wielding sharp instruments is the stuff of nightmares. The emotional experience of surgery is stored in the body long after the intellect has dealt with the literal event. Compliantly, unconsciously, the body carries the weight of the experience. It is a mistaken notion that the anesthetized person has no memory of the events that take place during surgery. They absolutely do. The memories are stored beneath consciousness and can be influential in a myriad of ways.

For no reason I could recall, in my forties I began having a recoil reaction every time I saw a hypodermic being administered on TV. The reaction was autonomic and viscerally painful. When I did a little research, I found out that during a surgical procedure several years earlier the anesthesia had worn off and I had recoiled and cried out as a catheter was being inserted into an artery. At first I had no clear recollection of that event, but my bodymind certainly did.

Have you ever considered contemplatively dancing to the experience of your hysterectomy, mastectomy, or cesarean, or even more important, your own birth by cesarean delivery? Moving with the sensations of who you become when the unconscious influence of a memory of dismemberment overtakes you can be cleansing and enormously freeing. Just as every thought translates into an emotion, every emotion translates into a subatomic biochemical physical response. These responses form clusters of subliminal affects that limit our natural physical expression. Your body can form a blockage of feeling-laden experiences (Jung called this a "complex") just like your psyche forms. Surgical residue can provide an unconscious magnet that will attract a group of similar experiences to it. This body complexity can trigger a psychosomatic response to even an anticipation of a similar occurrence.

One friend tells me she used to feel queasy every time she saw broken glass on the highway until she allowed her body to move with the image of "broken glass that sickens me." She then remembered cutting herself badly on a piece of discarded glass she picked up from the street when she was a preschooler. The next time she saw a piece of broken glass she intentionally picked it up, tenderly remembering the little girl whose emotionally laden memory of fright at the sight of her own blood had stayed tucked away in the adult's unconscious. She smiled when she said, "I told myself that I am not a child who picks up things that can hurt her—today I am a woman who knows what is safe and what is harmful." Repressed discordant memories are not sweet music for the bodymind to move to. Yet move us they do. Static-laden, they keep us on edge, creating a bodymind tinnitus, a constant distractive hum. It is up to us to recreate the insight that will remove the din.

Bodymind's sensate realm thrives on its own natural rhythms. When you are exploring the hidden truths of your body, you want to chose music that will not superimpose a psychological or a physiological map over the movement. Otherwise your bodymind will respond in an adaptive way either to the beat, the social associations, or the associated memories. When this happens it is the musical equivalent of a restraint, in as much as the external event couples with a prior experience (belief), and the body responds unconsciously in an old prescribed way. So don't choose the soundtrack from a favorite film or the music with which your husband or lover courted you to contain you when you get

Women's
Intuition

ready to move. You want music that is as pure as possible, without associations or vocal accompaniment. Vocals, like associations, can and do interfere with the spontaneity of the movement.

Music without a familiar melody or a predominately controlling beat allows the body to adjust to a natural aerobic balance. Classical and some New Age music most closely fills this bill. The interaction of breath with the sensations of the body blend with the rhythms of the sound. We feel the centerpoint of nature when we relax into the natural ebb and flow of the ocean or the swish-hush-swish of the wind through the forest. Nature-centered societies have rhythmic rituals that reenact the *anxiolytic* strains from the environment in order to prepare the community to face a stressful event such as the relocation of the camp or a change of season.

Intentional harmonies rely upon evoking a certain tension. There are times when these intentions are precisely what is needed. A march quickens the heart's beat, energizing the listener or the soldier about to march off to war. Lullabies are designed to induce slowed respiration and lowered blood pressure as a preparation for sleep. The notes of a solitary bugle poignantly sounding "Taps" evokes the solemn singularity of death. Repetitious sounds such as drumbeats are intended to provoke an altered state of consciousness. Interestingly, anxiolytic music includes harmony judiciously in order to alleviate this possibility. According to Linda Rodgers in "Music for Surgery," psychospiritually this genre of music encourages spirit (breath) as it enters matter to soothe the body in a rhythmically nonobtrusive way. In the same way, carefully selected music, quietly focused breathing, and contemplative movement are the ingredients for a nonintrusive ritual—a body prayer. A time of somatic communion while sharing the bread of Soul and the wine of Spirit.

Movement has the healing capacity to allow a memory from the past to exist in the moment of reenactment with the same vitality as it had originally, but without the original impact. While this is going on, the mover has the opportunity to become a co-creator in the recreation of an event from the past.

In SCM done for healing, the dancer *intentionally* evokes the old experience and *intuitively* engages with the energy in order to rescript the emotional memory. The movement becomes the metaphoric bridge between the past and the future. Memory evoked by movement is less stress-producing than memory evoked by talking, because the innate intelligence of the body instinctually balances the stress, awakening the possibility for healing on a visceral level. This shift in perspective transits the separation between fate (that which cannot be changed) and destiny (that which is always unfolding). What seemed chiseled in stone dissolves into the finest granules of sand to mix with the yielding clay of matter. The trauma is transformed from that which was done to me into this which I can handle myself.

Translating image into affect and feelings into motion the contemplative dance of embodied soul sketches out the complex interplay between body and soul *in this moment*. Intentionally (consciously) allowing yourself to be led by the spontaneous sensations arising from within your body, your soul's journey unfolds as each succeeding pulse of movement holds the history of the preceding one and the transformational promise of the next. Thoughts are held in obeisance as the liquid streaming of the Ineffable bathes every cell, baptizing the union of body and soul. The sweet safety of the pregnant silence that fills the room as a woman's contemplative trust in her body wisdom matures and deepens is *anxiolytic*. Her movements are contained by her breath as it harmoniously guides the natural rhythms essential to body wisdom.

The silence contracts and expands as the dancer's inwardly directed attention intuitively perceives the symphony her body is creating from old memories, new attitudes, changing perceptions, and true sensations. What was once held together by muscle, tissue, and bone is now held together by love.

The Sweet Safety of Matter

The authenticity of Spontaneous Contemplative Movement creates a sphere of safety for the bodymind to expand into as you remember your true purpose in life. The feeling most often expressed after a session is "centered." Intuition is easily accessed when we feel centered and at home in our own matter. Close to the end of a movement group, I ask participants to find a partner and stand quietly before one another with soft eyes. As they drop inward on the breath, I ask each one to note a part of her own body that she is most aware of and tuck that to one side of their consciousness. Then, I invite them to allow their intuition to scan the partner's body energy and note where they "see" the most energy in the partner's body. It is remarkably reassuring when the energy that is personally noted is intuitively recognized by the partner and vice versa. In this kind of exercise there is a very real possibility that they are picking up telepathic signals from their partner. But this is not the point. I want them to experience that intuition comes from many sources, multiple directions. Our consciousness of its presence makes the difference. I've never known anyone to develop an intuitive relationship with the bodymind that didn't marvel at the wonder that is the human body.

As Jill Mellick quotes Marion Woodman in their book, *Coming Home to Myself: Reflections for Nurturing a Woman's Body and Soul,*

> If you can listen to the wisdom of your body,
> love this flesh and bone,
> dedicate yourself to its mystery,
> you may one day
> find yourself
> smiling from your mirror.

Chapter Six

THE SELF-BETRAYAL
IN DISOWNING
OUR MOTHER

Healing may flow from the places we least expect it.
—*Marc Ian Barasch*

L IVING IN A SOCIETY THAT WIELDS THE YARDSTICK of experience and
accomplishment as the final measure of personal validation, a
woman begins to rely as much upon external validation as upon an interior sense of knowing. It becomes all too necessary for her to minimize
the lessons that are formed in the crucible of her belly, her breasts, and
her blood, explaining them away as symptoms or complaints. When she

does allow her body to orchestrate homage to these lessons, she is danced with the strong energies of intuitive knowing. Yet all too often these occasions are rejected as confusing because of their refusal to fit the norm. To avoid suspicion, ridicule, or interference, she simply keeps these resources to herself—or she avoids them altogether. This contract is an agreement to disembody, disempower, and disown the most valid and vital aspect of incarnation—the body. Further, it is a compliant agreement to muffle or silence the body's most profoundly spiritual spokesperson—intuition.

For many of us, our intuitive energy surges into our conscious awareness when we are too young to understand it. There is nothing we can do with it if we have no support in the form of teachers, role models, or mentors to help us anchor our insights with instruction and encouragement—and society refuses to cultivate this way of knowing. This can make the novice feel unstable and "crazy."

Many a woman, visited by her intuition, believes herself to be "strange" or "possessed," doubting yet discordantly intrigued by this other parallel reality. Often her insights are viewed as "hysterical" or irrational by those she trusts the most. She realizes if she is true to herself she'll be deemed out of synch with the consensus reality. Or, she makes fun of herself—turning her gift of intuitive "seeing into and beyond" into a shallow bit of magic. Most commonly, however, she learns to tune out the messages and live in the "rational" world, like a receiver that is tuned to only one channel and is completely out of synch with the satellite dish that is receiving a multitude of other signals. This sort of restricted reception may provide temporary relief until instinct takes over and the body spontaneously responds, stirring up the deep feminine whether intentionally called upon or not.

Out of Touch with Ourselves

Living in Central America in the '50s, in labor with our second child, I was a patient at Gorgas Hospital, the gemstone of research and medical care in the crown of government services for U.S. citizens abroad. My labor room shared a bathroom with an adjoining room, allowing the large staff that assisted with each delivery to move from my bedside to the next room regularly. As the evening wore on it was obvious the woman who shared my bath and I were going to be parents by midnight. Suddenly the heavy metal, hurricane-proof bathroom doors separating our rooms were slammed shut by my neighbor, who securely locked herself inside the bathroom. There before my eyes, as I continued to labor, an ever-growing group of hospital personnel begged, pleaded, threatened, and coaxed in their mounting desperation to prevent my labor-mate from delivering her own child—to no avail. After her baby arrived, a lusty nine-pounder, she bit the cord neatly in two, washed him off in the bathroom sink, and unlocked the door only after she had given him her breast. "Horrors, unsanitary, not sterile, contamination," cried the staff. "This child cannot go into the nursery with the others." And he didn't. Our son was born about an hour later, properly sanitized, and uncontaminated by suspect touch. He was quickly taken to the nursery, not to be returned to my arms until four hours later, the time deemed proper for his first feeding. As I was wheeled to the ward (no walking, I might get dizzy and fall, injure myself. I had, after all been through the "ordeal" of delivery) I heard loud sucking noises and there was my roommate, her son of two hours lustily nursing at her breast. The next day I learned the rest of the story.

Maritza (not her real name) was from the bush country. A native Panamanian, she had watched the women in her community midwife each birth as the expectant mother squatted over the earth and allowed nature and gravity to assist in the delivery. Intuition and instinct were intimate companions in Maritza's bodysoul experiences—instinct telling her when and intuition telling her how. Determined to avoid the steel stirrups and episiotomy of Western medicine, she took her son's delivery into her own hands. Instinctually she knew when and how to stay intimately aligned with her body and even more important, *in her body*. Labor pains were the instruction she followed to prepare her for this great event. "I don't like being treated like I am sick or helpless

THE
SELF-BETRAYAL
IN DISOWNING
OUR MOTHER

when I am going to drop my baby," she said. "What they do to you here is black magic—put you to sleep and tie you up and cut your body—so there is no *madre* at home when the *niño* arrives." No contest. Maritza was fully at home, in her body, when her *niño* arrived. Maritza was non-plused that the medical staff shunned her for her "aberrant" behavior, while the other mothers envied her because her baby was the only one allowed to stay at his mother's side to be held, rocked, touched, and fed anytime Maritza and the little one felt the urge.

Men and women alike have suffered the black magic of technology and disembodied cultural norms. We've been tied up with the unending quest for an ideal body—a "ten." We've been put to sleep by the deadly drugs of perfection and eternal youthfulness. We've been cut, slashed, and scarred by the cultural contempt for the feminine. Treated as an unruly visitor, an uncivilized interloper, we shun our depth of feelings, reject our matter, and live disembodied lives. Treating our body like rental property, we live as absentee landlords blaming the tenant for each disrepair.

We as women have all taken a profound devaluing of the feminine into our bodies like mother's milk. A witches' brew, it has soured our joy and turned us against ourselves. Unless and until we examine this unconscious distrust of the feminine, we will never inhabit our bodies fully and never trust our intuitive wisdom. Distrust is an insidious assailant, eroding our sense of now. Distrust keeps us vigilant lest we be overtaken, cautious lest we risk too much, hyper-vigilantly prepared for the other shoe to drop, the trick behind the reality to disclose itself.

But there is an instant cure for distrust. Refuse to devalue the feminine—trust your instincts, your intuitions, your feelings, in the here and now. Take up full residence in a fully conscious body. All else will follow.

Authentic Resonance

Every woman must find a clear and clean connection to her body and the full range of her feelings before she can trust her own intuitive capacity. A woman must learn how to give voice to her emotional position without the messiness of an undifferentiated mood—or the fear of revealing her power. We have to learn to like the sound of our own voice, teaching ourselves not to allow it, neglected, to become wistful, strident, or faint. We have to develop the courage not to apologize when we realize that others disagree or know more. As females in a male-oriented culture, we each must learn how to recognize and value our own genuine innocence without trading in the counterfeit coin of seductive stupidity or contrived helplessness to conceal our fear of rejection.

At times, we simply will not know how to articulate what we are truly feeling until we express ourselves *exactly* as it comes out. It is a gift of maturity to be willing to assert yourself, name your feelings, and then say, "No, that is not exactly it. I want to restate myself." No apology, no embarrassment, no defensiveness, no lies.

The tight body and rigid psyche of a woman who has no way to revel in her own womanliness guarantees a restricted un*ex*pressed voice—fertile ground for *de*pression. When there is no voice flexible enough to articulate authentic expression, the bodymind will protect health and sanity by *de*pressing the energy until there is an outlet. Seen from this perspective, emotional depression is one side of an ailing bodymind, where the rigidity, constriction, and tightening up of matter diminishes Spirit, dismisses Soul, frightens and confuses the ego, and paralyzes hope. On the physical side, there are the repressed energies of words eaten, stuck in our throat, lying like lumps in our stomachs. Unexpressed emotions turn our energy back upon us and pull us into a depression, where we symptomatically embody the very emotion we are trying to avoid emotionally.

We must be willing to face what we feel, to develop a vocabulary that clearly, definitively, and appreciatively expresses how we feel, if we are to loosen ourselves from the popular opinion that women are more emotionally unpredictable than men, and therefore deficiently unstable. Our emotional perspectives are *real,* but when they are disembodied they lose their integrity. Our focus becomes scattered, we misdirect our energy and inappropriately spill perfectly appropriate feelings all over the place.

The expressive language of the feminine may appear disorderly or messily inclusive when contrasted with the deductive skills of the masculine. Feminine perceptions are nature-centered and are, innately, encompassing. *Mater,* Latin for "mother," is the root of the word *matter.* Matter, Earth, the maternal, and Mother Nature share the relational attributes of the feminine. Nature, that which is most basic in each of us, resonates with a fiercely honest instinctual energy that ferociously protects what it loves at any cost. When this energy awakens in the body, we feel the undulations of emotion and the vibrations of feelings that connect us relationally heart to heart and soul to soul, not only with others but with the web of life.

It is a rare woman who does not first and foremost think and feel relationally. Linking threads of DNA, birthing, parenting, coupling, gathering, creating, and relating, without the contamination of politics or institutions, is innate to a female. Because a woman's psychic pull is toward connections—relating simultaneously to both her inner and her outer reality—her scope of inclusion is often broader and more diffuse than that of a man. In his classic book, *Men Are from Mars, Women Are from Venus,* John Gray juxtaposes the energy-attracting Venus-like qualities of female energy with the more penetrating Mars-like singularity of the male. Gray's description of the sweeping embrace of the feminine as compared to the purposeful reductions of the masculine has clarified many a marital communications conundrum brought on by the male's frustration at what he perceives as the female's diffusely encompassing viewpoint.

Mother Nature is at work here. Molecularly a woman *does differ* from a man in the way her body is *designed* to relate to intellectual stimuli. The corpus callosum, that wide band of connective tissue between the two hemispheres of the brain, is measurably wider in a female brain. This additional width allows her to make many more neuronal connections between the two hemispheres than most of her male counterparts. When she shares problem solving with a male, more areas in *both* sides of her brain will be innervated. When a male exhorts a female to "Please, get to the bottom line," she is; however, the route to her bottom line encompasses far more scope than his, literally. A woman is far more likely to consider feelings when coming to a point of logic. Not because she is irrational, "neurotic," or hopelessly indirect, but because she naturally employs nonverbal resources as easily as verbal ones. The possibility for pregnancy and childbirth hormonally prepare a woman for this expansion—for flexibility, for mystery, and for paradox, in a way that a more masculine logic and bottom-line mentality cannot.

Feminine energy is reflective, receptive, relational, and multidimensional. The process is spiral, seeming to diverge, wander, and reconverge at any given stage. Feminine energy abhors being pinned down, limited, or prematurely birthed. Feminine energy is full of paradox—incubating and seemingly inert one moment, it can move through us like lightning the next. It is the nature of feminine energy to entertain many possibilities before choosing only one. Nature loves all her creations equally.

The gifts of the feminine are a reservoir of paradox. Until we can come to love both the sheer beauty and the imperfections of our matter equally, our intuition will elude us because it can sometimes appear too paradoxical and imperfect to bear. Intuition is never logical, seldom absolute, and often just beyond our grasp. In many ways, it is the epitome of the Feminine, and as such, it has been denigrated and dismissed by male culture and, because we are products of that culture, by ourselves as well. Nowhere is this profound ambivalence more obvious and difficult than in women's relationships with their mothers, the primary symbol of the feminine in both body and soul.

I believe part of the reason we women have been willing to treat our intuitive skills so lightly is because of the strong psychic link they give us to our mothers. Stories abound about the results of a woman being receptive to this mother link. Mothers report that they have felt their expectant daughter's labor pains even before the call that she is in labor was received; daughters describe that they have known intuitively that their mother was ill or in pain, through a dream, an image, or a literal symptom in their own bodies. The most recent and startling example of this happened for me with the early pregnancy of one of my daughters. I was driving home from the office when clear as a bell I simply "knew" the baby's gender. This insight was a surprise, since up until that moment I'd felt the baby would probably be a girl. Two weeks later I mentioned this to our daughter who said, "Well, you're right. The sonogram confirmed it, and I knew also the same afternoon that you did." This psychic-intuitive connection seems especially strong between female family members—sisters, mother-daughter, grandmother-granddaughter. When a woman is struggling to "cut the cord" and claim her own identity often she has to close this door.

Our Mothers, Ourselves

While a man can take pride in his obvious physical difference as he becomes his own person, a woman often rejects her body because it is so like her mother's. Confusing the psychic necessity to grow beyond her mother bond and into a unique individual, with succumbing to the cultural disdain for most qualities of the feminine, a woman can easily learn to hate those parts of herself that remind her of her mother. In particular, a woman who wishes to become highly intuitive needs to reconnect with her love for the female body. For until a woman can come to terms with her physical and emotional bond with her literal mother, she will have to mediate her relationship with her body through an unfinished mother complex. This will keep her from ever becoming fully embodied, rending her therefore perpetually out of touch with her body wisdom.

The word *complex* is a bit of psychological shorthand meant to describe a commonly experienced developmental process. As we grow psychically and socially, we are inundated with ideas, attitudes, experiences, and rules about life. In order to develop some sense of autonomy, we choose certain things to hold in our consciousness and others to let fall away into unconsciousness. As the repository of the personal unconscious increases, the psyche creates a sort of filing system where similarities attract one another and form a field around common themes, called a "complex" in Jungian psychology. These rejects tend to form categories—like attracting like. Hence we say all material about the feminine is a mother complex and all about the masculine a father complex, and so on. When any of those things we relegate to unconsciousness are too threatening to the ego to allow back into consciousness, they often signify their presence by returning disguised by an exaggerated emotional charge. When a complex is activated, some repressed and emotionally laden memory triggers a response that takes us quite off guard. Our first clue to the unconscious nature of the material is the intensity of the feeling.

Everything that an individual associates with the feminine, females, and mother that she cannot handle psychologically is repressed and stored in the mother complex. At the center of this complex is the universal (it is called archetypal because humans everywhere share some aspect of this) image of the Great Mother, the Goddess, or Nature. The magnet that keeps this energy alive within the unconscious is the fact that these memories, perceptions, attitudes, and experiences associated with the feminine and mother carry an emotional energy too hot for the ego to deal with. Tucked away in obscurity, deep in the hindmost regions of the psyche, this emotional charge can be set off without any conscious warning. Since the triggering event is equally obscured by a delayed reaction, the resultant eruption takes us completely by surprise and is unnerving. Any or all of the associated thoughts and feelings captured by a complex can be hurled into consciousness and out into the world like shrapnel. You know you are in the grip of a complex when you are experiencing a mystifying surge of emotion that is far greater than the occasion calls for and you cannot slow it down or deter it.

I'm certain you'll immediately recognize what I'm describing from the following example. Basically I am an introvert. I prefer to listen, not talk, to be introspective and quiet. My mother, on the other hand, is vivacious and energetically engaged in life. She, by her own admission, "never meets a stranger," finds "everyone has an interesting story," and loves to chat. As a child, I'd be quietly lost in my own reverie when

Mom would enter the room talking and full of energy. Loving her, my ego would respond but internally my emotions would be in disarray. I'd attempt to listen and keep up—to meet her energy with some of my own—but in no time I'd feel depleted, compromised, and worn out.

I stored the conflictual feelings I couldn't decipher in my Mother file, in that old box of complexes. As I matured I found myself doing two things. First, I could get really upset with anyone who pursued me with too much vigor or too many words—even when I liked them a lot. Secondly, I became my "Mother" whenever I was in the presence of a silent person. I had an uncanny urge to talk too much.

This is how a complex affects us. What we have stored away reaches a critical mass, the file gets full, pops open, and, since every complex is emotionally based, rushes willy-nilly over the ego with a surge of intense feeling. If the surge doesn't get our attention, a symptom or a dream image may magnify the impact. If we are wise enough to know what is happening, we can do something about it. There are many ways to resolve the conflicts stored in a complex.

No matter how we resolve the experience, consciously or uncon-sciously, the natural desire to be loved by Mother forces us to either identify with her or disagree and suffer the fear of alienation. Complexes are inevitable; everyone has them. In order to create some manageable modicum of psychic balance, something has to be chosen and some-thing gets filed, as in this case in the Mother Complex file. What no one tells us is that the things we push into the back of the file as most repul-sive can turn us against ourselves. The day then arrives when we dis-cover that loathing our own femaleness is costing us too much and we have to free ourself somehow. So we project our unconscious self-hatred out into the world as if this will absolve us from hating ourself. We do terrible things to ourself as if "the devil made me do it." You know the shock of discovering that your own worst persecutor is none other than yourself! To further complicate things and obscure the quest for our own feminine identity, our mother complex is also influenced by tribal norms.

Southern women in particular have to deal with the weight of being a "lady." Taught to be nice, courteously indirect, and self-effacing, the "Yes, Ma'am" of Southern gentility leaves little room for a woman to find, much less express, her own voice or her own identity. Looking more closely we find the cultural paradox that the Southern woman lives with. The South's plantation history cannot disguise the strong leadership of these "magnolia" women who, in the absence of their men, ran the farms, birthed their young, and in crinolines and corsets went to the slave quarters to assist with births and deaths there, only to return to the main house and become a self-effacing, dependent female once more. In the epic *Gone with the Wind,* Scarlett and Melanie are two sides of the same woman—the strong-willed rebellious one and the long-suffering acquiescent one. Every woman has to come to terms with whether she will acquiesce and be like mother, rebel and defy that role, or grow up and find her own version—the one that suits her best.

When a woman comes to me hating herself, I teach her to realign her relationship with the feminine through the sounding of the name she wishes to be known by. Intuitively a woman will choose the name that fits with her deepest love for the unnamed in herself.

NAMING YOURSELF—CALLING HER FORTH

This exercise has its roots in the sacred naming practices of prehistory and deserves to be treated with ceremony and reverence. Read this through before you begin so you can focus your full attention on the ceremony when you do it. Many have found it helps to take a bath or shower before beginning, since water changes the ionization of our subtle body's vibrational field and awakens a deeper sense of receptivity. The texture, fragrance, and images of water, candles, oil, and incense deepen our interior experience. You'll want to arrange a quiet uncluttered space, with enough room to be able to walk around. Light a candle, arrange flowers, or do whatever you usually do to evoke the sacred. Be certain you have a hand mirror also. Give some thought to what you wear. Come as a woman of free instincts, unrestrained by tight clothing, restraining belts or jewelry, or a closed mind.

Select a relaxed standing posture, feet about shoulder width apart and knees bent enough to soften their stance but not so much as to create a fear of collapsing. This posture will align your body naturally with gravity and your relationship to the Earth. Turning your attention inward, allow your breath to become the focal point, breathing in and out through the nostrils as you imagine a tiny elastic cord between navel and spine that tightens with each exhale, creating the barest of pelvic tilts. After a few minutes of rhythmical breathing, begin to sound the name you wish to be called by in syllables. If your name is Susan, sound it as *Sue-san*. As you proceed, the syllables will create a rhythm and melody all your own. Follow your body's spontaneous directions as you walk, pause, sway, whatever. You will want to stay on your feet, since you are embodying a conscious standpoint about your name—your personal relationship to yourself. The innate homeostatic intelligence of your bodymind will lead you. At a certain point you will feel your body relax and a quiet vitality will begin to express itself through other spontaneous movements. Follow your movements, contemplate the sounding of your name until you sense intuitively you have filled every cell of your body with the resonance. Then, with softened eyes, pick up the mirror and gaze into the eyes of your true Self. Welcome her and pledge to call her name often and with loving respect.

A note of consideration: If you have an urge to name yourself metaphorically, for example, "Woman who has wings on her feet," reconsider this. Yes, of course, you'll want to deepen your relationship with the winged feet part of your deep feminine. For now I am inviting you to bring the deep feminine into your conscious body in the most ordinary and practical of daily experiences by embracing how you want your given name or names spoken. I have found our most familiar name usually carries a lot of relational energy. Our surname holds, archetypal energy, and the name we seldom speak carries unexplored energy. Reclaiming the full depth and breath of our energetic legacy is what we are about. To fully incarnate means to be fully conscious of each of these energies in the present, as they inform us here and now.

It does feel wonderful to drop into *kairos* time and allow our imaginations to teach us about the depths of our experiences. However it serves no purpose if we are avoiding the tough work of reeducating our ego about our self. Only the ego carries and identifies with a body image. More often than not the image is distorted and faulty. How often have you felt perfectly fine about yourself one moment then had a critical perception about your weight or appearance take over and nothing seems right—not your self-confidence or satisfaction? The resonance of the name we recognize as "me" when sounded appears to set up a homeostatic tonal vibrational field throughout the body that I believe diminishes and heals the jarring affect of a complex about the body. I have found that sounding your name even subliminally when in a crisis of confidence can be more reassuring than words, especially when combined with contemplative movement. You will come home to your Self. The psychomatic responses to naming yourself are instinctual, but the choice to commit yourself to this level of self-love is pure discipline. Your ego must be willing to pick up the flaming sword of your integrity, place itself at the entrance to your inner chambers, and bar the approach of any critic—literal or imaginary.

The Three Mothers

One of the real trials of conscious embodiment for a woman is the inability to separate the literal mother from the mother complex and these two from the archetypal mother. The confusion among these three differing states of emotional relationship can get a woman into emotional deep water. Attitudes and opinions that spring from our feelings about the feminine are often confused with the literal woman we project them onto. A faulty projection assembled from the bits and pieces stored away in a mother complex, disowned and inaccurately aimed toward another woman, can rob us of our own birthright by convincing us of our feminine powerlessness.

Janet, recently returned from a trip to see her mother, voiced her continuing regret that she doesn't have an independent feminist mother. "She is so agreeable and weak that I feel I have been robbed because she is my mother."

She writes in her journal: "All my life—all my life—I've struggled against some great implacability, some block against standing up for myself. It's difficult to be vitally alive, hard to see things through, to care when the way is hard. I go to meet my mother on her terms and I come home feeling as if I'm up against some huge barricade. I feel that because I have her for a mother I am defeated from the start. No one can really understand what I go through, it's so complicated, so demoralizing."

Janet's mother is in her small hometown a well-known, accomplished musician, who never pushed her daughter into music because she wanted her to find her own life's work. Widowed after twenty years of marriage, she remains independent, active, with her own circle of friends. Janet says her mother is bright, well-liked, and has a fiery temper but a quick recovery after she gets angry. Janet relishes how wonderful she is with grandchildren. So who is this crippling, inadequate, internalized mother that stymies Janet's growth?

Then Janet had this dream: "I am with a little girl who is about six or so. She looks something like me. She has just caught a big silver fish which she proudly places on the picnic table where we are going to eat. A stranger, a woman dressed in old-fashioned clothes, takes a flyswatter and knocks the fish off the table and into the dirt. 'Don't you know that you're too little to bring scales to this party?' she sneers. I am appalled. Then the fish starts to rot but it grows wings and flies into the sky like a beautiful Mylar kite. The little girl is dumbstruck."

Janet is at a crisis of collision between her feelings for her literal mother, her mother complex, and the Great Mother. Using the images from this dream, Janet used contemplative movement to allow her body to intuitively express the child's energy first, then the big silver fish, followed by the flyswatter woman, and eventually, the flying fish.

As the dream child huddled in the corner of the room, Janet's spontaneous movements were reminiscent of swimming. Later she said she couldn't tell whether she was the fish or the child, she only knew that she intuitively loved the rhythmical motion of being in the water. The emotional beauty of spontaneous movement lies in the body's capacity to express the blending of what on the surface appear as completely differing viewpoints. This paradoxical illusion creates an emotional tension of opposites. Janet felt nurtured by the competent repetitious motions of breathing and stroking as a fish would while simultaneously feeling little and undecided as the dream child did. Her stroking, swimming motions turned into self-stroking and she began to cry—softly at first and then with abandon. By using SCM, her internal conflict began to transform into a union of the two—a balance. Clearly the instinctual body (the fish that *knows* to breathe and swim beneath the waters of the unconscious) is not so unlike the emotional body (the child) that instinctively knows something is amiss. Maybe this dream child's emotional "incompetency" is seeking to express her intuitive solution in order to regain the natural rhythm her fish knows so well. Later Janet said that she was mourning, swimming her way through the sorrow—mourning the way she had swept her best offerings away over and over again in her life. For a period of time she sat with her legs drawn up and her chin on her knees, silently facing the wall. After a while, she began to make the swimming motions once more as she began to move in a spiral on her side on the floor. This spiral unfolding eventually brought her to her feet, where she allowed her entire body to follow her breath into a graceful and fluid expression of the dream kite's dance.

In talking about what she had learned as she was danced by her dream, Janet said she realized she wouldn't allow herself to see her real mother through the eyes of an adult. She kept wanting to blame her mother for her own vulnerabilities. Her dream underscored this mother complex artfully, creating a flyswatter female who "knocked my silvery dreams and big catches" right out of the offering. "That swatter," muses Janet, "is me also. I go back home and see my mother's happiness and I want her to be proud of my life. Then I return home resenting her because I'm not happy with my own life. I verbally bat down all the strengths she has given me. I tell myself that I'm glad I'm not stuck, settling for a second-rate life like she is. Baloney. Pure crap! Mother is really happy. I'm the one that is settling for compromises in my job, my marriage, and with my health. God! What a projection! Thankfully the Great Mother hasn't given up on me. She takes my silver fish and sets her flying."

Fortunately the body has a long and unwavering memory. Deep within the tissue and bone there dwells an unrequited yearning for the sweet unimpeded relatedness of the Great Mother: of Her. Of Sophia, the Great Mother of our collective histories, of our *Mitochondrial Self.* Even the smallest fragment, the briefest moment of unconditional love and acceptance, stays stored within your body's memory bank urging you to seek more. Covertly the search for the Beloved never ceases. We can best recollect these revitalizing fragments in the company of a loved other— best recognize them through the empathy of that other for ourself. If we grow up alone and unrecognized, unmet, the way is infinitely harder. When we feel loved or loving toward the literal mother, our love for Archetypal Mother—the deep feminine—is stirred into action, filling our psyche and our soul with renewed energy for living freely and well.

I believe that empathy is to the adult what mirroring is to the infant. Empathy soulfully relates us to our Self and to the Self of the other through a bond of mutual recognition. For one brief moment, we feel held next to the compassionate heart of God the Mother, yet completely at home in our flesh-and-blood body. We feel Her presence within. We are heart of her heart, intuitively linked, eternally held. In that instant, no matter how brief or infrequent, we feel a blessing of grace that can't be put into words. Turning inward, we are taught by images from a distant forgotten time. We can sing or dance or paint the expression of its imprint; we simply can't do justice to it with mere words. Naming ourself and then really embracing the sound of that name until we love the total being the name represents is an empathic response. Unless we are willing and able to look openly and compassionately into the eyes of our reflection in a mirror, we are fooling ourself that we are embodied. We are still governed by some insidious form of shame and self-hatred about the feminine.

For a woman to become fully embodied, with access to her full intuitive powers, she first must find the courage to grieve her own unique portion of the inevitable losses every human suffers with her biological mother, withdraw the mother projections she has thrown out into the world as she searched for an altar onto which she could lay her grief, and open herself to the fierce compassion it will take to forgive her fury about those losses while she learns to love her matter, to re-mother herself.

The majority of us had mothers who both loved us and wanted to mother us. They did the very best the could without even being aware of their own estrangement from their bodies or their emotional deprivation without a circle of elders with whom to celebrate this profound coming of age. Their intentions were sincere and often well thought out. Thought out, but not felt through. They, like us, are victims of the culture. Getting pregnant is instinctual. Knowing when and why is intuitive. Conscious embodiment opens us to the union of the animal and the angel that live side by side in every cell.

The Archetypal Mother

There can also be no grounding in the body, and therefore our intuition will always be chaotic and random, until we can discriminate between the literal mother who birthed us and the Archetypal Mother who lies at the center of our very nature, at the core of our essential self. Because the archetype represents a universal representation found in every culture, her countenance is reproduced in every culture. The Black Madonna or Sophia, Isis, or Grandmother Spider Woman, she walks among and in us. You must find the image, claim the attributes this image holds for you without trying to identify with it and cut it down to human size. This is a grave error. Every archetype has multiple attributes representing both poles of the human experience. Each positive non-requiring attribute is counterbalanced by a demanding and off-putting one. An archetype can teach us about the full range of our spiritual and emotional lives, but since no human is ever able to contain all those attributes and survive, we are to learn from them, not foolishly pretend to be them.

A conscious awareness of the presence of the image and the energy of the Archetypal Mother in her guise of the ideal maternal bonds a woman with her body even when she has no memory of a bonding with her biological mother. Grounded in the unconditional love the archetypal feminine has for all matter, the conscious body opens and opens and opens—to a deepening of self-understanding. Absorbing psychic strength from the deepening spiritual relationship with the Archetypal Mother, an internalized image of a human-sized ideal (good enough) mother forms.

At the center of every issue you have with your biological mother, or with any other aspect of the feminine, lies an unexplored relationship with the archetypal feminine. As Marion Woodman so eloquently demonstrates in *Addiction to Perfection,* unless you can meet her on her terms you will project that energy elsewhere, squandering your innate capacity for an embodied spirituality on poor substitutes, even muffins, leading to addictions (not the least of which is the patriarchal competitive one of perfection).

Bogged down in the attempt to intellectually concretize our desire for a spiritual mother or snared by our grief over what literally never was, we are blind to the rich multidimensional wisdom of the consciously embodied symbolic feminine. Blindly, without recognition, we become antagonistic toward our own genuine feelings, as if they come not to teach us about our truth but to seductively betray us by their truths. Casting blame upon how we were mothered, we excuse our part in the major disappointments we feel about our own femaleness—as if this alone will absolve us from the tough work of individuation. Leaving few stones unturned, some of us further thwart emotional independence by blaming her for the partner she chose to father us. Stuck in the past and suffering with unfinished business, we ignore the symptoms and images that can carry us beyond this stalemate.

In our unending cultivation of the thorny unfinished business we have with our literal parents, we neglect the more fertile dimensions of an intimate personal relationship with the spiritual mother. The two go hand in hand. Every tired complex, ridden like a worn-out steed, takes us to the bog of a neurotic hell. Round and round we go—sinking deeper and deeper into the benumbing satisfaction of suffering with our own sweet suffering. Meanwhile, the key to release is just a dream, or a symptom, away.

Marley couldn't bear to even hear her mother's name spoken aloud. She was so dependent upon her relationship with her mother that it had cost her the alienation of her two brothers. She had lost four jobs in seven years, due, she said, to her mother getting her so upset she couldn't work. Her mother lived over a thousand miles away, but Marley kept her psychically alive—very present—magically influencing her thoughts and moods.

Many of us do the same with any number of things onto which we project an unwieldy and unwarranted amount of external power and control so that they influence our choices and their outcome. My friend, the Jungian author Robert Johnson, calls this "giving your gold away." I've chosen an example of a mother-daughter relationship to describe this folly, but it can just as easily happen with a woman and her job, or her beauty, or her possessiveness. As we become sensitized to the number of surreptitious ways we give away the best of ourself in order to get our nurturance needs met, we are appalled.

After a bitter series of letters in which Marley mourned her mother's lack of empathy when Marley told her mother she was unable to have her come for a visit, her mother accused Marley of too much self-importance to care about others. As angry as she was, this was a blow to Marley's sense of herself as a misunderstood but long-suffering daughter. Marley had the following dream.

Marley's Gold

"A huge car is blocking my driveway. It is black, highly polished, carefully cared for, with bulletproof windows outsiders cannot see through.

I am intrigued, there is a kind of honor in this, even though I can't go anywhere unless the owner moves it. I am in a hurry so I decide to ride my pet goat up to the driver's window. Hopefully he will be fooled by my innocence and roll the window down, offering to move.

"The goat smells bad and the ground is covered with a gluey sap that pulls at her feet. A huge woman, with skin as black and as shiny as the car, gets out of the trunk of the car. She laughs at my predicament, but I can tell she is not really amused. Her face is glistening like patent leather, her hair ropy, unkempt, black. Her feet are like owl's claws and she smells awful. 'Well,' she says, 'are you going to stink too?'"

In Einsiedeln, Switzerland, standing in her own niche, enveloped in the waxy smoke from an endless array of prayer candles, the Black Madonna receives all who come her way. Housed in an elegant medieval cathedral, she is lovingly and ritualistically attended by the nuns from the adjacent convent. In the background, monks chant much the same as they have for centuries, as prayers wend heavenward and supplications are laid upon the altar. Communicants finger rosary beads, knotted sashes, and prayerbooks. Touch, sounds, smells, and images reflect the multidimensional languages offered to Spirit in behalf of the soul. Resonantly, the entire cathedral is filled to the uppermost arcing of its peaks with petitions to the shiny-faced Black Mother of Matter. Is she painted black, or blackened by smoke, or is the whispered story true, that she was turned black by the intense grief she carries for the pain and suffering inflicted upon the feminine? The stories vary, such is the desire of humankind to explain how and for what purpose this potent black representative of the archetypal feminine came to be. No matter. It is enough to awaken to her presence, in out-of-the-way chapels, magnificent cathedrals, dreams, iconography. When one opens to the intense love of the Mystery in the body, her reflection appears unbidden yet abiding. To ascend to Her is to first descend into matter, into your own body; to allow your heart to open and break a thousand times over until you love your Self as she loves you. Guardian of nature, she displays the claws of the owl when she comes forth as Lilith, the teeth of the predator when she emerges as Kali, the supple beauty of the gazelle when she visits us as Shakti. In her bounty, the polymorphous bounty of nature, the Black Madonna comes to us in as many different guises as are needed. The fragrance of her mystery permeates all of nature. Ignored, she is even willing to stink.

Marley recognized the bulletproof huge black car as the faultlessly armored mother complex that both intrigued and blocked her. In her ineffectual struggle to get away from her mother complex, she let everything her mother said and did to, as she said, "get my goat." She was shocked to realize that she was "riding that goat and getting nowhere." Meanwhile the work she had been doing with her dreams and movement was beginning to change her addiction to bitterness.

There in the trunk was exactly what Marley required. Another, larger-than-life, transpersonal mother who could cut Marley's mother complex down to size. Sometimes the only way to work through a psychic mess that stinks is to be assailed with a more powerful stench. The stink of a rancid or rotting psychological perspective can burst upon our consciousness like a violence—saturating the illusion of our entitlement, our victimization, helplessness, or superiority.

If Marley persists in thinking her mother is her biggest detractor, she will have to come to terms with what this dream has to say, since she is both the author and every actor and object in it. This dream points out that this displaced stench is hers, and hers alone as a result of her sticky standpoint, her putrefying energies. She can choose to remain defensive and defeated or chose to allow her dream to teach her another, more individuating way. The work of disentangling the web of the feminine, separating the strands of the biological mother from the knotty mother complex interspersed with the tinsel strength of the Archetypal Mother's cord, is crucial as a woman matures.

Intuitively Returning to the Source

Some of us were birthed by mothers who were so disconnected from their relationship to the experience that they were Medusa mothers, stony and cold. For these women the Great Mother has retreated, and the only trace of her presence is in the instinctual imprint of maternity.

Rena felt she had had such a mother. Rena learned to mother herself by duplication; by being like her mother, becoming emotionally inaccessible herself. She despaired of ever having the depth of relationship she yearned for from husband and friends. During her second year in a body and psychotherapy group she uncovered an aspect of her motherless child she called the Fundamentalist. The Fundamentalist protected her from rejection with opinions and judgments that kept her aloof and separate. She had an arsenal of well-chosen words to hurl in indignation at anyone or anything that breached her carefully constructed defenses. Afterward she would feel a piercingly pervasive sense of loss undergirding her "successful" rebuttals—a keening, a yearning. Then during a pre- and perinatal workshop she participated in a rebirthing experience. She writes of her experience:

> This experience took place after the leader had given a lecture focusing on the possibility that the experience could be traumatic because it would literally regress me back to my own birth memories. Since I had been prepared to expect a less than positive experience I was totally unprepared for what occurred.

> Trance was induced. I was brought back to a time before time, before conception. I have to pause here because this part was an experience in itself. . . . The only way I can explain it is to say it was like being in pure gold. Ecstasy. Totally infused with light, clean. . . . Words fail. . . . I can still reexperience this in varying degrees when I go back to it in my mind.

> Then I was asked to see my parents as they made love. See the sperm and egg as they meet and become the gateway for me to enter into form as an embryo. I could feel the transition between living in the gold and becoming "form." I did not want to go, but I was not forced. I think, as I write this, that the *battle was in me.* I was therefore surprised that I began to feel warm, and, at one

point early in the pregnancy, welcomed. Almost as if I could tell when my mother realized she was pregnant. I felt such warmth and joy. I felt as if I were in a cocoon, totally safe. I could feel myself grow and experienced my mother loving me (not so during my lifetime). I have concluded that my mother loved being pregnant and really wanted me, and that is what I felt during the whole experience.

As I write this I am realizing how much of the imprint of the battle is within me still. The remembrance of my mother's pregnancy with me was one of feeling unconditional love. As the birth process proceeded, I felt an anticipation rather than a dread (which the leader had prepared me for). The birth was easy, just a pass through, a push, unencumbered. When I came out I was overwhelmed by a feeling of abandonment.

Afterward I was reminded that I was actually born in the labor room because the attendants didn't listen to my mother when she told them I was coming. In those days babies who were not born in the sterile delivery room were assumed to be "dirty" and were put in a separate nursery. When the attendant handled me she then had to scrub up, so I am guessing that they avoided handling me except to bring me to my mother every four hours for a feeding, and if she wasn't up for it someone would have to go out of their way to suit up and feed me in the "dirty" nursery. I probably had to endure this ostracism and minimal contact for the two weeks of postpartum hospital stay that mothers received then.

Since my rebirthing experience I have felt I was brought back to my roots. I have found more confidence in myself. It has been an expanding experience that is changing my sense of who I am, and it continues to change me. The sense of knowing for *myself* that life as we know it is merely one dimension and there is so much more. I have grown beyond the Fundamentalist because now I can imagine that the only thing holding me back from knowing the breadth of my own capacity to love myself is *me*.

Rena discovered the origin of her inability to trust acceptance in a relationship by anticipating rejection instead. The beginning of her distress originated in the crucible of her postnatal experience. Remarkably, her body's prenatal cellular memories help her recall the embodied truth of that first deeply imprinted relationship. The love that was revealed to her during her rebirthing experience refutes the absolute nature of the deprivation recorded by the "dirty nursery" infant—alone, unwanted, with no mother to receive her. Tucked deep within her cellular recollections there is a crucially different story of anticipation and tender acceptance. Rena reports she now has a growing sense of living life on an accelerated curve, open to the magnetic pull of new experiences inspired by a genuine resistance to any pretense. Her feelings are more accessible, and she trusts them. She feels more vulnerable, yet she is clear about the value of "this new softness."

Tender yet strong self-acceptance appears frequently when a woman discovers she does indeed have a reservoir of compassionate love for herself that is hers alone to draw upon. The "cocoon" of love and acceptance that Rena experienced with her return to the womb is the "fire within the rose," the luminous love of the Archetypal Mother that passionately embraces the new soul and welcomes her into the chalice of the human body. At the end of life this strong steady flame will intensify to illumine the path: to point the way Home.

The energy represented by the Fundamentalist is an example of how an attitude or a feeling can influence a major part of our life. As long as an emotional block remains active, the energy invested in keeping the emotions associated with it depletes all of our remaining energy with a symptom or a self-defeating bit of behavior. This is why it is not only healing but also practical to use your intuition to bring the meaning behind these blockages into consciousness and free your body from the symptom or your psyche from distress. Today Rena's body no longer tenses in the presence of this energy, her adrenals no longer respond with a fully armed endocrinal barrage, her mind no longer spins in defensive mobility. These days when the Fundamentalist comes calling, Rena is able to say, "Now we both know the enemy is not 'out there somewhere,' it's in me, so I have work to do." This is a far cry from the old days when she felt she had to get sick because she couldn't bear the message.

Dream symbols, personified images like the Judge or the Gambler or the Fundamentalist, can provide you with an entry point into the nonverbal collective history of a particular energy when you are working with intuitive messages. On the shelves next to my writing desk are several volumes that I find irreplaceable when I am looking for the symbolic connections that will deepen my personal understanding of my intuition. Barbara Walker's *The Woman's Encyclopedia of Myths and Secrets* is one such beginning point, as is Clarissa Pinkola-Estés' work with fairy tales in *Women Who Run with the Wolves* and her many teaching tapes. Jung's *Collected Works* are invaluable but often difficult to read or understand. However, there are many who write from a Jungian perspective, clarifying his work for those of us who want to understand it. Inner work always benefits from historical, crosscultural, and mythological amplifications.

Marie-Louise Von Franz, one of the world's most gifted interpreters of dreams, says we cannot understand the symbolic language of a dream unless our inquiry is grounded in at least two cultural perspectives. The reason for this goes back to our clan or our ethnic roots. None of us has escaped a multicultural history. Scratch the surface of any genealogy and another culture rears its head. Our psyches know our symbolic genealogy, and our imagination draws upon a lexicon that reaches back, back, back in time and history.

During a seminar with Jungian analyst Dora Kalff, founder of sandplay therapy, in her home in Zollikon, she told of a case where a child with an Eastern mother and a Western father dreamed of two rabbits guarding a significant passageway. The child was depressed and too young to talk about her grief about moving away from China, leaving the only home she had ever known. Frau Kalff was able to reach her and help her heal when she recognized the child's psyche had chosen a symbol (rabbit) that carried the same meaning in the East as in the West. She realized this child was trying to convey that she had to pass between the two cultures represented by her parents if she was going to move on. The task was almost more than she could manage. Frau Kalff's knowledge of Asian and European symbology was the key to unlocking the young girl's dilemma.

In Rena's case, how has the motherless child been represented across time, across cultures? Some have been wolf-mothered, their inner strength giving rise to the rule of a nation. Some have found nurturance from a stone, a rag, a bit of this or that. Others, orphaned or rejected, have wasted away to skin and bones. There are exquisite tales of how the alchemical brewing of witch mothering, the heat of stewing, or the temper of the hearth has marked an infant for a destiny that first required the deep pain of orphanage. The abiding myths and folk tales teach us about the psyche showing us, through their metaphors, how to discern the seeds of strength, of leadership, the apprenticeship of healer or warrior, that lie buried beneath the pain.

Seeking the bits and pieces of myth and story and fact sets your imagination cooking, stirs the cauldron of your inner work, tempers the chalice of the bodymind. Uncovering a metaphor or movement that sets the body ringing or ignites the imagination is but the first step. Beyond that initial uncovering are treasures yet to excavate, rooms yet to explore, paths ever unfolding.

Beheading the Inner Critic

Once we have the courage, or the desperation, to enter into discourse with the sacred feminine, we change. The fear we have of being seen as fierce as the goddess Hecate, who guards the crossroads and transits from Earth to Hades as needed, of being labeled as defiant as Lilith, who as first woman refused to diminish her stature by lying beneath Adam, or of being experienced as furious as the Hindu goddess Kali, who can devour the darkness herself, we shift from the polar good or bad cultural judgments about the feminine into a delicious, if painful, discovery of the rich spectrum of emotional expression of which the authentic woman has full charge.

It should come as no surprise that the metaphors of the goddesses of the deep restlessly reverberate in the innermost chambers of our matter, charging our intuitions with their ancient instinctual energy. The West is a culture of comparisons. When judged not good enough, the rejected parts of ourselves are either forced into oblivion where they are repressed and denied, or into purgatory where they are given an exaggerated position in our psychic life. We, too, go on intrapersonal psychic witch hunts and relegate our own witchiness to the unconscious. Hung on the pegs of our self-styled purgatory, we fret, stew, worry about our deficits, our mistakes, as we avoid the rich and fomenting intuitive energy trapped in those aspects of ourselves we struggle to keep securely hidden.

However, you can not relegate anything to the unconscious without losing the rich vitality that is associated with it. These repressions are like little emotionally charged time bombs ticking away, waiting to be set off. None of us can escape the ticking, especially when we are ill or aging.

Within the psyche of every woman there is an arrogant patriarch who disdains the imperfect body or the inept intellect and torturously criticizes a woman's every attempt to come to terms with her own limitations. There also, in the region of the unloved and unlived parts of ourselves, dwell the goddesses of the deep. Moving among the shards of our neglect, their viewpoint is never polar, seldom static, and certainly not romantic. Their wisdom is ancient and irrefutable, intuitively coming forth again and again during Spontaneous Contemplative Movement to illuminate the darkened corners of our innermost chambers, showing us the beauty and the contrasting malevolence hidden there.

As I continued to witness the depth of body disconnection women suffer from, I wondered why the presence of these old goddesses, especially, afford such appreciable relief. Looking more carefully into what these myths recount, I realized theirs is the metaphoric retelling of the pathos of the disembodied soul. These goddesses are disdained not because of malevolent intent but because they reside in matter. The intensity of their vitality has the capacity to awaken and flesh out the essential bone-bare nature of the listener. Because their messages arise from the oral traditions of voice and movement, their stories engage us viscerally, evoking a profound, nonverbal, intuitive understanding of the sacred dimensions of the fully embodied self.

For over 5,000 years the rituals and the principles created to emphasize the spiritual relationship between human life and nature have been eroded, diluted, and expunged from conscious commerce with the culture. Male and female alike, we have suffered the loss. The goddesses who personify this connection are not lightweight. Their imprint is deep, their message sonorous. Bury them and they will exhume themselves: Medusa, Athena's snaky-locked nemesis, with the tenacity to bear the disfigurement unleashed upon her by the competitive feminine maddened with an addiction to power. Eriskigel, the underworld goddess of Sumer, whose presence teaches a woman the forfeit of denial, the blessings of depression. Hecate, goddess of crossroads, whose serious commerce with the gates of Hades can guide a woman back from a psychic abduction, and Lilith, Adam's first mate, whose inexorable autonomy terrifies those who would demean a woman's birthright. These mythic representatives of the collective unconscious have equal representation in our personal psyche.

Equivalently, they appear in nature when they speak to us as tidal waves, earthquakes, mud slides, and all the great heaving and pitching of the planet midwifing herself in spite of the determined intention of humankind to abort her regeneration. Modern humankind continues to search for the meaning of life in all the wrong places while neglecting the wisdom of the heart, the intuition of the bodymind, or the fundamentals of natural instinct that begin in the womb.

Shared Womb Consciousness

Ultimately, as women, we must accept that we alone are the guardians of the sacred mystery of life. Through this shared "womb consciousness," we must consciously acknowledge our deep connection as one who is capable of mothering our own mother without rancor or blaming. Essentially a man must find his independence from his mother in order to claim the physical and psychic differences inherent in his maleness, however this process is far more complex for a woman. She must come to terms with how identical she is, psychically and physically, to the one from whom she must also differentiate herself, without accepting the patriarchy's cultural disgust for the feminine as a necessary part of the seamless nature of the mother-daughter mystery. This is no easy task. So many of us want to distance ourselves psychically from our mothers by idolizing our fathers and demonizing our mothers.

We can never be the male our culture accuses us of not being— never! We cannot but suffer self-degradation when we persist in aligning ourself against the feminine, because no matter how we keep our guard up, secure our arguments, every time we look in the mirror there she is.

No matter how minuscule, any positive memory of the sweet sacred community of the womb is precious beyond measure. Our dreams offer us every opportunity to come home to these memories. Regrettably, disembodied dream *interpretation* can disguise the infant's remembrance of ecstatic love for the first mother sapping that memory of its purity and joy. Spontaneous Movement replaces words with energy, interpretations with body wisdom. Misinterpreted, the fragile link between belonging and bereavement can be obliterated by too many words, too much logic. Every adult must have access to whatever fragment of good-enough mothering she is able to recover in order to banish the deep pain of emotional orphanage. And if there is none there she must have equal opportunity to own the strength it has taken to survive such a deficit.

One woman said, "Here I am, the president of a multimillion-dollar enterprise, and the inside of my body feels like a cavern with a bleak landscape and a dry cold wind ceaselessly blowing through me every time I have what others call a 'big success.' I absolutely don't know who the hell I really am or, even worse, what I am seeking way down in there. Last month my company was awarded a contract that guarantees me a sizable bonus and a very secure retirement. I went home after the announcement with the praise and the envy of my colleagues still echoing in my ears and cried. I sat by myself in the darkened room and whispered like a confused two-year-old—what's the point? Who really cares? I am so alone. What's the point? I felt like my heart would break. Now here I am telling you I have just had my first attack of angina and I feel scared to *death*. Well I won't live this way. If I'm to die soon I am going to love myself and this life I have left with all my heart and all my soul."

So, do you have to be on the verge of losing it all before you are willing to say, "I am going to love myself and live my life authentically, intuitively attuned to my heart and soul"?

Chapter Seven

MEETING THE
LOATHLY LADY
Coming to Peace with
Our Female Bodies

Consciousness inhabits even the humblest quarters
of our flesh.

—*Marc Ian Barasch*

THAT WHICH I HATE LOVES ME AND WILL NOT LEAVE ME ALONE and
that which I love kills me, letting me down over and over again."
So began Evangeline's first words to the movement group one
December evening. "I hate my inability to lose weight and I love the
food that is taking me down. I LOVE, LOVE, LOVE, THE FOOD
THAT IS KILLING MY SELF-RESPECT. I HATE, HATE, HATE

MY LUMPY BODY—MY FLABBY BELLY, MY GIGANTIC THIGHS. Oh God, I'm such a mess!"

While not all of us have feelings as strong as Evangeline's, I have never met any woman who is totally happy with her own body. Somewhere, usually between the ages of seven and thirteen, we begin to adopt a standard of comparison that guarantees we cannot measure up. This false standard is fueled by the fashion industry, reiterated by the media. Our personal dissatisfaction becomes localized and projected onto a part of our body that we then reject. This is not a modern phenomenon; however, it has become more pronounced in industrialized societies.

Indigenous societies rely upon their bodies to lead them, to teach them, to comfort them, to bring the entire community new life, new leaders. In Aboriginal Australia, after death and a year's interment, the bones are solemnly dug up and honored before being placed in a final resting place. History and the embodied spirit is being remembered. In Hawaii, the entire body is used through dance and movement to transmit the lore of a culture that finds meaning in movement, remembrance in embodiment. In Tibet, urine is smelled and the multilayered pulses of the heart are listened to through the healer's touch in order to determine what is ailing the bodymind. It is unthinkable in these cultures to blaspheme historical wisdom by hating this exquisite instrument of truth.

For those who seek conscious embodiment and the intuitive rewards it offers, modern culture's hatred of the female body presents real problems. For nowhere has the Western contempt for women's ways of knowing had a bigger impact than on our ability truly to embrace our intuitive knowing by having an ongoing, interactive loving relationship with our bodies.

When we begin to love the wild creature that is our body, the imperfections become the gateway to the deep feminine and all her diffuse energy has to offer. Make a list of everything you dislike about your body, and there before you, you have a map to your soul. Love these parts of your matter, and everything will begin to matter to you in a tender yet fiercely honest way. These rejected parts of your physical self are sources of intuitive strength. We can't honor the wisdom of Soul if we are wasting our energy rejecting our own incarnation.

Turning Up the Flame

At a workshop I was leading several years ago I asked the question, "When did you first realize that you could not feel at home within your own body?" Most reported somewhere before the age of nine. Many said by age three. Most said they had never discussed this feeling with anyone but had written a lot about it in their journals. Frequently a fear of betraying one or both parents by even writing this feeling down was expressed. Everyone had a specific memory of the first time she became aware of her sense of alienation from her own body, a sense of body betrayal.

MEETING THE REJECTED
PART OF THE BODY

Following is an exercise I have done with hundreds of women and men to help heal our relationship to the body.

Choose a comfortable space on the floor where you can stretch out and begin to work with the rejected part of your body. Place your journal and several sheets of blank paper near by. This experience will teach you what this business of the unconscious is all about by locating a complex in the body and following how its presence shapes and limits who you believe yourself to be.

Recognizing how cleverly the unconscious can disguise itself from our attempts to bring it into the light of consciousness, first take a sheet of paper and draw a simple picture of your body. Now, focus on the part of your body you don't like or that disappoints you, and add anything to that part of your picture that feels appropriate. Remember, I repeat, with this work the truth is everything. Lie to yourself and you may as well not do this exercise.

Stretching out on the floor, drop into your body by following your breath, moving deeper with each inhalation as you turn your attention to the rejected part or feature of you dislike. If you have no rejected part, then focus on the one feature you are most proud of. Become that and only that part of the body. Breathe into whatever you most dislike and allow yourself to feel yourself becoming the fat thighs or the family nose or the thin hair, or the great pecs. Then, with soft eyes, slowly come to your feet and allow the rejected part of your body to teach you. Focus only upon the way the rejected part moves, feels, needs you to feel for it to influence your life. Attentive to your breath, intensify the feeling and allow this energy to walk you. How are you moved by this energy? Can you move? Continue to breathe and intensify the experience as you consciously allow what has been moving you unconsciously to teach you about this neglected truth's impact.

Be a fair witness, open and nonjudgmental. Keep an open and curious mind. Return to your paper and redraw anything that is different. What have you found out about yourself? How does it feel to walk through the world defined by an interior identification with the part of your body you have rejected? Do you want to live this way? Are you willing to risk loving this part of your body no matter what?

Bringing a complex lodged in the body into consciousness by working with the rejected part of the body provides a way to dismantle the darkness by bringing it into the light a little piece at the time. That which we reject always draws a larger share of energy from us than it deserves, because it takes a lot of energy to keep it hidden, in check. The energy we invest in the rejection unconsciously shapes how we perceive ourselves from every angle—physical, mental, emotional, or spiritual. Without any conscious effort, every attempt at change or risk or creativity is weighed against the deficits we believe restrict us due to the handicap of this unloved body part. Your soul cannot fully occupy a bodymind that is so displeasing to the ego. Psychically the rejected part of the physical body becomes a living paradox. It is simultaneously the most adamantly rejected and ferociously protected part of what matters most to you. Once a personal introduction to the influence of an unconscious bodymind relationship has been made, each part of the bodymind must be explored to determine its capacity for consciousness in order to support work with the more rejected parts.

Evangeline, walking around the room while chanting, "What I love hates me," began to feel the weight of her feelings toward her thighs. At first she seemed to be heavily stamping each foot as she ponderously swung each leg forward. As her voice got softer and more rhythmical, she began to talk to her thighs softly in Polish. Moving to the floor she seemed to be planting her legs in imaginary soil while she sang a Polish children's song. Evangeline sat quietly for a long time. At first I thought she has fallen asleep. Then she slowly uncovered her legs, stroking her thighs and calling them "Grandmother and Grandfather."

A second-generation American, Evangeline wanted to be thin and "lovely" like her American playmates, not sturdy and stocky like her family of origin. Her body complied everywhere but in her thighs. Evangeline is an athlete. Her strong legs make her success in her sport possible.

By moving, Evangeline discovered it was her shame about her Polish ancestry that fueled her overeating. She made a bundle of rags which she draped over her belly to emphasize how she asked her belly to sag with her depression. Walking around the movement room, she allowed her belly to teach her about her unconscious self-abuse in order to avoid being fully aware of her pain. She found when she was in despair about her "flabby thighs and belly" she could not say No to her boyfriend's abuse. "Those two, my self-abuse and his deprecation of me, fit like a hand in a made-to-order glove."

Contemplative embodiment allows the damaging distortions and inaccurate beliefs we hold about our body image to be explored, experienced in our bodies, and accepted in a nonthreatening way. The pain still present has an opportunity to emerge, highlighted as a clearer, more authentically articulated self-image. Psychologist and yogi Jon Kasik reminded me that resistance is but the other side of resilience. Joy, relaxation, self-care, and a capacity for self-compassion lie weighted down beneath the resistances we maintain in order to avoid what we perceive as weaknesses or threats to well-being. When we confront our assumptions, we find an even increasing sense of authenticity, of strength and resiliency, to be mined and embraced.

The Loathly Lady

The myth of the Grail Quest, of King Arthur and the Knights of the Round Table, is probably the best known myth of Western civilization. Written from the perspective of a masculine quest, the myth has much to teach us about compassion and the no-nonsense acceptance of the feminine

King Arthur was out hunting and, fixed on the pursuit of a certain target, he overstepped a boundary and trespassed onto another's land. (A king, in fairy tale or myth, represents the ruling consciousness, the ego.) The knight who owned this land was incensed, demanding retribution—Arthur's life in exchange for his unconscious blundering about. Even the ego, we're to learn from this tale, makes blunders, takes far too much privilege for granted, and is not immune to punishment. In a burst of contrived and malevolent "fairness," the affronted knight agrees to give Arthur a fighting chance with a test. He must pass this test if he wants to keep his land and his life. Arthur is told to go out and within a limited amount of time return with the answer to the age-old conundrum, "What does the feminine want?"

Now here we have a pretty graphic picture of one of the terrifying ways a complex can affect us. The ego sets out feeling completely in charge of the world, goes unconscious, and makes a mess of something. Then another part of the unconscious roars forth and emotionally demands recompense, with threats, doomsayings, anxiety, or depression. In a flash, the world becomes a scary place, leaving the ego cowering and attempting to mobilize some protective defense. Confidence plummets, an emotional alarm sounds, and we are left quaking and in disarray. No matter how often this happens, each time is as awful as the last until we begin to recognize that this is not an unknown visitation but rather a disowned and unclaimed part of the Self demanding to be heard.

Arthur, the story tells us, approaching the deadline and grasping for the answer that will save him from a most unpleasant fate, passes a horrendously ugly hag known as the Loathly Lady squatting by the side of the road. She accosts him and chides him for his insensitivity—for ignoring her because she is not attractive. To his amazement, he discovers that this apparition claims she is the sole guardian of the answer. She alone has the power to save him from the deadly result of his overreach. Ah, yes. Poor, poor ego has to give up the illusions of power and entitlement and get down in the dirt to be redeemed.

It's a terrible moment when we realize the only salvation for our egoistic stance in life requires us to embrace the inner horror we have been trying to avoid. We want no one to even suspect that we harbor such foulness, yet it is this very aspect of ourselves we have to cozy up to if we are to survive. We cringe, get sick, get angry, plea, bargain, and still our hideousness waits, clutching the key, the answer, the pardon we yearn for while making it clear it is not to be ours unless we genuinely recognize that the hideousness is our hideousness. Our fears are valid. If an exchange is to be made it won't come without the ego paying a price.

Arthur, recognizing the seriousness of his plight, strikes a pact of honor. If she'll provide the answer, Arthur promises her marriage to his most innocent and unblemished knight, Sir Gawain. That's the arrogance of the ego, believing it only takes the sacrifice of some part of the psyche that isn't too important to get itself out of escrow. We'll soon see the surprising outcome of this maneuver. For one thing, Arthur has taken the better part of himself (his innocence) and offered to wed it to the more reprehensible part of his psyche (the hag).

Individuation, the process of deepening consciousness by integrating the unconscious while taking full responsibility for the underdeveloped parts of our personality, always exacts a sacrifice from the "fairest knight," from our innocence, our naiveté.

Gawain, as we might expect, does honor to his king by agreeing to wed this eminently repulsive creature. His act of honor pins him to the horns of a profoundly requiring dilemma. Facing the ritual of the marriage bed, he is confronted with an impossible choice from his bride. With hideous countenance and emanating the foulest of smells and sounds, she asks, "Shall I be fair for you by night and foul by day, or fair by day and foul at night?" This question succinctly sums up the ongoing ambivalence of modern humankind toward the feminine. We malign and ignore her by day and then court her each night in our dreams.

For Gawain, her question represents the conundrum of the insecure ego—be true to my deeper Self and appear loathsome in the eyes of others, or suffer the loss of my Soul in order to garner the approval of others? One way or the other, this resolve guarantees half the time is spent in the hideous grip of self-contempt.

Gawain's answer surely sent every bell in the halls of the Mysteries pealing. "*You choose,* my Lady. You choose, for it is *your body* and *you alone* know what is best for you." In that reverently intuitive instant of consciously honoring the instinctual wisdom of the feminine, as it ranges from the naturally winsome and egoistic vitality of youth to the blessed involution and withering of aging, the loathly lady transformed into a figure of rarest beauty. A fully enfranchised embodied woman, she no longer needed to live out the pretenses of others. She became her true Self.

This tale has profound implications for women. Fastening upon our loathliness, we become disembodied, disenfranchised, disillusioned. Meanwhile the unblemished (the soul) is evicted by our ignorance of its presence. Intuition, insight, imagination have no resonance when Soul has no birthright, no body, no home. Loathliness or loveliness is not the scale upon which a woman can confidently weigh her own inner worth. Nor is the degree of youthful beauty as laid up against aging valid either. Rather, Queenship—authority, sovereignty—over one's own authentic embodiment is the Grail from which the elixir of life is drawn.

What does the Sacred Feminine want for all of matter? Sovereignty. Reverently, honorably, vested authority over the realm of all that is natural. In her domain there will be no evaluative contest between lovely and loathly. Love's delicate touch and rage's cumbersome armor are each breathtakingly correct in the eyes of the feminine. Intuitive wisdom and well-honed logic are equally well met. The newborn's pristine beauty and the grandmother's well-worn countenance each need the other to complete the cycle of life.

One of my friends speaks lovingly about her participation at an annual gathering of older women. She describes that sacred moment when by the light of a nighttime fire she watched women dancing, touching, parting from, and rejoining with one another. The waltzing light of the bonfire dissolving the shadow forms of young bodies into the oldest among them, the elders then dissolving into a living mandala, of maiden, mature woman, and crone, each dancing, weaving her own presence into the shadowlight fabric of the moment. In the muted glow of the flames all were as one—lined and unlined, well-lived and infirm—beautiful in the complexity that is lovingly reflected by each incarnation.

YOUR LOATHLY LADY

In order to heal our relationships with our bodies and access our embodied intuition, we need to work with our own Loathly Lady. You can do this either by choosing a body part you hate, or by taking some chronic symptom you suffer from—a bad back, carpal tunnel, whatever. That's because a chronic symptom also carries an emotional charge and all sorts of repressed or unexamined attitudes and ideas that shape and define your behavior when you are under its influence. The symptom or body part is then referred to as the Loathly Lady.

Before you begin, chose a piece of music such as a Mozart violin concerto. Place your journal nearby and, as the music begins, go inward, following the pathway of your breath. As you begin to relax, scan your body and loosen or remove anything that is distracting you. Now allow your attention to go to the symptom or the rejected part of your body. Continue to breathe deeply and evenly, focusing on that place. If a sensation develops, intensify it without injuring yourself. Often the focus alone will provide enough of an increase in intensity. Allow yourself to hold this focus until a spontaneous movement arises from the tension in your body. Allow yourself to follow that movement until you are so inwardly focused on the experience that you become defined by what you are feeling. Allow your body to shape itself into the posture, the attitude, the energy as it unfolds.

Now experiment. How do you move when you are using only the energy of this symptom, this disliked part? Does your posture change? Are there images or sounds you want to make? What about your balance, your body image? Walk, crawl, roll up into a fetal position—whatever this part of your body leads you to do as you allow yourself to feel the shape you are in when your unconscious focuses is on this symptom or this loathly part.

Once you have a conscious sense of how you are being affected, allow yourself to move with the music as you get to know and respect, if not have compassion for, this loathly lady. You can use your journal to record your experience as you allow this symptom or this part of your body to teach you about self-hatred and self-love.

I've yet to meet the woman who is not moved by the Loathly Lady. After telling her story, I usually receive a swell of "confessions": "I can't believe how I've treated my thighs. Hating them I've hated myself." "I have always raged against this brown stain on my arm until, in today's workshop I remembered it's there as a badge of courage. As a kid I was badly burned in a fire and the scars on my upper arm represent a life saved, not ruined." "I am mourning how I have hated my own mud, my own body." One participant who had lost a leg in an accident said she wept with joy when she confronted the hatred she harbored for the stump that remained and heard an inner voice say, "Suit yourself. I've never let you down and I've watched you learn to do more with a prosthesis than most two-legged people. I've been right here all along." Later she reported that she still mourns the loss of her leg, but she no longer hates her body.

Every one of us carries some mark of courage, some scar of contest with the world stamped upon our body. These insignias are yours to claim in deep appreciation for a body that would not collapse under the weight of its marring. Bearing stretch marks, birth marks, skinned and scuffed, burned and beaten, our body sustains the blows and resiliently renews itself every seven years. An unmarked body houses an unlived life. Focused upon with compassion and benevolence, these marks are intuitive touchstones with a language of their own. Even a missing limb will arrest our attention and turn us inward with phantom limb pain. The woman with the missing leg says she has learned that when her missing leg "speaks," she listens and finds that almost always she was about to make a choice or decision without the counsel of her intuition. Shyly she says, "When I go unconscious and there's no me to speak for myself, my soul speaks from the leg that isn't there. I guess I can call it my phantom intuition."

The unnatural social judgments about acceptability demand a sacrifice of the natural order of life in the quest for perfection or competition. They create an artificial priority that wounds us personally, rupturing our relationship with matter. Strip mining, strip shopping, deforestation, littering, insecticides—each reflect how deeply entrenched the antirelational prejudices of our forefathers have become. The planet is fast becoming a tortured Loathly Lady as the body of an unconscious humankind absorbs the deadly blows it inflicts upon nature. Personal symptoms only differ in scale from the global symptoms of neglect.

Waking from the Spell

There is an urgent summons for the modern woman to release herself from the spell of ego worship, entitlement, and white-knighted maidenhood. The dragon that must be slain is our personal indifference and hatred of our own embodiment. The gods and goddesses aren't out there somewhere. They are images lodged in our imaginations, describing the prescriptions for what most ails humankind. The god of wind is the guardian of breath, the goddess of love a guide to the heart's energies, the furies, the muses, are all personifications of the variety and complexity of the psychomatic state we call incarnation. They do not speak to us in well-ordered, logical syntax and theory. They beg our attention irrationally, symbolically, symptomatically, and imaginally via intuitions, hunches, insights, and dreams. Ignored and ignorant, we lose—and life goes on.

Our compliance with the unconscious brutality that we allow to be inflicted upon the feminine by brutalizing ourselves rests as surely in the unconsciousness of women as of men. One of the most wicked contracts struck between patriarchal history and modern woman is the belief that in order to be found pleasing in the eyes of men, a woman has to best other women first, beginning with her own daughter by teaching her self-hatred and self-denial. Buying into this toxic contract for competition with our sisters, we utilize the defense of suspiciousness in order to overpower our innate capacity to trust from the heart. It is not too late to identify your own Loathly Lady, intuitively face that part of yourself, and humbly listen to what your sacred feminine has to offer you.

Resacrilizing the Body

Hating a part of your body is madness. It saps the creative capacities of life, reduces every joy to a base comparison between the pleasure of embodiment and the disparagement of the hated part. The sheer joy of embodiment is constricted by the weight and measurement of living in a body marred by self-contempt. The abhorrence that inhabits you— whatever the drug, relationship, complaint, or remorse might be—is the demon that keeps you "deliciously" locked in a deadly dance with the body part you hate, and that can kill your creative relationship with the feminine. All that matters is the deflation and despair that seeps in as you feed off the hatred.

In a talk he gave several years ago, Andrew Harvey said we can't know the world, the sacred feminine, without loving the world. No surprise then that you can't surrender fully to a love affair with matter without loving your body—your own personal portion of this world. When the archetype of Spirit, the basic, elemental, becoming energy of the universe, enters the matter's realm, it becomes the zygote that becomes the fetus that becomes the matter of your embodiment.

Birth brings consciousness with it, and the spirit of that consciousness is potently embedded in every molecule, every atom of matter. When the energy of your destiny, your nature, gets split off, only the soul's metaphoric language will retrieve it. Awaken the metaphor that is hidden within the rejected part of your body, and you will feel its presence releasing blocked energy as it links your neural network, your immune system, and your endocrinal pathways with your intuition, imagination, and emotions. The indwelling spirit that has been locked away by your disdain will metamorphosize exponentially. What once appeared as a dark stormcloud will reveal itself as a creative thunderhead.

Every bit of consciousness is garnered at the expense of letting go of the security of your unconsciousness. The core issue of trust in or fear of your embodiment will go with you in some form to the grave. Individuation, consciously doing your inner work, will not eradicate that which has wounded you. What it will do is heal the distances between the fragments that form the gestalt of your life, so that you feel the creative interweaving of your psychic life with the waxing and waning of your physical body and the rise and fall of your psychology.

Psychosomatic individuation, embodied wholeness, releases you from the illusion that Spirit, Soul, bodymind, and the complexes are separate unrelated entities. The intuitive body brings all the disparate parts of the Self back into the alchemical community of mattering. To heal the psychic, somatic, and spiritual wounds of our lives we must uncover the rejected parts of the Self, name them, and learn to love the lessons each and every incident has brought.

Together as if with a silent summons we
stand in witness to the fire.
Nine will own not one degree of heat,
Or care for nothing, no, nothing.
Yet one,
that certain singular distempered one
in homage to a skewed rapport,
Will yield.
Tempered by the flame,
the stone of her desire pouring as liquid,
Slaking the firebrand of her searching.

—Becca, 1991

Women's
Intuition

Chapter Eight

TRUSTING INTUITION TO LEAD US

Through the lens of intuition all things reflect
Vitality.

—[pmr]

ONCE WE BEGIN TO CLEAR AWAY MUCH OF WHAT HAS STOOD in the way of conscious embodiment, we begin to feel, see, and hear the murmurs of our intuition more clearly. We must pay heed to these whisperings or else they will again disappear. These faint signals come from the essential Self, urging us to be true to ourselves and the changes authenticity brings. But we face many challenges as we learn to listen in—for example, what if what we hear is disruptive to our lives? How do we differentiate between "true" signals and those that should be ignored? These are crucial issues, particularly for women because our desire to please is so strong.

Our strength not to succumb to the fear of rejection, alienation, or abandonment by those who want us to stay the same will be tested. This can be very difficult, for the urge to change may bring us into conflict with the others who share our lives. Whether we wish it or not, as females, our primary core desire in life is to relate genuinely, at a soul level. Connections, relationships, unions, and weaving are what the feminine is all about. The threat of a loss of relationship is no small thing.

Because of this, it is inevitable that we will feel a conflict between what our intuition is telling us we want at the deepest level and our wish to avoid a disruption in the expectations that we have been carrying for those we love. Listening to our bodies, we may even realize that we have agreed to things not because we truly felt them, but to guarantee that we will not be abandoned or rejected. Revisiting the many barters made under the guise of only wanting to avoid conflict or not make waves in order to belong, to be acceptable, to be thin enough, or bright enough, or to avoid gossip, we may discover we really don't give a damn about an antiseptically clean kitchen floor, parenting, marriage, or the latest fashion.

We live in a culture unprepared to differentiate between being female and the issues of the feminine. Female roles and tasks, whatever they might be, are not always reflective of or conductive to the full expression of the deep feminine. A woman can feel deeply fulfilled by motherhood, yet mourn in silence for the loss of her truer self—for a return to her deepest yearning. We can reach our ego-driven goals, in jobs, professions, or marriages, and still awaken each morning with the tracks of dried tears etching our faces. In our sleep we are weeping for a return to the deep feminine. We silently yearn for the freedom to come home to our essential being.

These two, fulfillment and mourning, are neither exclusive nor incompatible. Every time a woman gives of herself to create life for another she also must grieve the loss of time and solitude for inner life. Every woman who gives birth to a child or an idea or a dream must also come to terms with what she must lose if she is to say Yes to this new energy. It is the way of the feminine that each springtime advent heralds also the coming fall and winter.

Each compromise that we make to conceal our feminine essence in order to avoid rejection will have to be renegotiated before we can claim the psychospiritual truth of our genuine feelings and the spiritual compass of intuitive knowledge. We must learn how and when to yield to the opinions of others and when to stand firm even though we feel desperately inadequate and alone.

You may remember Jodie Foster's character as a scientist in the movie *Contact,* who is awakened to the reality of universal love, saying, "We feel so cut off, so lost, only we are not." And being told by an "alien" that humans are such a paradoxical species—"capable of such beautiful dreams and such terrible nightmares." Living the paradox of a beautiful dream and a terrible nightmare is an apt metaphor for the unholy union of the deep feminine attempting to dream a woman into full embodiment when the woman is living in a culture that devalues her especially because she is female. Psychologist William James echoed the profound plight of the disembodied human life also when he penned, "The hell to be endured hereafter is no worse than the hell we make for ourselves in this world by habitually fashioning our characters in the wrong way." What women are taught to care about the most often leaves no room for any care for the soul. Our first loves often teach us to ignore our deeper need for self-love. So we learn to please others and in the process abandon a precious part of our Self.

For a woman, one of the first and more difficult stages of psychological independence is learning at an early age to discriminate confidently between what Mother thinks is right for me and what I know is right for myself. Holding to that position in the face of a feared loss of her love and an innate terror of abandonment takes fortitude. Yet it is only when we discover that we are lovely in spite of our "rebellion" can we feel the strength of our uniqueness, our individuality, our selfhood.

That being said, it is no easy task for most of us. I have exquisite empathy and respect for the tension contained between the instinctual urge to live life more consciously and the emotional pull to maintain the status quo. I, personally, am especially susceptible to physical problems every time I am called to extend myself beyond where I feel comfortable and predictably in charge.

This manuscript originally began with a central theme based upon a dream I had at the age of four. As it was written and revised, it metamorphosed into something less poetic, less mythic. As I have taken a leap of faith following my editor's guidance, I have had mild but persistent acne for the first time in decades. I felt protected, and secure allowing the mythic to protect me as I related intuition to the gods and goddesses of mythology, not to myself or those I have worked with. These lines feel bold, bald-faced, and without disguise. Facing this risk has not been easy. Yet these revisions feel deeply correct.

As an intuitive, my body has carried the tension of the risk in this transition. For others the tension may result in emotional distress—in depression or agitation. Determining what is correct for you is between you and your inner wisdom, you and your confidence that there is a higher purpose, a benevolent energy, at work in your life. Wasn't it Einstein who said the ultimate question is whether or not we believe that this is a benevolent universe? When our external systems fail us, when beloved others die or leave, there has to be a steadfast inner retreat to return to, to move out from. There has to be an unshakable ground of being.

For some of us a leap of faith may leave us disoriented, "cotton-headed and forgetting who I am." Others become disembodied, detached from everything but necessity. And for others the experience is more tragic—too fearful to continue, they return to their depression or addiction or painfully shallow out their desires. The choice points often come without preamble, catching us in mid-stride.

One morning while on a trip to the central desert in the outback of Australia I was flooded with the quiet, absolute realization that I was happier and more creatively challenged than I had been in years. There

I was, awake, alive, and vitally engaged by the awesome impersonal power of nature as I never have been before or since. I made a life-changing decision that I was going to close my therapy and lecture practice in the States, and return and spend time in Central Australia. The decision felt deeply satisfying. Then I began to fret about the complications my desire would create. I felt ambivalence seep in, but I brushed it away. Within hours I was ill. So ill I had no choice but to leave the desert if I wanted to live. Emotionally I was unprepared for the radical shift in consciousness my decision engendered, so my body carried the shock.

I will be the first to tell you that knowing the message between the covers of this book and learning how to live in this manner is an ongoing discipline for me. For most of us, our childhood leaves us ill prepared for the kind of sturdy soul-reliance that would encourage us to find security and spiritual self-fulfillment in a radical change based largely upon instinct or intuition. And I can tell you also there are those of you who will read this book and know that for you, like me, there is no other way.

Most of us have to wait for a serious illness or a catastrophe before we listen to Spirit's relationship to Soul. Beforehand, if we turn to Spirit it's as a New Age delight, a magical plaything, or a disembodied power out in the vast reaches of the unknown and unknowable, whose guidance and benevolence seems random and elusive or girded with daunting requirements. Instinctually the deep feminine urges us to plumb our very depths. Emotionally we are torn by how daunting acceptance can seem. Once we are more embodied and listening to our intuition, we are guided by the deep feminine's sense of morality. This morality can't be legislated.

Essential Morality

A collision between instinct and emotion usually indicates a clash between a strong unconscious (and therefore unexpressed) desire and an equally strong conscious resistance. Consciously exploring the relationship between these two seemingly oppositional urges can uncover the revitalizing roots of your own *sense of essential morality*. This level of morality can't be legislated by church or state. The principle of essential morality the feminine lives by is an instinctual inner principle: an embodied sense of what must be and a standpoint of personal cellular-level authority strong enough not to yield to anything less. It is out of this source ground that a woman can develop an unshakable trust in the wisdom and strength of her personal choices.

Of morality, feminist thinker Carol Gilligan writes in *In a Different Voice:*

> The essence of moral decision is the *exercise of choice and the willingness to accept responsibility for that choice* [italics mine]. To the extent that women perceive themselves as having no choice, they correspondingly excuse themselves from the responsibility that decision entails. Childlike in the vulnerability of their dependence and consequent fear of abandonment, they claim only to wish to please, but in return for their goodness they expect to be loved and cared for. This then is an "altruism" always at risk, for it presupposes an innocence constantly in danger of being compromised by an awareness of the trade-off that has been made.

The deep desire for acceptance when combined with no choice except to fear and repress any conflictual message from the body that tells us we must step out on our own can smite us with paralyzing emotional jolts of inadequacy and undermine the development of instinctual morality. The unedited emotions that erupt when a social compromise conflicts with a deeply held intuitive truth are the bodymind's primary method of arresting us in mid-stride and jarring us into a reevaluation of what really *matters*. Complying unconsciously with whatever we perceive will alleviate the unwelcome feeling and thereby reduce the terrifying innate fear of abandonment affects our nervous system like a deadening drug, and we go spiritually limp, losing our psychological footing and our somatic ground. The emotional stupefaction severs our innate intuitive relationship to the body and disarms our instinctual capacity to protect ourselves. Bereft of self-confidence, we relinquish our connections to our personal convictions and collapse internally.

When we are so challenged, if we are able to pause and turn inward, our intuition can and will save the day. Anxiety, agitation, excitement—the full range of emotions and sensations that have us in their grip during a denial of instinct—are signals from our intuition. They mean something, if not at times everything. One of the reasons we avoid our intuition at a time like this is because our culture teaches us to think these responses are pathologically female—hormonal, hysterical, or flaky. No one has taught us that what we are more likely experiencing is the vibrational energies of our moral compass realigning us with a deeper and thereby essential truth that will not tolerate diminishment any longer.

Off-balance and misguided by cultural and social standards that deny the influence of the deep feminine, we are pulled into an unconscious competition with our true Self. Torn between the deep desire to protect our vulnerability at any cost and the yearning to make the choice that may lead to spiritual independence stirs up an internal war. The clarity of focused inquiry—What do *I* want? How does my body feel? What are my dreams trying to tell me?—flees, lost to the fierce emotional competition such an unspoken battle engenders. In the end a migraine, fatigue, depression, eating—anything seems preferable to the tension.

Choices based upon personal authority can't, after all, just be pulled out of thin air or thinner information. These more definitive choices that form the basis for a moral imperative, a keen sense of knowing who you are and what you are about, require a sense of discernment and discrimination. Otherwise, even you will soon be skeptical about the benefits of knowing yourself well, of seeking intuitive insights as guidance to live and grow old by. Intuition is a distillation of the vast repository of spiritual wisdom that saturates the universe. We would be swamped by the muchness of it all if we didn't learn to take our time, to listen, to focus, and to choose what we can respond to and what we cannot.

Discernment and Discrimination

Not wanting to displease is only one of the challenges faced by those wishing to become more intuitive. Another is learning to decipher and decode the messages from the body, to recognize when they should be listened to and when they are to be overlooked. One woman I know who attributes emotional meaning to everything is reminded often by her best friend, "Sometimes a headache is just a headache." True, but often it is a message, and the ability to discover the difference is a crucial skill in accessing intuition.

One of my favorite people is a computer wizard. She designs complicated programs that run several large corporations. "Phooey, so much hokum" is her generic dismissal to any mention of her intuition. One day she was laughing about how she had a hunch about a program and made an uncalculated change "when my hands just itched to try it" that turned out to be a "brilliant solution. But who," she laughed, "would have thunk it! Dumb luck strikes once again." In mock dismay I put my hands together over my heart and said, "Forgive her, Soul, she's a nonbeliever and has no idea the debt she owes you for tweaking her hands." My friend stopped and sat with her mouth open: quite a sight from one whose quick wit and electric intellect is seldom stilled. Then she said, "So that's what you've been talking about! Now I get it. I've done this all my life. It got me through exams and all sorts of tough quandaries. I've always said I have a tiny librarian running around in my head that can download what I can't remember or figure out and put it at my fingertips." "Yep," I said "and her name is intuition." Later I made her a little card that says, "In or Out I'm intu-it." We may not have the map to our intuition, but the territory is always there. It's all a matter of perception.

Discernment, the ability to perceive differences, and *discrimination,* the capacity to differentiate between which of those differences is correct for you and which is not, are the twin pillars of the portal into conscious embodiment and higher intuitive functioning. Both require focused commitment and the disciplined practice of listening to and learning from your particular intuitive style. We tend to avoid anything that smacks of discipline as too patriarchal, rigorous, unyielding, or stifling. That's discipline done from power. The discipline of commitment is done from love. Love allows you to open to the deep feminine as a teacher, and you, her disciple, hand yourself over to the conscious discipline of your novitiate as you come before the altar of your soul and are taught the story of your life yet to be lived.

In this book I am talking mostly about intuition at an intrapersonal level, a dialogue between you and your soul about your Self. But there is also the work—the discrimination—of sorting out the difference between an intuition about someone or something outside yourself that does not impact you or your life directly, and an intuition that is specifically about you. When you follow the lead of your body about your intuitions, you will always be doing your own work first. Even when your initial intuition is about another, your somatic responses will quickly tell you the difference. In *Awakening Intuition,* Mona Lisa Schulz has many fine examples of how she learned the difference between her symptoms as hers and those of her clients. Belleruth Naparstek, in *Your Sixth Sense,* clearly defines and then gives many examples of this also.

As Carol Gilligan so succinctly reminds us, as we become conscious of the difference between living to please and taking pleasure in our own life, then we alone have to develop a sense of discernment about what we choose to commit to and to what we cannot. Intuition can be very helpful in the development of confidence that our choices are our own and not just another way to please. Choice demands discernment and discrimination; otherwise we will accept what others choose for us and lose our moral footing—parroting the opinions of others, we'll have no true compass of our own.

Discernment comes first, since it is the capacity to observe, notice, and select what you are drawn to, what you focus your attention upon. Discrimination is the next level of this process, as you decide how little or how much of something, as you sort through the many possibilities and allow yourself to choose what feels correct, what seems to matter the most. This isn't a scientific process, nor is it random. Rather it is a complex multilayered sensorial experience that becomes increasingly natural with practice. Once begun, you'll discover you'll no longer be willing to settle for being silent, or cotton-headed, or whatever you used to rely upon to get you past the tension. You'll value your capacity to change your mind or your direction in mid-stride, mid-sentence, or midway if your intuition tells you to.

My dreams and my intuition are my spiritual gyroscope in the most practical sense. They guide me and I listen, working many hours a week with my dreams and using SCM daily. My closest friends will tell you, "Paula will cancel a trip, change her plans, or even hold still if her intuition or a dream interrupts her course in life." That's true. I count myself fortunate that I've never had to cancel a speaking engagement or make a change that seriously affected others. This would be very difficult to do if I felt I had to, yet I would. It's the risk we take. A commitment to conscious choice is quickly trivialized by indifferent misuse. What begins as a foundation for a clarity of essential moral conviction becomes nothing more than a casualty to our emotional ambivalence. Lo, we return to asking others to tell us what to believe in.

Developing Your Own Gyroscope

Once, at a conference, a woman came into my workshop holding a feather she had found on the lawn. She was sharing her find with others when a man said he too had found a group of three gull feathers on the beach at dawn that very morning and he pulled them out of his journal to display. A third person spoke up and inquired, "What does this mean? What do feathers stand for? What is going on here?" I told them I had no idea, but each of them did, and I was confident each one of them was attracted to the feathers for their own unique reasons. Each had been discerning enough to notice and pick them up. Now it was up to each one to discriminate between the feather, my feather, what is feathering in me—what this symbol evokes and attracts. Asking someone else to give you their answers is begging the depth of the spiritual summons your feathering evokes.

Paraphrasing the words of a poet, what we love is so small, yet that which loves us is Infinite. Our inclination is to follow the small, the generic—to go to a symbol dictionary for a quick solution or dilute the intrapersonal experience by seeking to compare our particular feather with what a feather means to another. Meanwhile we miss the infinite source of our own feathering—as our imagination is awakened today to this feather, in this place, at this time.

At this same workshop a woman said, "I'd like to know the meaning too. I've been collecting stray feathers for years and I don't know what they mean, only that I always feel happy when I find one." Several years later she wrote me a letter telling me that she had never accepted my invitation to allow her intuition to guide her on her quest for insights about those feathers. "Last summer," she wrote, "I lost my best friend and lover. I was ruined by the grief, and one night to comfort myself I took out my feather box. When I opened it I was horrified to find the feathers were riddled with mites. Eaten up, powdered, destroyed. I laid them out on the floor and asked my bodymind what does this mean to me? After a week of spontaneously moving to my sorrow, painting, and writing in my journal daily I am at peace. Feathers no longer attract me. I smile when I see one now. I've gotten the message of the feather and it had nothing to do with feathers—it had to do with loving myself."

The practice of choosing to take your life seriously takes willpower. At times it will feel as if you are going against all guarantees of security as you break your familiar patterns of compliance—the expected postures of agreeableness. Yet it is from the relentless sorting and distillation of the ferment of embodied choice that true conscious embodiment emerges.

Intuitively informed choices are not random guesses. What informs you from the depths of the feminine must be heard, must be respected, if you are to know your Self fully. Self-respect leads to the principle of self-love. You cannot disrespect your personhood and love the soul that lives within you. The principle of self-respect requires that choices be made between the immediate demands of the instinctual life (the automatic response to just survive) and the more refined purposes of self-reflection (what *I* want in order to spiritually thrive).

The laser energies of focused, discriminating love for the embodied soul burn the heart's chambers clean of diffuse feelings of fear and powerlessness. Focused self-respect crystallizes a well-articulated sense of personal authority, of what I call the "standpoint." Standpoint is a metaphor for the ground of being: a conscious claiming of who and what you are willing to stand for, up to, and upon. Consciously claiming and embodying a decision, a change of attitude, or a deepening of consciousness by ritually getting to your feet declares your commitment to putting your foot down and allowing your truth to stand under you. Yes, it's true that we can scare ourself into abject submission when we claim a personal conviction and don't have a clue about what to do next. It helps to know this and be prepared. These changes may not come easily but they come with a lifetime—maybe a multi-lifetime, who knows?—guarantee.

One woman told how after much soul searching, she finally gathered up sufficient courage and conviction to face her domineering father's demeaning criticism and tell him she was leaving the family business to go off on her own. She said her father listened, scowling. When she was finished her dad raised an eyebrow and condescendingly asked, "So? What do you want from me? A bouquet?" "I collapsed," she recalled later. "I hadn't considered anything but relief and I felt his disdain like a knife through my side." Only partially prepared, she didn't know how to protect herself from an unimagined outcome. Depressed, she used his emotional response to validate how dangerous her conviction had been and decided maybe he was right. Maybe she was being premature.

Can we ever be totally prepared? Sometimes. More often the best preparation we can make is to take each feeling seriously one by one as we play out every possible outcome in our imagination, first. Notice which outcome really stirs you up or leaves you numb or cold. Instead

Women's
Intuition

of interpreting the feeling or, worse yet, ignoring it, turn inward and allow your bodymind to speak to you about your fears or your strengths. You'll be better prepared, feel far more protective of yourself, better able to maintain your standpoint even though you can feel the ground shifting beneath your feet. The admonishment to "be as strong as the mighty oak" is not the way of the feminine. She is as bamboo. Flexible, bending, and moving as would an aikido master who watches the blow come toward her and moves slightly; she remains on her feet, well-balanced and grounded, as the blow passes her by.

One way or another a woman cannot avoid the tough task of soul searching and discrimination if she is to determine which is more authentic for her—who she wants to become, or who society tells her she must be. The difficulties of claiming authenticity in the face of conflicting demands are often described in early mythology. Looking at the Greek myth of Athena and her dark sister Medusa, we quickly see how personal authority can be a strength when used consciously and a handicap when taken to extremes.

Athena and Medusa

The goddess Athena, unrelenting representative of a strong feminine standpoint, is said to have sprung fully developed from the head if her father, Zeus. With such a beginning, she merits her reputation as a goddess of purposeful intent. As a guardian of clear thought and focused creativity, her energy mentors those whose cognitive skills augment decisions (like my computer genius friend). This energy is present in your life when there are tough decisions to be made and you choose to contain your emotions while you think through your options. Her behavior is never ambiguous. A consideration of feelings is never her preference. Her resolve is always well thought out and pointedly executed. Rational and "heady," she is reputed to have intellectually distanced herself from the embodied affectual concerns of sensation and emotion. Choice benefits from clear thought. The risk here is relying too heavily upon good sense and forgetting or deleting the emotional input from your body. Athena's brand of conviction can provide confirmation and courage during the initial cultivation of a woman's own intellectually creative actions.

Every woman who has gone into graduate school or climbed the corporate ladder via skillful strategies and intellectual enterprise can sing Athena's praises. In mythology, Athena was an advisor, mentor, and protector of those who approached the battles of life with intellectual heroism. It is said she was a weaver also, turning to the loom to weave together the variegated threads of her creative logic. Her competitive nature in the mental realm is legend. In her presence a woman is offered the gifts of clear vision (focused thinking) and well-honed insight (self-reflection) as prerequisites to choice making. She is the goddess of assertion, not ambivalence. She will not tolerate a woman bewitching herself with either a paralyzing ambivalence or an altruistic barter with her soul.

When you are torn between two possibilities, allow your clear-thinking Athena energy to follow each possibility to its endpoint. This is one of her gifts. Do I get pregnant or not? Well, if I do what will happen after I get the news? And then what, yes, and then what? To the endpoint. All the while stopping periodically and allowing your body to move spontaneously into an embodied awareness as you come to each discriminated choice point. Your Athenian nature will assist you in staying conscious, aware of how you are proceeding and what the process means to you and you alone. Your body will send you the messages from your intuition about the soul implications of each choice. Athena teaches us to appreciate our capacity to recognize conflictual choices as *possibilities,* not *problems.*

It is pure foolishness for a woman to ever pretend that she can neither reason her desires through to a meaningful endpoint, nor does she need to. When coupled with self-reflection, emotional integrity, and intuitive awareness, reason and resolve are the markers of a creative, well-focused, consciously embodied intellect.

Like Athena, born from her father's forehead, we too are intellectually sired by the patriarchy. If we remain headstrong and disembodied, our thinking is shaped by our cultural context, our emotions conscripted by a culture that values concepts over relationship. Conscription legislates bondage. Such a restriction of emotional integrity will force the shadow side of a bright goddess to reveal itself in a corruption of unclaimed and unrefined feelings.

When Athena's bright energy turns dark it reveals an intellectual aggressiveness, whose bludgeoning judgments can block a woman's fluid sensuousness, her intuitive knowing, and all flexible receptivity to relationship by turning her, or anyone who displeases her, to stone. How many times have you rehearsed what you intended to say or do, only to be overtaken by a scathingly judgmental energy that leaves your best intentions in a shambles?

This darkness is primitive in its instinctual drive to be embodied also. Unfeeling, stony decisions are disembodied decisions. Medusa, Athena's mythological counterpart, is the snaky-haired representative of totally disembodied feelings. Barren of any emotional input, this energy is capable of ruthlessly paralyzing any who attempt to offer a differing perspective. Head wreathed in snakes, she telegraphs the viperous potency of rigid opinions. Medusian assessments eradicate all connections to feeling. Compassion and empathy are summarily disallowed. This energy carries the seeds of a vindictive instinctual ruthlessness that we often use to ward off any who would sense our emotional vulnerability. Oddly enough, when this energy captures you, the eruption of fury may be chilling and frozen, but it is still a supercharged withering emotional blast. Medusa's wordless alienating fury is in stark contrast to Athena's creative patronage, whose inspiration can elicit uninhibited artful expressiveness.

Medusian energy leaves us feeling estranged—cut off—while Athenian energy leaves us receptive—securely related. From this emotional vantage point, your Athena energies provide the constancy necessary for weaving together relationships imbued with focused respect and caring, not compliance and indifference. And your Medusian energies are equally useful in their force and impact. It is impossible to be in the grip of such stoniness without at least one fragment of curiosity about "Why?"

These two metaphoric figures are but reflections of a shared dynamic: one pole clear, purposeful, mentoring; the other cold, defensive, alienating. Both of these attitudes reside side by side within the range of every woman's susceptibility either to be influenced by focused desire or to be ruled by diffuse emotion.

When these two metaphoric aspects of the feminine are forced into opposition within the psyche, a woman can suffer bone-chilling periods of stony silence or icy mean-spiritedness in which a precious idea or an anticipated connection is aborted in a frozen and abrupt manner. If you've ever had this experience it's rather like watching your alien "sister" take command of your life.

When I lived in Panama, I had a neighbor who periodically would alienate the majority of her friends and her family with a haughty judgmental style that could pierce the most armored of hearts. One day after a particularly ruthless bout of attacking her friends during a birthday party, I found her standing by the seawall crying. In a moment of rare disclosure, she revealed that just when she felt closest to everyone she got scared that she was imagining the warm reciprocal feelings she felt. Exposed and needy, she felt she had to push everyone away before they rejected her. Unable to speak up and check out her perceptions, she projected her own critical, opinionated inner dialogue onto them. Believing in this falsely orchestrated interior scenario as her only option, she reacted with a ruthless defensiveness. Others, baffled, were frozen in their tracks.

When a woman, unable to speak for herself, feels harshly judged by her own inner authority, she is in the presence of Medusa, the petrifying underdeveloped aspect of Athena. Medusa's thoughtless, unfeeling opinions fill our heads and are capable of rending a woman or her target immobile. In this guise she is an energetic guardian of self-effacing disrespect.

Medusa appears when we are competing against ourselves, and the soul is the pawn. Serpentine, she represents the fury of the rejected feminine grown desperate in her starvation for genuine contact. Deadened to the ecstatic body, emotionally walled off, your Medusa energies are

180

Women's
Intuition

starved for authentic relationship. About this psychic posture Marion Woodman writes, "One aspect of the dark cave is the unconscious body, frozen as an iceberg, without personal feeling, made rigid by stress and drivenness: work harder, achieve more, get money, gain power, drink more, smoke more, eat more, have more sex. Any male or female existing in a frozen body (symbolized in dreams by freezers, snow scenes, and impenetrable glass) is Medusa's victim, gradually turning self and loved ones into stone. Nothing has personal value. All the senses are partially closed down because to open them is to open to a volcano." In Medusa's grip there is no room for intuition, just rigidity and control. Many of us take our Medusas to the workplace as an underdeveloped feminism, thwarting male and female relationships alike.

Medusa energies influentially reside in our bodymind and must not be ignored. Our task is not to attempt futilely to eliminate them, but rather to bring them to consciousness so they heal, not sicken, us, our children, and society. Medusa energies keep us rigidly opinionated without the balanced rationality of Athena. This stance is the downside of too much unfeeling intellect, too little emotional clarity, and even less of the healthy and creative awareness of bodily sensations and feelings that would help us use our intuition.

Medusa energies are not all bad when seasoned with a big dollop of conscious choice. A woman can benefit from her Medusa energies when she is confronted with evil. Facing the virulence of such things as child abuse, battering, crippling addictions, or destructive societal practices, she will be able to protect herself or those whom she loves by consciously turning the perpetrator to stone. The capacity to voice a dispassionate and implacable "No way!" is Medusa's irreproachable purview. "Stonewalling," "stony gaze," and "stone still" are all metaphors for the conscious standpoint that is etched in stone. Both Medusa and Athena know that the word *No* is a complete sentence!

After Medusa's death, Athena wore Medusa's severed head on her breastplate, as an *aegis,* a symbol of strength and authority. Jean Bolen points out in *Goddesses in Everywoman* that this defense will protect a woman when she fears the valance of her own vulnerability. Thus well protected, the same woman must remember that it is a symbol only and can be put on or taken off at will; otherwise she can get captured by the unmitigated power inherent in such a highly defended attitude and betray herself by becoming a caricature of the very evil she wishes to defend herself against. The flexibility of will, to know where your Medusa resides and summon her if needed, belongs to the development of conscious choice and a grounded sense of personal integrity, of soulful morality and self-reflective intuition.

Backwash: Self-Betrayals

Alix has struggled for two years with a left knee that gives way under emotional stress. Her physician can't find anything remarkably wrong. Feeling betrayed by her weakened knee and remembering the first time she felt she betrayed herself, she recounts this story:

> I am five and I am making my very first cake. It is a sheet cake for my grandfather's lunch. The women in the family are helping me and I feel so grown up, a real part of their close knit kitchen club. Just as the pan is readied for the oven, my aunt says I have left out the baking soda and that the cake won't rise. Distressed and embarrassed, I am frozen by my ignorance. In a flash I have been reduced from full and joyful membership to an inept fledgling. She tells me it will be OK if I stir it in as long as I don't scrape the grease coating the bottom and sides of the pans. I do what she tells me to do, even though something tells me to pour it out and stir it all together. I feel bruised by my oversight but happy again.
>
> Filled with the most delicious anticipation, I am stunned when the pan is withdrawn from the oven and the cake is flat on one end and about four inches high on the other. I had carefully stirred the leavening into one end only, not knowing it would not spread throughout the batter. I felt awful. Weak in my knees, I wanted to flee. Then I heard two differing layers of conversation

swirling around me. One: the reassurances of the women that any-one could have made such an error. No problem. A great first effort. Won't ever harm the taste. Grandfather's piece will be from the risen end. And the other: an amused commentary on my mis-take with smiles and chuckles and smug remarks about teaching a five-year-old to bake something so complicated. Their ambiva-lence stung; a snaky betrayal. I felt enraged that no one had told me what everyone else so obviously knew. And I felt really sad that I hadn't poured it out like I thought I should.

But the worst part came as I compounded my pain and confusion by letting *myself* down. Listening, as if for the first time, to my own competitive internal discourse between my desire to be a good girl and the newly emergent, but angry and hurt, betrayed woman-child, I gave into the good girl and was silently compli-ant. I told no one that I really wanted to pour the batter out and then add the soda. I ignored my instincts because I was embar-rassed and afraid that they knew better. That compromise wrecked my self-respect. It damaged my own sense of morality, of *personal integrity.* I wanted that cake to be wonderful. I wanted to follow their instructions so well that they would be proud to have me as one of them, and now everything was ashes. I had listened to them and I pushed down my own intuition and still I ended up feeling awful. In order to not burst into tears I turned my heart to stone, but I wanted to really hurt those women as they had hurt me. I felt confused, unable to tell if I'd tricked myself or been tricked by their unrealistic expectations. Instead I pretended none of it—not the cake, nor the pain, nor the excitement—none of it made any difference to me any longer. I withdrew emotionally and kind of numbed out. Strange, isn't it, how a seemingly innocuous event can change a woman's sense of security? I remember sitting at the table no longer able to be just a little girl waiting for the cake from the oven. Nor was I a grown woman who could speak up in my own behalf. I had nowhere to go emotionally or spiritually.

Tragically, for a woman, self-betrayal is usually preferable to being betrayed. Make no mistake, *any* betrayal always compromises embodiment. A betrayal can turn the heart to stone, but a self-betrayal obliterates our individuality, undermining our connections with the essential Self. Self-betrayal corrodes our standpoint with the acidity of a Medusian alliance, which in turn weakens self-esteem, self-confidence, and self-respect. Betrayal, especially self-betrayal, causes the soul, your essential Self, to shrink. When we've betrayed ourself so often what we do with our intuition is to stir it, like leavening, quickly into one end of the situation and if it helps, fine. Relieved, we then go unconscious, once more failing to consult ourself and explore what happened, where the strength or insight came from.

Numbed by impotence, even your instincts can appear to let you down. An intuitive capacity is a special salvation when a woman feels emotionally paralyzed. Stand up and fight? Cut my loses and flee? Yell out or keep silent? Jean Bolen describes the Athena-Medusa relationship in a woman's psychology thus: "Living in her head, the Athena woman misses the experience of being fully in her body.... Athena keeps a woman 'above' the instinctual level, so she does not feel the full strength of maternal, sexual, or procreative instincts." This is such an obviously mental place that you can become so compromised by a point of logic that no other information can improve your discrimination.

One way to understand how this happens is to recognize that Athena's position represents the intellectual activities of the left hemisphere. Dark as she is, Medusa, on the other hand, represents the banished or pathologized activities of the imagination, of the right hemisphere. Intuition transits both hemispheres, making use equally of both intellect and imagination. Every attribute has what appears to be its opposite when the two are isolated from one another. Actually, every opposition is really a complement—a balance of the total range of possibility. Intellect without imagination is dry and devoid of expressive vitality. Imagination without intellect is swampy and devoid of focus or purpose.

Concerning Athena's dark side, her Medusa energy, Bolen continues: "An Athena woman has an ability to intimidate others and to take away the spontaneity, vitality, and creativity of people who are not like her." This is Athena's Medusian side. Then no amount of intellect will suffice for the loss of relationship, to herself or to others. When these seemingly opposing energies are blended, there is no need for intimidation, only empowerment, no place for entitlement, only peerage.

When even a small portion of the Medusa effect is turned on a little girl who is only beginning to form a sense of her own creative vitality, she can be knocked off her "feet," as happened to Alix. Cavalier insensitive opinion can be devastating to the unwary recipient. Emotionally bound to those upon whom she is relationally dependent, a child has to decide—either to agree with who they tell her she is, or risk a differing viewpoint which may alienate her from the others.

Age five is an exciting time of fledgling autonomy. It is a crucial time in the beginning stages of a woman's developing her interior sense of what is most important to her, of her *standpoint*. In other words, she is just beginning to explore ways to increase her focused thinking, to value her own experiences while staying well grounded in her instinctual relationship with her feelings. All this—without succumbing immediately to the fear that her differences will cause her to suffer abandonment. Alix remembers her feeling that she could just pour everything out of the pan, add the baking powder, and pour it all back in again. "Even back then my intuition was coaching me—running out ahead of the outcome and then running back to give me options to create a better ending," she said. "At five I followed the lead of others. At fifty-five I follow an inner guide. Now I blend experience with intuition, instinct with choice."

Prior to age five, most of our introspection is spontaneous and unfocused, so that it appears to be imaginal or fantasy. By our fifth year we are beginning to have enough of an appreciation for our own capacity for self-reflection that our observations contribute to the genesis of personal opinions about our feelings and our own lives. When he was three, Christopher told me something I was about to do wouldn't work. "How do you know it won't work, Christopher?" I asked. "I know because I tried it and it never has, Grandmother." There you have it—experience, reflection, opinion, standpoint—at age three.

The courage and hard work of practiced conscious discrimination (seeing choices and making decisions) is always undergirded by the genuine spontaneous sensations of the bodymind. A commitment to respect rather than resist this spontaneous feedback as it confirms or refutes each choice can create the vitality that is experienced as "Knowing unequivocally what I stand for and standing up for my Self." Then a woman can ask for and actively seek acceptance for her genuine convictions based on her intuition and her intellect, rather than assume a protective adaptive posture that masks her fear of criticism and rejection.

Standpoints: Emotional Safe Harbors

When a new or different perspective about you and your place in the world accessed through the body's wisdom becomes real to you, it gives you a new way of standing up for and to yourself. Calling this change of emergent consciousness a shift in standpoint is metaphorically descriptive of the literal physiological change that takes place as the new awareness is consciously experienced. Not infrequently posture improves and stride lengthens.

Rebecca struggled for years with her desire to create a close-knit relationship between herself and her much older sisters. She was born well after the others were in their teens and older.

Her task was made harder by a mother whose strong matriarchal presence prevented the women from speaking their minds or disclosing their true feelings. Caught in the middle, Rebecca found herself with two physical complaints—an unpredictable rash and chronic discomfort because one leg was slightly shorter than the other. After a series of long and painful events where Rebecca tried in vain to reunite the family, her mother became ill and it was left to Rebecca to be the caregiver. Her mother's health continued to fail, and, as she was dying, Rebecca brought her sisters together and asked them to join her in healing themselves by loving their mother until she took her last breath. Rebecca went to her mother, told her how much she loved her, and asked her for her blessing. Her mother, whose last years had been filled with bad humor and complaints, told Rebecca that she too loved her. Her mother died surrounded by her daughters, who, in accepting Rebecca's invitation to gather to love their mother, found a renewed love for one another. Rebecca was deeply affirmed by the experience.

After her mother's funeral, while at her chiropractor's office for an adjustment, she discovered her legs are now of equal length. When she told me this, we celebrated the wonder of Rebecca's experience. Following her deepest sense of how to approach her mother's dying as an opportunity to heal the family alienation, Rebecca found her own spiritual standpoint. Up until then, no matter how she tried, her mother's dismissive and controlling attitude left the little girl with only one full leg to stand on. The other leg couldn't lengthen into its full stature. The difference was very subtle, yet her bodymind structurally demonstrated her lopsidedness—one leg an adult and the other arrested in an unrequited childhood.

Rebecca has always sought her identity outside herself—first as her father's daughter and later as her husband's wife. Today she stands on her own two feet. Her legs stand under her, expressing her full *understanding* of her place, her birthright. A vital and highly relational woman, Rebecca is well known for her penchant in putting the right people, the best ideas, and the most creative resources together for the benefit of others. Now, blessed and more consciously embodied, she can do this for herself as well.

FINDING YOUR STANDPOINT

Try it yourself. The next time you have an insight or a decision that is significant, stand up and consciously declare that you are taking a step forward in your own behalf, that you are stepping into a new standpoint that you will not forget. Then walk around consciously feeling your own authority, your renewed, or new, sense of self-confidence. If you find yourself filled with doubt later on, put your feet firmly on the ground and step into your truth, renewing your commitment to yourself. You will be surprised at how powerful the acting of stepping into the full power of a feeling or a decision can be in cementing the relationship between intention and conviction.

....

Consciously incarnating a standpoint is useful in many ways. The next time you want to be listened to, try sitting with *both* feet firmly placed upon the floor, your back straight, and your head raised. Lowered eyes, a tucked chin, feet askew, and back slumped is not a convincing stance, it garners no respect or reassurance, internally or externally.

Movement can also help you figure out whether to follow an intuitive decision.

WALKING YOUR INTUITION

If you have any doubt about an intuition, sit quietly and focus on the details or the feeling that tells you what to do. Now direct your consciousness to your feet and walk around the room reviewing the feeling or the details. Remember to breathe deeply and soften your eyes, allowing your intuition to fill your bodymind. Notice how your feet strike the floor, how the ankles flex and your legs move. Note any difference between how you walked before you gave your attention and your respect to your intuition and how you are walking now. Pause and take an inventory. Does your body feel the same? How are you placing your feet now? Is there anything that your bodymind is telling you that will strengthen your intuition? Continue to move about the room as you grow more accustomed to the physical changes caused by an intuitive interaction. Some have noted subtle changes of balance; others, shifts in body image. Be imaginal, follow your energy; move backward and sideways to allow the bodymind to open up to and fully express the multiple changes your intellect may block or ignore. Take time to record or review your experience so you feel more at home, more closely and creatively related to your embodied wisdom. Now go about your regular life as you allow these changes to ripen and make more sense.

....

Remember, the body is at its core instinctual—to the bone, no-nonsense impulse, energy, and action. The imagination is more elegant, evocative, and relationally creative. The two will work in unison, and slowly you will incorporate the changes into the psychological and the somatic fiber of your bodymind. Your task is to respect your insight, stay conscious, awake, and aware. Don't go back to sleep.

Body as Teacher

Consciously relating to your physical body does not mean manipulating your body self-consciously. It means allowing your body's responses to teach you to be more aware of the full range of feelings the bodymind is capable of expressing each time you are willing to make a choice, to express a standpoint.

Psychologically the establishment of a conscious standpoint grounds a woman, ensuring a sense of firmly rooted conviction. Physiologically our feet do stand beneath us and propel us forward or root us in place. Spiritually we must know who or what this embodied conviction serves.

Securing a safe metaphoric position as a home base, we can then return to an exploration of those issues that leave us on shaky spiritual ground or relationally isolated, high and dry. We can test them against the metaphor by asking, Where do I truly stand on this? Metaphorically describing work with the feet as *standpoint,* with the coccyx as *seedbone,* and with the throat as *true voice,* you can experience more fully the intimate immediacy of the interconnections of these three areas in the literal development and interplay of a woman's focused purposefulness, sexual energies, and creative vitality. The coccyx comes into play as the literal root of the spinal column, that bony flexible chain of intricate ivory that allows the standpoint (feet, legs) to radiate into an upright and full stature. Containing vestiges of the aquatic prehensile body—the primal relationship our body has with the ocean and the deep waters of the unconscious—the seedbone metaphor contains an invitation to get real about your own coccygeal nature. To own your own mud. To reassemble yourself from the root up.

Standpoint, stature, and rootedness go hand in hand. Finding your own intuitive truth and connecting with or disconnecting from the rules, injunctions, strengths, and deficits of your history is crucial to a fully embodied authenticity—basic to feeling awake and alive. Until this work is consciously embodied, by allowing the images, the sensations, and the symptoms to stretch you into a conscious connection with who you truly are, you will never establish a congruent intuitive voice that speaks of what matters to and for you. Each of these—standpoint, stature, and rootedness—lead to an opening up of the throat: the establishment of a more authentic voice.

The metaphor of the seedbone is particularly powerful for those who seek to become more intuitive. Honoring the bones returns us to the *mundo subteraneo,* our embodied source ground, our own psychic soil. Bones and bone fragments have always carried oracular powers among indigenous peoples and those given to seeing beyond the veil. I have in my possession a collection of carefully carved animal bones to be worn for ceremony and thrown for inquiry. Rattling old bones stirs the vapors of the past—wakens the voices of the Mystery. There is a shared agreement among storytellers that if you can salvage the tiniest fragment of the skeletal structure you can, with ritual and the right attitude, re-member (add the missing limbs) the individual.

For example, there is the Native American tale of Buffalo Bride. It seems the father of a maiden is stomped to death by angry buffalo. She, wed to a buffalo, follows the direction of Raven and resurrects her father by unearthing a single bone from his remains which she covers, waiting for the spirit of her father to re-member itself.

Clarissa Pinkola Estés writes of Skeleton Woman in *Women Who Run with the Wolves,* leading us, through story, to the realization that we cannot flesh ourself out without the capacity to resurrect the very bones of what is abandoned and nurture the reclamation back to vitality. To do so is to dive into deep waters and bring up the skeleton of what we've abandoned, and nourish it. When it is enlivened so then are we.

For Yourself Alone

When a metaphor carries an image's potency it awakens the collective energies that stand behind it. Female intuition has a history before mind and beyond recorded time. In earliest history midwives, healers, and women of law and authority relied as much upon their intuition as they did upon their intellect. In *The Woman's Encyclopedia of Myths and Secrets,* Barbara Walker has gathered and alphabetically arranged a wealth of information about this forgotten history of womankind. So also has Riane Eisler in *The Chalice and the Blade.* Metaphor bridges any gap between intellect and intuition, assisting the ego in intuitively allowing this forgotten history to have its due.

I've found the seedbone metaphor evokes a spiritual concentration of embodied historical energy that resonates physiologically, inspiring deep and lasting change. Working with this metaphor, a woman can begin to tease apart exactly what she knows intuitively to be true for herself alone while reclaiming her feminine legacy. Knowing that there is a tiny fragment of soul lodged within the depths of your self—a seed-bone—to be nurtured and re-membered is the equivalent of resacriliz-ing the body daily. Such a personally meaningful metaphor provides a unique zone of psychic safety. It offers a language that can be utilized without the fear of premature exposure. One can learn, by following an embodied sense of satisfaction or dissatisfaction, to discern a personal understanding of embodied *seedbone* wisdom.

Seedbone metaphors are deeply reminiscent of our origins. Learning to love one's own mud, return to one's own clay, find one's own deep-rootedness are all fertile images here. The capacity to claim your essential birthright, to be fully in your own body and trust your embodied sensations and feelings, opens the door to an ability to refuse to be an eternal victim of circumstance, even to the most degrading and destructive experiences of the past. The pursuit for eternal perfection inevitably leaves one at the mercy of shame. If we allow our intellect to lead us, forever reminding us of our regrets or our shame, we'll stay stuck, unable to allow ourselves to take strength or pleasure from our imperfections and the intuitive lessons they teach.

Remember Alix, the woman with the problem knee? Working with her body in a safe and nonjudgmental context, Alix's weak knees from her cake-baking episode at age five led her spontaneously and intuitively into what she perceived as "grasshopper" energy. Reflecting upon the memory of that day in the kitchen, she released herself to the movements the memory engendered. Lying on her back, she allowed her body to coil and stretch as a very active infant might. Humming to herself she then began to pull herself upright until she was making constant small leaping motions. She imagined herself leaping over all the emotional obstacles in the cake-baking kitchen of her childhood.

Eventually, tiring of having to be constantly on the move, her body signaled her with the beginning of a depressed mood, an all too familiar signal that a change was needed and her ego was not up to the challenge. Emotional depression can be a psychosomatic speed break. It is a bodymind summons to slow down, introvert, and be quiet; to wait and observe—to contain yourself, stop thinking, and wait to discover what wants to change.

At first Alix alternated between standing defiantly with locked knees and then wilting as if she had no bones. As the vulnerability of the betrayed five-year-old overtook her, she felt her legs tremble, she weakened and fell to her knees. The interplay between the locked defensive stance and the weak-kneed stance allowed a third, more congruent possibility to evolve. Moving spontaneously from defiance to vulnerability, and back to defiance once more, only when the energy for one dissolved into an impulse for the other, Alix concentrated on her breath as the sustaining thread to her deepening embodied consciousness as it led her through the pain of the memory and toward the wisdom her survival contains.

As Alix's example demonstrates, your body's natural impulses will inevitably guide you toward the intuitive resolution that will help you untangle the emotion that has you in its grip. Don't bother with interpretation. A good keen intellect is only an impediment here. You can assassinate bodymind's wisdom by attempting to interpret logically what is happening. The natural rhythms are all the interpretation you'll need. Deep sighs, bowel motility with soft rumblings and the breaking of wind, a sense of relaxation, are but a few of the many ways you'll begin to recognize your embodied sense of "Yes!"

Working with paints and clay, Alix created a figure of green grasshopper energy that evolved into a green man who "can compassionately stand up to me, refusing to allow me to yield when I feel inclined to betray myself by leaping forward instead of standing still and seeking my own truth." Alix spent the better part of the winter months watching how her emotional "grasshoppering" affects her stance in life. She consciously explored how her feelings influence her physical and her emotional posture and consequently, her ability to stand up for herself.

Mistakenly, we grow into adulthood believing that a heavy investment in thinking will override our conflictual feelings and garner us an ultimate reality that we can control. Shadows of the Athena/Medusa conflict lurk here. Since the ego carries the only formal awareness we have of the body, any battle waged with the intention of elevating intellect over feeling leaves the body's wisdom a maimed casualty. Citing the dangers of an *Addiction to Perfection,* Marion Woodman warns, "In the intellectualizing of a problem the body is cruelly left out." And, I will add, we become spiritually heavy handed, heavy hearted and heavy footed to boot, treading on the grace of our intuition like a clumsy two-year-old.

Self-Reflection

As we free ourselves from the psychological and social traps that keep us from our intuitive resources, what we discover is that we regain the direct access to an embodied wisdom that most of us were in touch with when we were very young. Learning to trust your own instinct for correct choices and your intuition about how to thrive is a direct benefit of learning to stand up for yourself. Living an embodied authentic life is freeing—and it is healing. There is a certain kind of joy that begins to color our experiences and bring us pleasure. Happiness is good for the immune system. Authenticity breeds security, self-confidence, and contentment.

Chapter Nine

REDISCOVERING YOUR
INTUITIVE CAPACITY

The weaver is as nothing without exquisite care for
the loom.

—*[pmr]*

I hope that by now you have begun to understand the blocks to
embodied intuition, the deep cultural psychological issues that keep
women from their bodies, and have begun to employ SCM to move
them, and in so doing, move through them. As you do, you will discover
that your intuitive knowings, the messages from your soul, will flow
more easily and become a more accessible guide. In many ways, this is a

process of rediscovering *yourself* as you awaken to and reclaim the intuitive nonverbal cellular wisdom of the deep feminine.

At no time in life has it been more important than it is today to establish a self-reliant, intuitive inner wisdom that will remain steadfast while most of the old systems we have relied upon are being deconstructed. Whether it's your health, and managed care no longer allows you to use the physician you rely upon, or the economy that no longer affords you the resources to live as you once did, or any other of the myriad social and cultural changes, now is the time to rediscover your inner strengths, to create and use an inner sanctuary.

In this book we've been focusing on your body, on bringing intuition home, back to its true birthright of conscious embodiment. Instead of directing our attention outward, I have invited us to take full ownership as stewards of an innate intrapersonal intuitive faculty. I've enjoined you to acknowledge the unique legacy of the deep cellular feminine that is innate to the female gender. In these pages you've been training yourself to wake up, be aware, learn the language and the syntax of your particular brand of intuitive communication. Now we turn to bringing this awareness more into the consciousness of everyday life.

There are a multitude of ways that we use intuition daily while calling it by another name. For example, I find prayer to be a highly intuitive sacred act. When a prayer moves you, or you feel it has been heard, or answered, you just know. There's no particular evidence, no specific rational process—you just know. Poet David Whyte says there is an intelligence in the universe that heals simply because that is what it does. It is present whether we humans relate to it or not. I have found this to be so. And further, this universal healing intelligence is unconcerned with our small pursuits but available always if we wish to pursue it. Access to this energy lies just beyond the edges of our rationality, yet the approach is unimpeded via contemplation and spontaneous movement.

It may offend some of you if you read this as a suggestion that prayer is a human device controlled and answered by the individual instead of a higher power. This is not what I am saying. Spirit is universal no matter what name or what religion informs you personally. Intuition is a faculty of the bodymind that is simultaneously both transpersonal and inherently personal. When we pray, we need some kind of translator to decipher the reply. I am suggesting that your deeper receiver—Soul—intuitively connects you to Spirit.

This is not Spirit's only translator. In the town next to mine is a woman who has visions of the Virgin once a year. She hears Mary's voice speak to her about the future of humankind. Thousands gather at her farm annually on the anniversary of her first vision with pleas and curiosity of their own. Afterward many people report that they have had an insight, or a prayer answered, or an intuition about what they must do next. The contact is nonverbal, but the affirmation is nonetheless real. As one participant said, "No, I didn't hear voices or have a vision as I prayed, but I was answered. I just knew it in my heart."

As this person acknowledges, embodied intuition is more than an affair of the mind, it is an affair of the heart, soul, and body. It is a total experience. At the most basic human level it is a daily experience, a convocation of the personal senses and transpersonal sensibilities. It is first and foremost personal because the only vehicle soul has in matter is the conscious personhood of each and every incarnation. It is universally transpersonal, because to be conscious is to be alive, spirit incarnate, connected to the *Anima Mundi,* to World Soul.

What I am asking you to do personally is to step back in time and reclaim a prehistoric universal female skill. I am inviting you in so doing to consciously resacralize matter. All matter is energy. As you resacralize your bodymind by becoming awake, aware, and authentic, *your* field of consciousness will spread and touch the planetary consciousness so sorely in need of a reawakening. When you are awake, aware, authentic, and true to your intuition, you cannot love your own matter without falling in love with the Earth: you cannot genuinely love the Earth's great body without falling in love with your own body.

I have not talked about or encouraged you to call your intuition psychic, or to use it to diagnose or understand others. Psychic capacity does rely upon a keen sense of intuition also, along with a variety of other skills. Intuitive diagnosis is yet another way to use your intuition to uncover what ails another. I feel, however, that first and foremost it is essential that you become the subject of your intuition, since it is your soul and your conscious embodiment that is at stake.

Using your intuitive wisdom to understand yourself is, at first, a far more difficult task than using your intuition to understand someone or something else. Inner vision has its price. A blind pilgrim has only to rely upon the generosity and protection of others. Blind, we eat what we are fed, we go where we are led. We are, however, left to the mercy of other people's viewpoints, perspectives, insights, and visions. We can't be held accountable for what we cannot see. You may find relief, even exoneration, in your blindness, but you are blind nonetheless.

Personal insight, on the other hand, places the onus for change squarely on you, and you alone. You can walk away from an insight about someone else or a blind spot you wish to ignore, but you have to find a way to live with a deepening of consciousness about yourself. I saw a cartoon in the paper—a little boy is watching TV and there is an insistent loud knock at the door. He ignores it but it continues. His younger sister asks him why he doesn't answer the knock. He says he can't be sure it's someone he wants to see. But suppose it's a surprise, something unexpected and wonderful like a big present, she says. He shrugs off her enthusiasm and says it's not worth the chance—it could be bad news too.

That's how many of us approach Soul's messages. We want to be pilgrims, but prefer to remain blind because dream work is so confusing and symptoms can lead to a frightening diagnosis. Even intuition is unreliable. We suspect that at its bedrock life is complex and will elude our most vigorous inquiry. If we delve too deeply we may not like what we find. We are reminded that there is pain as well as joy—why rock the boat, open the door? There are no guarantees, yet if we ignore the knocking there may be no consciousness either.

So I offer you five knocks at your intuitive gateway. Five practical ways to continue daily to learn more about your life, your destiny, your Self. You have to answer the knock, step across the threshold to recover the gifts, the unexpected, the surprises. There are no guarantees—only the promise of a life more fully lived, a vitality more fully embraced, a wisdom more richly enjoyed. There is indescribable freedom in knowing yourself well, and knowing that you can rely upon what you know, because it is more than cognitive, it is cellular, tissue, and bone knowing.

The Five A's of Embodied Intuition

1. Awaken

To Your Dream Life

Keep a dream journal. Record any image or memory you have upon awakening. Dreams evaporate when they are interrupted by an alarm or getting up to go to the bathroom. However, they often flicker back into consciousness as a déjà vu—a feeling of re-experiencing something from an earlier time. Write your dreams in your journal. It is the nature of the dreaming psyche to respond to the ego's attentiveness. Recording even one line of a remembered dream will increase your chances of remembering more. Intuition is not unlike a waking dream since both states of consciousness lie just on the other side of rationality.

If you don't remember your dreams, then use your journal to explore your imagination. Allow yourself to write letters to your interior three-year-old, the friend who left you, the lover you miss; write those unspoken and unfinished communications that persist within you. Then read the letters and reply. Be candid and real. Do not allow an imaginary editor to curtail your conversations with yourself.

To Your Body's Metaphors, Your Symptom's Wisdom

Your physical symptoms—an aching wrist, an itchy foot, a rash—will teach you a fairly specific metaphoric lexicon that works for you alone. Once you become familiar with the signals beneath the symptom and do some SCM, you'll be able to respond as if you are receiving a verbal suggestion. Approaching a chronic symptom intuitively can teach you more about yourself than you ever imagined when you were limiting yourself to the symptom's obvious affects. Take time to recognize and follow your spontaneous movements, always asking yourself, What more is there to this symptom? Who do I become when I am affected by it? What do I have to give up or do to yield to it? Is there a hidden benefit or a wicked trade-off ? If you will not give your body a half an hour a day how can you expect your intuition to be anything but disembodied?

To Your Heart's Desires

Listen to what you yearn for. It may be something as simple as always wishing you could live a life without clutter or as complex as wishing you could return to your teenage years. If you'll honor your yearning by hearing the metaphoric message it conveys, you'll touch the deep feminine and learn significant truths about your unclaimed vitality.

Essentially we know what is best for us. Our heart's desires keep these truths alive. Unfortunately we mistake them for complaints or impossibilities, when in truth it is our intuition urging us to wake up and embrace life fully. Yearning to return to your adolescence may be your soul's way of reminding you that you have unclaimed youthful energy begging to be noticed. Why not set aside a day and live as if you are whatever you are yearning for? Listen to what you tell yourself, to how you feel and what you discover. Each one of us lives by two different chronological ages anyhow. There is our literal birth date and then there is an interior age that only we know about. Try asking yourself what that interior heart-filled age is, and then live with that vitality one day a month. Go to your journal and record what you discover about yourself.

To Your Negative Thoughts and Expressions

It may surprise you to know that negative beliefs have a potent effect on your physical health. Expressions like, "That breaks my heart," "It sickens me," "It's killing me," suppress the functioning of the immune system so effectively that the *Journal of the American Medical Association (JAMA)* has reported its deleterious effect on health and well-being. The term *nocebo* was coined to describe the influential power of negative suggestion. One twenty-year study of women ages 45 to 64 showed that those who believed themselves likely to suffer a heart attack, even if there was no personal or family history of coronary disease, were over three times more likely to die of coronary complications than others who did not believe they were susceptible.

Suggestion plays a significant role in the issue of *trust in* or *fear of* our body. Fearing it makes it inevitable that a relationship will break your heart; telling yourself "I may have to die to get out of this relationship" can become an embodied truth. There is a mistaken notion that positive suggestion in the face of "evidence" to the contrary is false hope and therefore unethical or dishonest. Books like Louise Hay's *You Can Heal Your Life,* Catherine Ponder's *The Dynamic Laws of Healing,* and others refute this. What you think, the words you use, and the beliefs you give lip service to affect your health and your capacity to thrive. Positive affirmations are healing, and negativity is not.

2. Become Aware

Of Your Inner Dialogue

Listen to and observe your behavior, your inner dialogues, your neglected feelings. Begin to find your inner dialogue interesting. If a song keeps tugging at your consciousness, go and look at the sheet music or write down all the words, chorus and verse, to really hear what you are telling yourself. Many a deepened insight has been inspired by following the trail of a melody that just won't go away. Treat the song like a waking dream. What is the theme, the images, the context? When did you first hear it, what associations do you have with it—all will lead you to the intuitive message.

Of What Is True for You

Learn to discern what is true for you and what is not. Learn to separate what really matters to you from what you've been taught should matter. Commit to breaking habitual negative thought patterns by interrupting them and telling yourself you will not think this particular thought any longer. When it returns, interrupt it firmly and consciously as many times as it takes to change the thought pattern. Take your positive thoughts seriously, especially if they are about unexplored desires. Your intuition is coaxing you to be real, intentionally.

Of the Effects of How You Live

Notice how your daily habits affect you. Careless eating, prolonged inertia or boredom, mechanical behavior—all will impede body consciousness. Experiment and pay close attention to what your body wants and reacts to. Many women I know have discovered they have much more access to their intuition if they avoid caffeine and alcohol. Throw out or get rid of those things that cause you to feel distracted or disembodied. Clothing or shoes that are uncomfortable, clutter, furniture that is of no value any longer, things you have inherited that are not you, or things you have kept too long that prevent you from living a conscious life must be cleared away. Stop saving things because you may need them at some later date. You'll find when you release yourself from anticipating the future, you'll reduce the poverty mentality that is afraid to let go in case there is no replacement. One of the basic laws of energy tells us that to make room for anything new, we must first release something that is no longer useful.

The careful and caring attention to the needs and desires of your mind and body is not self-centered, it is Soul-centered: you are consciously caring for your essential Self.

Be selective about what you acquire. Ask yourself if you are willing and able to be the guardian of this acquisition. Do not burden yourself by concretizing your symbolic inner life. One icon well used and well visited is worth far more than a pile of crystals, symbols, and gewgaws. A single meal well prepared and savored is worth far more than an assortment of junk food or freebies at a party. Whether you are purchasing a piece of fruit or a loaf of bread, do so with care. Conscious embodiment is an act of loving your matter. Offer your body the most careful selections possible.

As within, so without. As without, so within. How much clutter do you want within?

3. Be Authentic

Be real, be honest, and love yourself and others with humility. Do not lie or avoid the truth. Even if there is danger in speaking the truth aloud do not lie to yourself—ever. Pledge to know yourself from the inside out. Be willing to admit that for every positive, generous, and well-intentioned motivation you have, there are other desires and attitudes that you keep hidden away. For your soul's sake get to know each aspect of this undisclosed Self.

This is one of the more difficult lessons a therapist in training has to learn. Until she is willing and able to know herself inside and out, she cannot listen to another with integrity. What we deny or attempt to keep hidden will, inevitably, be projected onto another or overtake us, creating all sorts of messy interpersonal tangles. When a client who exhibits the shadow side of the therapist enters the room, if the therapist doesn't know how to recognize that the "Loathly Lady" sitting before her has many of the therapist's own "loathly" attributes, there's the devil to pay. She can find herself angry for no apparent reason, or doing everything to avoid being direct with her client because she is unconsciously attempting to avoid her own inner discomfort.

There is great strength in uncovering and embracing the rejected parts of your psyche. Jung says that everything you find stuffed under the rug of denial and repression is at least 95 percent pure gold. Lying to yourself may seem a simple harmless solution to avoiding discomfort until you realize you not only can't escape yourself, but what you are pretending not to see is very apparent to others.

Have Integrity

Self-discovery merits integrity: a conscious commitment to make and integrate each change. Refuse to disrespect, denigrate, or abandon yourself by being unfaithful to your inner processes. Take pleasure in your developing clarity and focus. Do not allow yourself to avoid time for self-exploration and gratitude.

Do not use your intuition to inflate your power or your self-worth—that's a barter of Soul. Intuition is not a parlor trick or a fortune-teller illusion. The envy or admiration of your friends may be tempting, but it will dilute the depth of honesty you are capable of. You don't have to do this alone. Be willing to seek help when you need it, say No when you don't. If you can't look into your own eyes in the mirror you'll know you are missing the mark, that you are not taking your inner life seriously. Authenticity is an ongoing endeavor that becomes a trusted essential principle—a spiritual standard.

Trust the Messages

Trust your symptoms, dreams, focused impulses, and hunches to teach you what is authentic in your life. Depression will let you know when you are letting yourself down by returning to a less authentic way of behaving. Note this, and be appreciative that you are being held to the highest standard possible not because someone else requires it of you, but because you have asked it of yourself. We are not humans attempting to live a spiritual life. We are spiritual beings dedicated to living in a human form. Know this and invest the remainder of your life becoming what you already are.

Laugh

Learn to laugh at yourself. Humor heals. Learn to play. Imagination delights in the open joyful freedom of creative play. Do something physical where you refuse to compete with yourself or others but do it just for the sheer pleasure of the movement, the game. Laughter and spontaneous play are to the body what prayer is to the soul. There are so many ways to be real, to express the deep feminine cleanly and clearly.

4. Hold Yourself Accountable

Take Yourself Seriously

Take yourself as seriously as you want others to take you. Be mindful of who and what you love, who and what you allow to love you. Do not confuse romantic love with love of the Self. Guard your heart's desires as you would your most precious possession.

Take Time Alone

Establish a daily contemplative time apart. Create a sacred space you can go to, and maintain it. If your options are limited don't ignore this need. Many have created portable altars in a dresser drawer or a small box. One woman I know has a tiny four-by-three-by-four-inch lidded wooden box. There is a mirror on the inner lid, and inside she has a picture of herself as a child, a small icon of the Black Madonna, a stone from her birth place, and a pouch of incense with a few wax-coated matches. Each item is lovingly and consciously chosen—to be used and replaced as needed. No matter where she is she can spread a scarf or a napkin and set up her place of sanctuary. Another woman, living with roommates and sharing a bedroom, has no privacy unless the apartment is empty. So she uses the front seat of her car to meditate and journal every morning before others are awake.

Intention is everything. Later there will be other options. If we ask our soul to wait until conditions are right or we have more time or space we may lose the very thing that we yearn for, the capacity to know our Self well and love the woman we have become.

5. Be Articulate

Speak Out

Develop your own voice, literally. If you feel lost from yourself, disembodied or distracted, sing and listen to your words. If you've been told you can't carry a tune, baloney! That's a cultural curse. Westerners are fond of telling children such nonsense. Every infant hums and babbles in harmony with her body harmonics. We all can sing. Sound your name and play with the harmonics of the syllables. When you are sitting quietly and attuned to your breath, chant any sound or single word that pleases you. Soften your eyes as you attend to the wash of sound as it rises and falls. As your embodied consciousness deepens, your voice will become more natural. It too may deepen.

Try changing the pitch or tone of your voice. Really hear yourself, as if for the first time, and take pleasure in the sound of your voice. Contemplate what feels most natural to you. Trust your feelings, not your interpretations. If you feel your voice is less than you wish it to be, find the voice that suits you and then use it until the shape and the taste of it are as familiar and as pleasing as a comfortable garment, a well-used old shoe.

You can use Spontaneous Contemplative Movement to find your true voice. As you move, allow your breath to express the sound that wants to come up. Walk contemplatively or move with this sound until another takes its place. Pause as the first one fades and reflect upon how you feel, then continue, repeating this process until you intuitively sense that this sound harmonizes with your breath and feels congruent with your body's sensations. Breathe deeply while you quietly gather your energy and speak your name using your true voice. Repeat your name as often as you want to while you follow your breath and the spontaneous movements that echo the vibrations of sound. Fill the room, wall to wall and up to the rafters. Then pause and savor the echoes that surround you, declaring that this name is my name. In the following days consciously adjust your voice to express the voice that you've uncovered. In no time at all you'll notice a variety of changes in your energy, your authority, and your self-confidence.

Remember Medusa's positive energy? Stop anyone who mocks your changes or questions your sound with the authority of a stone wall—do not allow it. Your voice transmits empowerment. Your name defines a boundary. Finding your true voice gets you back in tune with your natural rhythm. It harmonizes your bodymind. Finding your own voice is part of learning to clarify what you want, what you stand for, what your limits are, and where your focus lies in preparation for speaking up and out. The way of the feminine may be less direct, more spiral, but it never need be unclear or too diffuse to make sense.

Claim Your Own Authority

Learn to speak with the authority of your standpoint instead of always quoting others or waiting until you are certain you know how others feel. When you really want to be heard, plant both feet firmly on the floor and remember to breathe deeply and slowly from your navel, up and out. Intuition and breath go hand in hand. Consciously breathing deeply opens the channel for your voice while energizing your entire bodymind. Holding your breath will cause the power of your voice to diminish and grow thin and reedy.

Breathing, pausing, and contemplating what your embodied intuition is saying is an articulation, a refinement of your inner strength and wisdom. Articulated sound is healing, articulated breath is harmonious, articulated voice is enlivening.

Intuition thrives in a bodymind that is aware, awake, authentic, accountable, and articulate.

HELPFUL DAILY PRACTICES FOR DEVELOPING AN INTUITIVE RELATIONSHIP TO YOUR BODYMIND

1. Learn to love and respect the rejected parts of yourself.

2. Love someone or something openly and unconditionally once a day.

3. Believe in something greater than yourself—God, Buddha, meditation, prayer, nature.

4. Create an altar, a sanctuary for yourself, and go there regularly, especially when you can't sleep or feel vulnerable.

5. Journal, paint, dance, become the poet, dancer, or artist of your soul.

6. Stay consciously self-reflective. Be lusty about what you enjoy, what you dislike.

7. Practice forgiveness daily.

8. Keep a pen and pad in your bathroom. Running water evokes intuition. Swim, go to the ocean or any body of water and be aware of your images, your inner dialogue.

In addition to practicing the Five A's on a regular basis, I believe it is very important to do an annual check-in with yourself on your birthday, just as you do an annual physical check-up. Always celebrate the day of your birth with some kind of personal ceremony. Plant an evergreen or bury a stone in remembrance of your incarnation. Review the year you have completed by appreciating your body for having carried your soul through to this day, this year. Write a letter to yourself about your intuitions for the coming year to be opened on your next birthday. If there is anything on your altar that is ready to be passed on, give it away or burn it as an acknowledgment to nature that seasons change, life moves on.

Review the previous year's physical highlights and record them. When and with what were you sick? Did anything change structurally? Have you changed your exercise or your sleep patterns or your food preferences? See if you can find a metaphoric description for each entry and then note if there is a theme or a relationship that may give you further insight about your Self.

Go into a private space and, using SCM, ask yourself for the one change you would like to gift yourself with in the coming year. When you know what this will be, step consciously into your standpoint and promise yourself to do it. Life is a celebration. Spirit is giving the party. You are the honored guest. Please don't neglect to attend since you have an open invitation.

How-To Basics for Unusual Circumstances

Intuition is an extension of your inner vitality. In order to access this vitality under difficult or unusual circumstances, I believe you'll find it helpful to develop a ritual for dropping inward to the deep feminine and refreshing yourself so you can rely upon it whenever you need to. I like to think of this ritual as a portable sanctuary.

Trusting your breath is always reliable. Recently I learned a breath ritual that will quiet the nervous system, even alleviating panic attacks, no matter where you are.

INTENTIONAL BREATH

This ritual is most relaxing when seated in a chair with arms. Sit upright and rest your forearms on the chair arms. Breathe in once or twice as you focus on relaxing your jaw and dropping your shoulders. Then begin to breathe in through your nostrils, filling your lungs from the bottom upward to the count of four. Hold for a pause and then lightly pressing downward with your arms against the chair arms, tighten your navel against your spine and release your breath to the count of eight. Do not collapse forward. Allow the chair to hold the weight of your body. Like the standing breathing I talked about earlier, tightening your navel against your spine as you exhale allows the lower lungs to expel all the air and to refill more fully.

After a few trials you'll find this easy and you'll be able to do it without thinking about the count. Then wherever you are you can use this breath ritual to recenter and relax yourself.

Make a point of doing this a few moments each day and you will soon be able to access your inner sanctuary at will.

After you are comfortable with the rhythm of your breath ritual, allow yourself to focus on any image or color that appears before your inner eye. Note that image or color and return to it each time you sit and breathe. Welcome the image or color as a guide to the deep feminine that you need only relax and follow as you descend deeper and deeper into that place of Soul.

In addition to this breathing ritual, there are a number of things you can do when you find yourself in a difficult or unusual place to maintain the balance needed for intuition to flow:

When You Are Swamped or Overwhelmed
Close your eyes and take a deep breath while repeating, "No matter

how swamped I am, I am never more than a breath away from my soul's renewing wisdom." Breathe deeply and do this as often as you are able. When I'm surrounded by people, I go into the ladies' room, lower the lid on the toilet, sit, and do this until I feel relaxed. Remember you can relax and renew your energy anywhere and at any time just by turning your attention inward and breathing deeply as you focus upon your personal relationship with soul.

When You Are Ill

Wash your hands and face as often as you are able and rinse in water freshened with lemon or lime slices if you have them. If there is no one to care for you and you are too weak or ill to do much for yourself, turn to your dreams and your images and trust that you are being watched over and cared for in spite of outward appearances. If you are in the presence of any energy that is unsettling, insist that that person or noise or whatever be removed. Ask for an image that will tell you what to do to get through to the next stage. If you are in pain and can tolerate focusing on the pain, do so and allow your bodymind to enter the pain and release whatever is blocking your healing. If you feel you want to make sounds, do so, while you listen and follow the energy as you are led to a release. When you begin to feel better, gently massage your body with sesame oil and take a shower or a tub bath.

Afterward treat your body kindly by using lotion and anything else that pleases you. Some women I know prepare their body after an illness as carefully as they would if they were going to meet a lover. Do this for the love of the feminine and you will realize a spontaneous quality of self-love you never knew you had. Compassion for the body is healing. Love stimulates the presence of the holy. Intuition is one of the soul's truest expressions of love for matter.

When You Are On Vacation

Too often we think of a vacation as a time to break the rules, overextend our eating and drinking, and forget the daily routine. Give some thought to what you would really like—how you want to spend your time, what you'll do if the experience isn't what you anticipated or your travel buddies are disappointing.

Always consult your Self first about your unspoken expectations. If you have a hunch or an urge about your plans, listen to it. You may be telling yourself something that will change what you are about to do and deepen the experience in a more meaningful way. One woman reported that as she was packing for a trip to the beach she kept thinking about her raincoat and fretting about whether to take it or leave it. When she sat quietly, slowly breathing and allowing her mind to drift to her raincoat, she realized that she had an unspoken desire to hike in the woods to a series of waterfalls she had been told about. She canceled her beach trip and went to the woods instead where she had a richly rewarding week of hiking while staying at a beautiful lodge just inside a national preserve.

Another woman remembered the time she was on holiday in Canada and decided to follow her yearning to stay inside for the day and paint. She had no supplies so she went to a local shopping center to buy a few basics. There she met two women from Alaska who invited her to join them at their wilderness home for a week of watercolor and landscape painting. They had lunch and talked well into the evening hours. Feeling comfortable in their company and interested in their offer she accepted their invitation. Consequently, the three of them have become fast friends who get together annually to paint and explore new territory. If she had ignored her urge to paint, she may never have realized that her intuition was running out ahead of her, preparing the way for a fortuitous meeting.

When You Are Rearing Small Children

Remember that even the most demanding child can be taught that at a certain time Mother takes a break. I used to tell my small children that I wore an invisible Mother button. At eight o'clock, I turned it upside down and that meant I took some time for myself. I taught them to stay in their room, in bed, and not call me with any last-minute requests. I've taught hundreds of women to do the same and it works—if you mean what you say.

Be creative. As the children became more self-reliant I used to go out to my car parked in the driveway and stay for ten or twenty minutes while they were happily occupied inside. I would focus on my breathing and simply relax and let my mind wander while I listened in.

Another curious place to recharge your inner battery is in a line— at a supermarket, bank, or elsewhere. If the delay is inevitable, accept it as an intuitive moment, an opportunity to listen to the other voice, to tune in to yourself. This same principle works for me the many hours a week I commute to and from my office. As I inch through traffic I focus on my breathing and allow my intuition to reappraise my day. Often after one of these "auto sanctuaries" I tune to National Public Radio and note the first words I hear. More times than not they carry a most particular meaning for me while confirming that I am being taught how to live if I will only listen.

Be innovative. Find those moments and carefully cultivate them. You will be teaching your children the invaluable lesson that motherhood isn't all about service and martyrdom. It's about consciously relating, first to your inner wisdom, then to the tasks at hand.

When You've Suffered a Loss

Often a loss can feel like a personal failure or a rejection. The most important aspect of loss to the deep feminine is that you not ignore or deny how you feel. Now, if at any time, it is essential that you not betray yourself by collapsing with your loss. Even with the practice of using your intuition and listening to the yearning of your heart, there are limitations to your sturdiness when you are grieving. Grief has its own rituals and its own images. Don't be in a hurry to skip over your pain. Eat what comforts you as you deepen into the life lesson of your caring.

An authentic emotional life hurts. It must be nurtured and fed and held gently when there is grief work to be done. Wear what soothes you. While you are grieving you may not be able to bear the touch of clothing on your skin, or you may want to be wrapped up and securely held by an afghan or a favorite shawl. Follow your embodied intuition and learn to accept the compassion of the Great Mother to whom your grief matters.

Most of all be true to yourself. During this time you may feel vulnerable and childlike. Be attentive to these feelings. Leave a light on at night. Follow your impulses and don't force yourself to say or do anything that doesn't feel authentic in order to protect someone else's feelings. If there has been a death, do not be surprised if your intuition is more accessible than usual. You may remember your dreams more or you may have images or memories of the person who has died. Your psyche is attempting to show you how to heal. You are in good hands. While you sorrow, use SCM and allow your grief to dance you. When there is a literal death of a human life, the ending of a marriage, the loss of a job, time is the true healer and Soul your guide through the days and weeks that follow.

I have found that ritual allows me to heal when grieving in ways no other process does. Even after attending a funeral or other ceremony, be sensitive to what your energy wishes to do or say and how your imagination is teaching you to create it. A woman's body knows intuitively the instinctual expressions that will heal her, the community and the tribal history. One woman I know felt called to mourn the war in Bosnia and took ten days to alternately fast and pray and dance. Her neighbors thought her strangely excessive. I was humbled and in her debt for speaking for the few to the many. Do what your grief tells you to do, with no explanations, no apologies, no excuses.

When You've Received a Diagnosis

Speak your fears aloud. Write them in your journal, bring them into the light of day. Fears are real but they do not merit being literalized. A repressed fear is like a volcano, rumbling away internally while every cell in your body is desperately trying to avoid the inevitable eruption.

Talk to the part of your body that is ailing and ask your bodymind to teach you what you must do to help yourself heal. Use the healing energy of your hands to channel the instinctual healing of your immune system by placing your hand over the area that is not well. Forgive yourself for feeling weak or vulnerable or scared out of your mind. This is the ego's natural response. Don't compound it by going unconscious or by exaggerating what you feel. Do some soul searching and ask yourself what you truly feel, what you truly want to do next.

Prayer and affirmations are another way to keep yourself in your body, connected to your inner wisdom. An affirmation I often use is "Spirit is my health; I am being healed even as I speak."

Laugh often, whether you feel like it or not. Even a forced laugh will turn into a pretty good belly laugh if you do it intentionally. Laughter is healing because it connects us with the delight of the universe. Laughing is an alchemical act—an embodied shamanic ritual. Chemically it improves everything, especially digestion. Cry when you want to and yell when you feel the urge. Trust every spontaneous desire as an emissary from your intuition. Remember—intuition arrives first, instinct follows.

Answering the Knock

Everything you have been learning in this book has been in preparation for your being able to embrace living consciously with yourself and finding your own companionship deeply satisfying.

I hope that you now recognize that healing BodyMind and Soul is often thwarted because of unconsciousness. Selective embodiment sickens us. You can't choose where to be conscious and guarantee that all the rest will obediently stay unconscious. The little boy was right when he speculated that he couldn't predict what was on the other side of the door without having a look and once he does he'll have to deal with that knowledge. When our unclaimed life-force is awakened and moving once again, it too will knock loudly at any barricade of indifference or unconsciousness. In our attempts to ignore the knock at the door of consciousness, to barricade ourself against the urgency of a symptom or a dream, we end up tripping over our Loathly Lady time and again.

Women's
Intuition

Listening to the body's intention seems such a simple task, then we find that there is much to be learned, much to explore. So we get impatient wondering when we can divert our attention, ignore the daily summons, and just rely upon habit to keep the process alive.

But nature will not be ignored. Our body untended becomes identical to a garden abandoned to nature. Weeds flourish, vines grow wildly, sunlight is obscured. In a single season of neglect, the weeds can take a purchase upon untended soil. If you intend to become serious about your incarnation you must be prepared to commit to all the seasons, not just spring, or autumn, or winter, lest nature present her bill for your unconsciousness.

When I began to exercise for the first time after decades of being sedentary, I despaired about the requirements of time, trips to a gym, and boredom. Then I hit upon a solution. I'd try several different alternatives until I found the style and the rhythm that suited me. And so I began with only ten minutes a day of walking and later added five of stair climbing. I decided that if I could not give my body ten minutes a day I was a charlatan—fooling myself. Well, ten minutes a day has grown into a daily routine that feeds me deeply, but only after I uncovered several other clues about my relationship to my physical body. Walking is, for me, a chore done as exercise but a joy done as meditation. I have a mantra that carries me along on winged feet. I can walk, meditate, and be creative in a deeply intuitive way—or meditate and allow Spirit to walk me.

There are so very many ways to consciously relate to your bodymind. Your uniqueness is a gift of Soul, and I invite you with whatever you do to consciously find your path, your joy, your essence. There are many paths to intuition also—many ways to open a doorway of perception and find that of all the doors this is the one you hold the key to. There is an unplumbed depth of potential for deep healing and assurance contained within each of us. I urge you to step into the river of your intuition and claim your unique portion.

Chapter Ten

EMBODIED
RELATIONSHIP
*Intuition's Role in
the Healing of Humankind*

Whatever I do, the responsibility is mine,
but like the one who plants an orchard,
what comes of what I do, the fruit,
will be for others.

—*Naked Song,* Lalla

ZECHERIA SITCHIN, SCHOLAR OF ANCIENT HISTORIES and religions,
is credited with retelling this Arabic folk story. It seems there were
two travelers on their way from one town to another. Traveling on foot,
they eventually reached a crossroads. The post that held the signs for
each direction had fallen to the ground. The first fellow was filled with
despair. Crying, he wailed that they were lost, since neither of them

knew nor could they hope to know which set of signs pointed in which direction. The other fellow was nonplused. "We are not lost," he said. Picking up the pole, he replaced it in the ground facing the direction of the town they had recently left behind. Now they could see the direction they were to take. Turning to his pessimistic friend he said, "You see, you have to know where you have come from before you can hope to know where you are going."

Womankind has come from a long line of intuitive ancestry. The artifacts of this legacy are strewn, tucked, buried, and disguised in every direction, if we have but the eyes to see, the inner vision to discern, the wit and the wisdom to inquire. It has been the task of the feminine since time before time to sort instinct and intuition from ignorance—the wheat from the chaff, the peas from the stones, the seeds from the sand—to cultivate a harvest of earthy, embodied wisdom.

In fairy tales we find the many imaginal representatives of intuition tucked away as wee creatures, thumbalinas, dwarfs, animated dolls or other objects, each empowered by a knowledge that exceeds that of the hero or the heroine and belies their minuscule size. It is the wee bit, the tiniest of indications, the flash of insight, the whisper of truth that carries the energies of the soul. Spirit sweeps in with thunder and lightning, gale-force winds, or roiling waves. Soul nestles herself deeply within and pervades—not penetrates—our awareness with just the flake of leavening, the grain of courage, the flicker of endarkened consciousness that points us in the right direction. Not up and out, for that is not the way of Soul, not the intention of intuition. When we know from whence the feminine has come, then we can realign the signs of Soul so they point us in the correct direction—down to the realm of the Mothers, the Sisters, the Grandmothers. Down to the community of richly fertile embodied wisdom—the realm of the deep feminine.

Pure logic sticks in the throat of the feminine. She cannot digest what has not yet been thoroughly chewed, stomached, mixed with bile and juices, broken down, and taken on a spiral journey through the bowels of experience. Nor is she eager to call the outcome shit until she has poked and sorted, sniffed and handled what she finds before her.

Asking your intuition how a certain insight is formed, a conclusion gotten to, or a warning arrived at is like asking a rose how it knows to look and smell like a rose. It just does, for myriad reasons, created by an inexplicable imperative.

The world needs the wisdom that the consciously intuitive woman has to offer. For too long, society has overemphasized the rational, logical, and linear. These are all important. But for society to thrive, to prosper in the twenty-first century, we need the balance of the feminine—intuitive, encompassing, relational, and compassionate.

We need no longer speculate about a global community; it is now a reality. In the past, nations have been able to sustain differences as power and prejudices as proof of superiority. Wars have been fought on the basis of prejudice alone. Law and the principles of competition are always hierarchical, with someone or something on the top and all others lower on the totem pole of power and influence. The way of the feminine is to treat these differences as complementary, not oppositional, with honest inquiry, not defensiveness. From a feminine viewpoint, dominating power is disruptive and alienating, offering little of value to physical or spiritual livelihood. Empowerment, the capacity to learn and grow in wisdom and relationship, is a primary feminine principle. Power depletes the immune system with its alternating surges of exhilaration (when you're on top) and anxiety (when you're not). Empowerment balances the immune system with the steadfast psychic, physical, and spiritual reassurance that comes from self-assurance and an intimate relationship to something greater than the ego.

We are magnetically drawn to the activities of the feminine principle, whether we recognize them for what they are or not. The most frequently emphasized quality of Princess Diana after her death was her compassion for the unloved and unwanted—her genuine care and concern for humanity regardless of race, economics, or religion, her ability to treat everyone with respect and dignity even as she herself was being treated otherwise.

Does this imply that the feminine is immune to rebuff, that compassion requires self-denigration? Not at all. But it does highlight something that the world is sorely lacking today: disciplined self-sacrifice, individually and culturally. The feminine abhors self-aggrandizement at the expense of the soul, whether it is the personal soul, the soul of a culture, or the cumulative damage to World Soul. As the world shrinks and our future depends upon our willingness to share resourcefully with others, the era of me-ism and egocentricity must end. As the world grieved Diana's death, we intuitively were grieving for ourselves as well. Through her courage, her actions, and her personal pain, we had allowed her to carry a quality each of us yearns both to give and receive.

What each of us fears the most is that in the end we too will be left alone and unloved. Intuitively what we live for is a deepening of genuine relationship to ourselves and others. We yearn to link compassion with love, freedom with limits, work with play, and doing with being. Most of us, after generations of attempting to live by hierarchy, competition, and power, know intuitively that this is no longer worth whatever small benefits it provides. The feminine does not seek to elevate herself by standing on the shoulders or the prostrate form of another.

Public ceremonies or private rituals—whether laying flowers at the gates of Buckingham Palace, going to the altar for communion, placing a totem on our kitchen altar, or throwing salt over our shoulder to ward off bad luck—each is an outward expression of our deeper embodied wisdom. Each act began as an intuition, made manifest as the feminine conveys her desire to unite body and soul, consciously, relationally. Only yesterday I heard a news report that by the year 2002 over a third of the wealth in the United States will be owned and managed by women. Watch then and see who gets fed, what issues of human suffering will be alleviated, who will be educated and cared for, as women make financial choices, and run their companies and their homes with the principles of logic *and* intuition, competition *and* compassion.

The feminine moves in spirals, values circles, deepens by walking labyrinths. The feminine principle would never expect to find a balanced negotiation except from around a circular table. Nor would she seek to explore the pros and cons of a decision across the gulf created by two lines of tables or a raised dais. The feminine knows that integrity rooted in a genuine love for humanity can only be nurtured by return-ing over and again to nature and rediscovering the labyrinth of soul.

We're Working for All of Us

I learn much about embodied intuition by watching the ants that sud-denly appear in my garden each spring. Tiny creatures all, they approach a morsel of food, a dead bug's carcass, a bit of grass or debris, and then they begin a slow process of involvement. Sometimes the very thing I am positive they can not ignore or refuse they will give a wide berth to at 9:00 A.M., only to whisk it away rapidly at noon. I've watched them maneuver an object with all the vigor of a football team striving for a touchdown only to suddenly abandon the project as if summoned away by a knell of warning. What I have learned is how ants are governed by the instincts that guide them. Living on the edge of the jungle in Panama, I often watched in fascination as a colony of ants would form a bridge of living bodies across water that was blocking their path even when it meant that some of the ants would die, having no way to reach dry land when the bridge was dismantled. I've seen them industriously begin a bridge and then for no obvious reason abort the effort, leaving the bodies of the unfortunate ones strewn across the surface of the water.

As I watched, I began to realize all of nature has an instinctual pur-pose. Humans share this inner drive with all of nature's kin. I doubt that an ant has a sense of finitude or will or self-doubt. But we do, and this is where faith comes in. The human capacity to hold a balance between personal will and transpersonal wisdom gives us the courage of the ant that builds a bridge with its own body because it is the only thing its ant wisdom leads it to do.

Rupert Sheldrake has done groundbreaking work in describing the vast electromagnetic fields of influence that he believes contain all the knowledge of the Earth's past. All that lies behind humankind is still energetically present if we wish to use it as we seek direction for the future and a reorientation in the present. These fields of energetic memory telegraph not only the limitations of the past but the changes of the present. Bodymind's naturally intuitive energy field is an effective transmitter for these historical "morphogenic fields" of collective wisdom. Just as an acorn carries the energetic imprint of the oak to come, so also does the oak have within its genetic memory the imprint of the acorn.

When any woman brings something of her body wisdom into consciousness, she is connecting with the psychic history of the long line of women who preceded her as well as that of all who may follow. Christiane Northrup says, "When a woman enters into the work of healing her body and speaking her truth, she must break through the collective field of fear and pain that is all around us and has been for the past five thousand years of dominator society. It is a field filled with the fear of rape, of beating, of abandonment."

I tell the women who attend the groups I lead that they are doing this work for women and men everywhere. Like the hundredth monkey, once enough of us dare to bring bodymind's wisdom into consciousness, that wisdom becomes an accessible *conscious* domain for us all. This is the premise of truth behind breaking a cycle of abuse or addiction. It is crucial to name the "elephant in the living room," to name the secret or the fear that is robbing you of your destiny, your wholeness. In so doing you are releasing the community as well, which leads to greater truth and freedom from the weight of the past for everyone.

After reading *Women's Bodies, Women's Wisdom,* I find a shared experience with Christiane Northrup, who gives many examples of how the memories from childhood and collective memories associated with the repressed history of the feminine come into consciousness during pelvic exams, childbirth, and surgeries. Citing the work of Rupert Sheldrake, Dr. Northrup suggests that when a woman begins actively to engage in physical healing she has to deal with not only her immediate history but also with her own embodied connections to a "shamanic past." The collective experiences of all those generations of women who have preceded us are carried as shared memories by the interior healer that resides in our unconscious. Often our personal pain is intensified or amplified by our shared experiential "past." Who among us has not listened to a woman of the '90s talk about how, when visiting Holocaust Memorial Museum in Washington, her body had recoiled and she felt as if she had been present during the horrors of the Holocaust? Or after reading about the Salem witch trials has found herself mourning, with an inexplicable sense of deep familiarity, those who were murdered? Person to person, community to community, culture to culture, continent to continent, we are linked by a genetic web—a shared nonverbal heritage of intuitively embodied kinship. It serves no useful purpose to exaggerate this, only to simply and sincerely accept it.

As our personal pain is healed, others seem to benefit without doing the work. I have seen many an elderly mother, even when she is living a distance from her grown-up child, change as therapy changed her son or daughter. We of the West find the Aboriginal Australians' natural capacity for telepathic communications a curiosity, yet extrasensory relationships are basic to all sentient life. Our body transmits and receives more sensory information than we dare allow. I have chosen not to buy a house because my body didn't feel safe in an upstairs room. I could intuit a saturating sadness in that room. The transmission of embodied wisdom is not restricted to warm bodies. I have started my car's dead battery, and gotten a frozen automatic ice maker to release and produce ice by trusting that my hands "knew" how and where to touch in order to transmit the intuitive energy needed to "repair" the blockage.

All the natural rhythms of our bodymind are tributaries of Soul's great river. Spirit flows into and out of the sensate molecules of our matter, announcing its presence through the metaphors of movement and language that we have explored in these pages. Consciously stepping into this river connects each of us to the community of humankind and commits us to a shared responsibility for the evolution of the planet. This commitment is not the rigid or rigorous discipline of willpower but rather a quiet inner covenant with Soul to grow deeper and deeper in love with your own sweet matter, with the gifts of the feminine that you live through at a cellular level.

Soul and bodymind are inseparable companions in this life. The river of Soul waters the earthiness of body. The density of body anchors Soul in matter. Intermingle water and earth, and mud forms. Work it, refine it, shape it with experiencing, bake it in the light of consciousness, and Spirit's love affair with Soul emerges from the mire. Intuition is the clapper that causes the bell tones of Soul's resonant wisdom to ring out across the ages and stages of life.

Watering the Stones

In this book I have consistently invited us to step into the river and water the stones. I have coaxed us to move into the realm of mud, clay, matter; to get to know the Self incarnate, in matter, as tissue, blood, and viscera. I invite us to dare to listen to the voice that we fear, and hear what that voice has to teach us. I invite us to dare reawaken the divine seed that is planted in us at our conception, to allow that divinity to inspirit and ensoul our own matter as we rediscover our inner wisdom.

The older I become the more convinced I am that all of life is soul work. I've come to accept every act in life, done consciously or unconsciously, as either acceptance or denial of commitment to a higher order of wisdom, a divine consciousness.

I am convinced that for soul work to have any meaning at all it must be connected to an embodied, authentic ego. Soul must have a conscious bodymind to contain it and a strong clear voice in order to express the experience of being. We do not live through our soul. We live through the ego. It is your ego that got you to the store to buy this book and organized your life enough so that you can sit down and read. But it is the soulfulness of that experience that makes it meaningful. The most mundane act becomes a holy moment when done with conscious soulfulness.

The purpose of soul work is not to help us escape to nirvana or to elevate us to a state of godliness, but rather to allow us to function, day by day, with focused clarity and the security of knowing that life has meaning and your very existence is a constantly unfolding journey of a deepening relationship with Spirit. This is what I believe planetary consciousness is intended to become. When I am consciously embodied, I cannot deny that the River of Life that enlivens is calling out to me from every conceivable direction in the environment. Given this level of consciousness, it is impossible to feel disconnected and alienated from others. This is not an effortless journey. There are unplumbed depths to be sounded and navigated, sometimes to our peril.

Unfocused and indeterminate surges of affect, strong feelings, leave an indelible mark. They are like the glass beads dropped into the alchemical retort to force the liquid to the boiling point. Carl Jung says we have to be thrust into a conscious relationship with the divine. We do not chose the work; the work chooses us. We must, somehow, learn to affirm our own destiny, that unique relationship with the Self, so that when terrible things occur to us we have forged an ego-Self that does not collapse under the unendurable. And when joy arrives we can embrace it, knowing we are in the presence of the Holy.

The true Self is not an oppositional self. The rhythms of the body join the psyche in complete synchronization with the true Self. We have been led to believe that instinct is fit only to be shaped and tamed, but there is a deeply healing intuitive wisdom lodged within our atomic structure that informs us how to live fully and within the laws of our own nature. Living within the laws of our nature, we become stewards of the natural laws of this planet and all her creatures.

This wisdom has many names. The Vedic tradition calls it the Rishi. Western tradition speaks of God. Fred Alan Wolf writes of a shamanic belief in a Higher Power. Aboriginals of Australia call it the Dreaming. I call it Embodied Intuition.

To live a life of consciously embodied soulfulness is to risk living life as a spiral. It is not easy to give up the more popular mental construct of cause and effect, of beginnings and endings. We must find the courage not to despair or yield to the inner "voice" that disparages the process each time we find we must come back around a turn in the spiral and confront something we had hoped was integrated, or put to rest, or even something we had begged to be allowed to avoid. We must learn to value that the interrelatedness of mind and body, of Spirit and Soul, is not linear. Neither is it circular. These concepts simply will not fit. They squeeze the life out of soulfulness.

Forthright, uncomplicated, and nonjudgmental, your bodymind intuitively goes straight to the root of whatever is troubling the essential Self. Culture does not teach us to recognize this language. Many times what we take to be a symptom and rush off to find a cure for is divinity shining through—the energetic language of nature that, like the language of a nightmare, wants our undivided attention.

This other reality is what Francis Wickes in *The Inner World of Choice* calls the "X in the calculation." The X points us downward into to a deepening of consciousness in order that we might realize that there is an element of our being that transcends the ego and even the ego's carefully laid plans and purposes. Risking the move downward we begin to realize that this X has been with us always and cares for our well-being in ways we usually only glimpse in our dreams or later, when we are able to, identify in our projections. The realization that this presence, the Mystery, cannot be summoned to consciousness through power or by doing anything baffles the ego. Only love will do.

Learning to trust being in love with one's ground of being is the beginning. It is the beginning of the journey to God the Mother, the matrix from which all life is spun. Risking that to be in the experience is more meaningful than doing anything about the experience is a breakthrough.

When chatter is stilled and restlessness is subdued, then the higher Self speaks to us in our spontaneous movements, our skipped heartbeats, our symptoms, and our illnesses. At a certain age we are summoned to step into the river and become one with it. We are asked to dance with the divine, to be authentic, to be ourself.

The soul within us, the instinctual nature-centered deep feminine imbued with the love of the divine, embraces the stillness and feels the dance within that small quiet inner space. This is the X, the mystery, the *mythos* that is present even at our conception. The fragrance of the Mystery, once breathed in, once inspirited, never leaves us, and we, yearning for evidence of its presence, continue to search for it in our inner world. Intuition calls us home.

I have come to understand my earliest experiences of intuition as a crossroads experiences. Coming together of the events of a child's ordinary daily existence with the inner events of her spiritual development. This was the beginning of the weaving together of the tapestry of a requiring personal destiny.

Timelessly, the Self reaches out to the ego to affirm the presence of something worth living for, of something larger than the ego. That first arresting encounter with the inspiration borne by an image has continued to summon me time and again to dive deeply into the waters of the unconscious—to risk being irrational, to set aside power, and trust the depths of body wisdom that have been growing and maturing within me since birth.

The River of Soul

Soulfulness is only another way of describing the eternal as it manifests in the transitory. It is less that as human beings we seek ensoulment to develop a spiritual self than that as spiritual beings we must learn how to refine and live within the dimensions of our human selves. The River of Soul does not run through us. We are that river. The life-force that turns the planet on its axis, causes the tides to rise and the sun to set, is also in every cell of the body and every molecule of the bodymind. Soul is both our center and our surround. Mother-Father God, that eternal essence which is greater than my Self, speaks in every breath we take, and we, in our own turn, become what we eat, what we think, what we feel, and what we relate to. Our matter manifests a river of ever-changing, always-evolving embodied energy. Each intentional act of bringing consciousness into the body through movement, meditation, or touch is an act of *stepping into the River*. This is not a condition of genetics or achievement. It is a condition of stewardship. This is not a state of believing. It is an evolution of visceral experiential knowing.

Life is swift and precious while it's in our grasp. Loving yourself is such a small act of appreciation for the everlasting Love that has breathed you into being and on whose wings you will be carried when it is time to leave this life. The pulse of creation measures the dance of life. Join in, won't you? Say, "Yes, Yes, YES!" to all that is yours simply because you are a child of humankind, a child of Eternity.

> To occupy your body is to occupy your life.
> The body is everything in a way.
> —*Jacob Needleman*

Afterword

SOMEWHERE IN OUR ENTHUSIASTIC JOURNEY from agrarian to industrial life, we split mind from body. Entranced as we were with our wonderfully inventive brain capacity and awesome new mechanical toys, we lost our connection to our bodies. For this we've paid a high price.

When consciousness prematurely separates from the body (and by *premature,* I mean before death . . . or at least before sleep . . . in an unconscious, inadvertent way), we stop knowing when we're getting sick; we lose our compassion and empathy for others; our capacity for intimacy is compromised (after all, nobody's home); we destroy the Earth and still feel comfortable; and intuition becomes an unreliable, ephemeral sort of experience, instead of the grounded, solid body wisdom it was meant to be.

As a culture, we are vaguely aware that something is missing, that we are hungry for our birthright of sensation, feeling, and intimate contact. And, in its unconscious way, the culture tries to provide it. But a disembodied culture can only come up with offerings of pornography, violence, and the pseudo-intimacy of melodrama. Instead of The Goddess, we get Jerry Springer and Bruce Willis. These odd substitutes might capture our attention, but they just can't satisfy our hunger. We can't be nourished on empty, toxic snacks, and so we remain body-starved, a nation of questing, cranky addicts.

Even when we recognize this as the truth, we are still hard pressed to get back to our bodies, because we've forgotten how. Instead, we put more pressure on our heads; we talk more, and we talk faster.

But even in the psychotherapy chair, talk without the body's

229

engagement can only lead away from ourselves. The exercise is doomed to failure.

I remember an early research finding on the efficacy of therapy. The study's investigators were interested in predicting which clients would have successful outcomes from psychotherapy. The answer was simpler than they expected. Those who did well were the clients who, before answering their therapists' questions, paused, cast their eyes down, and consulted their bodies.

Ironically, those with the glib, articulate answers fared poorly at the "talking cure." The ones who stumbled around with their words as they immersed themselves in their emotions, feelings, and sensations were the "star" clients with the successful outcomes.

This comes as no surprise to the experienced therapist. We get those disconnected talkers in our offices, and inwardly we groan, knowing it will be a long haul. And all too often, try as we might to guide a person out of their head and into their body, they just keep bouncing back up into their heads, like one of those relentless pop-up clowns that won't stay down.

Luckily for all of us, and probably just in the nick of time, we are suddenly finding ourselves the recipients of scores of cultural invitations from books, movies, and TV shows, beckoning us back to our bodies and our innate intuitive wisdom.

Marion Woodman was the front runner (how lucky for us— what a passionate, inspiring, eloquent messenger!) issuing the call to embody our spirits and heal the artificial split created between our overtaxed minds and underappreciated bodies.

It has only been in the past few years that I myself realized how much of my own work with body-based guided imagery has been informed by the work of that beautiful, fearless, gentle warrior, shaping her gifted insights into a kind of audio-methodology.

And surely Paula Mumma Reeves has taken Woodman's insights into her own delicious methodology. Reeves gives us a road map back to our bodies through her simple but profound method of nonjudgmental awareness and movement, a kind of prayer-dance of the spirit that she calls Spontaneous Contemplative Movement. From the grounded base of her own psychotherapeutic practice, she tenders to us a safe and reliable pathway back to our buried treasure of body-based wisdom.

May contributions such as this one save us from our culture's inadvertent lapses and excesses, and bring us back to the truth and meaning of our lives. I'll let that be my prayer on this wintry eve of 1999. We still have time to get there.

Belleruth Naparstek
Cleveland, Ohio
December 30, 1998

Acknowledgments

FEW BOOKS EVER ARE WRITTEN WITHOUT THE CONTRIBUTIONS of an entire community of people. This book is no exception. It gives me great pleasure to extend my thanks to the following people:

The strong and creative women in my family who lived ordinary lives while never losing their commitment to an inner strength and wisdom, which they generously passed on to me.

My maternal grandmother, for her unquestioning belief in the non-ordinary experience and in God.

To my mother, who courageously rediscovered herself when widowed after more than fifty years of marriage.

To my deeply intuitive husband, for quietly and firmly urging me to pursue my dreams even when they took me far from home. Without his support I would still be at home reading, journaling, and yearning.

To my children, who refused to allow me to be only a mother. They have been both champion and devil's advocate, keeping me real and true to myself.

My deep appreciation for the mentoring of Annette Cullipher, who coaxed and coached me to present this work in the larger context of the Journey into Wholeness family and to the hundreds of lecture and workshop participants who have generously allowed their stories to be told.

To the open and inquiring spirit of the Tuesday Morning Group, without whom there would be no exercises, no experiential truths. To my dear friend and colleague George Williams, whose steady presence, direct talk, and great good humor have steered me away from the risk of a narrow gender bias, teaching me much about men's intuition and body wisdom. To Kimberly Cunningham, whose knowledge of anatomy and physiology inspired clearer thinking about the body metaphors that are most healing. To Al Pesso and Dr. Jackie Damgaard, teachers, theorists, and artists in the understanding and articulation of body's language. To Dr. Earl Brown, for his years of respect, honesty, and humor, a Virgil to my Dante, as I made my way—an introverted intuitive in an extroverted interpretative world. To Coleman Barks, whose translations of Lalla's poetry inspire us all and whose gift of these translations lends an inestimable richness and texture to these pages.

My ever-growing delight and thanks to Wendy Patterson, certainly for all she has taught me during our years of co-leading a women's group, but especially for the Cuban lunches where we have taken apart and reassembled many an intuitive experience between forkfuls of paella and black beans. To Jill Mellick, who never doubted I could write this book, and offered the kind of unwavering support that can only come from a caring heart. To Carol Barks, whose intuitive guidance lends poetry to this prose. To my editor, Mary Jane Ryan, who refused to allow the focus of this manuscript to be obscured by my tendency to minimize the potency of the work. To the staff of Conari Press, whose ease with e-mail and the telephone made our long-distance relationship work smoothly and well.

To the community of sisterhood; my Abraxas sisters, the Sha Sha circle, also to Jan Collins, Edith Sullwold, Eleanora Woloy, Marion Woodman, Mary Hamilton, and Ann Skinner. And to the sustaining brotherhood that has always been there—to Barry Williams for readily sharing his in-depth knowledge of indigenous healing, to Joe Selby whose keen inner vision has guided me more than once, and to Robert Johnson, dearest friend and teacher.

To Patte Buice Mitchell and Geneva Harbin, whose irreverent appreciation for my intuitions about our lives afforded us an embodied experience rich with humor, synchronistic guidance, and a decade of spiritual companionship.

Thanks to Dr. Granrose, currently Director of Studies at the C.G. Jung Institute of Zurich, for reading and commenting on the manuscript.

This book would be merely another how-to manual if it were not for the many stories freely shared by those with whom I've worked throughout the years. Some of these stories are verbatim, written by the author herself. Others are close approximations, with names and certain details altered in order to protect the deeply personal nature of the work. The stories cover a period of fifteen years and come from England, Canada, Australia, Latin America, Hawaii, Alaska, and throughout the continental United States. Since the emphasis is upon women's intuition, I have not included the experiences of the men whose work has contributed to my understanding of the similarities and the differences in body language.

Lastly, I thank you, the reader, for your interest and your time. I trust you will find something of what you are looking for within these pages and you will write and share your story with me if you wish.

> Let your body wear your knowing
> Let your heart sing songs. . . .
> —Lalla

Music Appendix

Don Campbell. *The Mozart Effect: Heal the Body.* Spring Hill Music.

Galway. *Song of the Seashore.* RCA.

Gabrille Roth and the Mirrors. *Initiation.* Raven Recording.
_____. *Totem.* Raven Recording.

Mike Rowland. *The Fairy Ring.* Music Designs, Inc.

Secret Garden. *Songs from a Secret Garden.* Philips.

Paul Winter. *Wolf Eyes.* Living Music Records.

Rob Whitesides. *Miracles.*

Bibliography

Books

Achterberg, Jeanne. *Imagery in Healing: Shamanism and Modern Medicine.* Boston and London: Shambhala, 1985.

Advances: The Journal of Mind-Body Health. John E. Fetzer Institute, 9292 West KL Avenue, Kalamazoo, MI 49009–9398

Andrews, Lynn. *Woman at the Edge of Two Worlds.* New York: HarperCollins, 1993.

Barasch, Marc Ian. *The Healing Path: A Soul Approach to Illness.* New York: Tarcher/Putnam, 1995.

Becker, Robert O., M.D., and Gary Seldon. *The Body Electric: Electromagnetism and Foundation of Life.* New York: William Morrow, 1985.

Bentov, Itzhak. *Stalking the Wild Pendulum: On the Mechanics of Consciousness.* Rochester, VT: Destiny Books, 1988.

Blum, Ralph. *The Book of Runes.* New York: St. Martin's Press, 1982.

Bolen, Jean. *Goddesses in Everywoman.* San Francisco: Harper & Row, 1984.

———. *Crossing to Avalon: A Woman's Midlife Pilgrimage.* San Francisco: HarperSanFrancisco, 1994.

Bosnak, Robert. *Tracks in the Wilderness of Dreaming.* New York: Dell Publishing, 1996.

Cameron, Julia. *The Vein of Gold: Journey to Your Creative Spirit.* New York: Tarcher/Putnam, 1996.

Campbell, Don. *The Mozart Effect*. New York: Avon Books, 1997.

Chamberlain, David. *Babies Remember Birth*. New York: Ballantine Books, 1988.

Chodorow, Joan. *Dance Therapy and Depth Psychology: The Moving Imagination*. London and New York: Routledge, 1991.

Chopra, Deepak. *Return of the Rishi*. Boston: Houghton Mifflin Co., 1988.
_____. *Quantum Healing*. New York: Bantam Books, 1989.

Choquette, Sonia. *The Psychic Pathway: A Workbook for Reawakening the Voice of Your Soul*. New York: Crown Trade Paperbacks, 1994.

Craighead, Meinrad. *The Mother's Songs: Images of God the Mother*. New York: Paulist Press, 1986.

Cunningham, Kimberly, and Debra Lancaster. *Human Anatomy and Physiology Laboratory Manual*. New York: William C. Brown Publishers, 2000.

De Beauport, Elaine, with Aura Sofia Diaz. *The Three Faces of Mind*. Wheaton, IL: Quest Books, 1996.

Dossey, Larry, M.D. *Healing Words: The Power of Prayer and the Practice of Medicine*. San Francisco: HarperSanFrancisco, 1993.
_____. *Be Careful What You Pray For. . . You Just Might Get It*. San Francisco: HarperSanFrancisco, 1997.

Duff, Kat. *The Alchemy of Illness*. New York: Pantheon, 1993.

Feldenkrais, M. *Awareness Through Movement*. New York: Harper & Row, 1972.

Gendlin, Eugene T. *Let Your Body Interpret Your Dreams*. Wilmette, IL: Chiron Publications, 1986.

Gleck, James. *Chaos*. New York: Penguin Books, 1987.

Gordon, David. *Therapeutic Metaphors*. Cupertino, CA: Meta Publications, 1978.

Gray, Henry, F.R.S. *Gray's Anatomy*. Ed. T. Pickering Pick, F.R.C.S. New York: Bounty Books, 1977.

Gray, John. *Men Are from Mars, Women Are from Venus.* San Francisco: HarperCollins, 1992.

Hartley, Linda. *Wisdom of the Body Moving.* Berkeley, CA: North Atlantic Books, 1989.

Harvey, Andrew. "Revelation and Revolution: The Renaissance of the Sacred Feminine." Keynote speech given at the Fourteenth Annual Common Boundary Conference, Washington, DC, 1994.

Hay, Louise. *Heal Your Body.* Santa Monica, CA: Hay House, Inc., 1982.

Hofstadter, Douglas. *Gödel, Escher, Bach: An Eternal Golden Braid.* New York: Basic Books, 1979.

Hutchinson, Marcia Germaine. *Transforming Body Images: Learning to Love the Body You Have.* Freedom, CA: The Crossing Press, 1985.

Gilligan, Carol. *In a Different Voice.* Cambridge, MA: Harvard University Press, 1982.

Griffith, James L., and Melissa Elliott Griffith. *The Body Speaks.* New York: Basic Books, 1995.

Hall, Nor. *The Moon and the Virgin.* New York: Harper Colophon Books, 1980.

Harrison, John, M.D. *Love Your Disease.* Santa Monica, CA: Hay House, Inc., 1984.

Houston, Jean. *The Possible Human.* Los Angeles: J. P. Tarcher Inc., 1982.

Johnson, Robert. *He!* King of Prussia, PA: Religious Publishing Co., 1974.
_____. *She!* King of Prussia, PA: Religious Publishing Co., 1976.
_____. *Inner Work: Using Dreams and Active Imagination for Personal Growth.* San Francisco: Harper & Row, 1986.

Journal of the American Medical Association (JAMA), cited in *Intuition* 17 (August, 1997), p. 7.

Jung, C. G. *The Collected Works* (Bollingen Series XX). 20 volumes. Trans. R. F. C. Hull. Princeton: Princeton, University Press, 1994.

Kalff, Dora. *Sandplay.* Santa Monica, CA: Sigo Press, 1980.

Kalweit, Holgar. *Dreamtime and Inner Space: The World of the Shaman.* Boston: Shambhala, 1988, Quoted in Robert Lawlor, *Voices of the First Day* (Rochester, VT: Inner Traditions, 1991).

Keleman, Stanley. *Your Body Speaks Its Mind.* Berkeley, CA: Center Press, 1975.

Koltuv, Barbara Black, Ph.D. *The Book of Lilith.* York Beach, ME: Nicolas-Hays, Inc., 1986.

Lalla. *Naked Song.* Trans. Coleman Barks. Athens, GA: Maypop Books, 1992.

Matzinger, Polly. "The End of the Self," in *Discover* (April 1996), pp. 80–87.

Mellick, Jill. *The Natural Artistry of Dreams.* Berkeley, CA: Conari Press, 1998.

Miller, Alice. *The Drama of the Gifted Child.* Trans. Ruth Ward. New York: Basic Books, 1981.

Mindel, Arnold. *Dreambody.* 1940. Boston, MA: Sigo Press, 1982.

Myss, Caroline. *Energy Anatomy.* Boulder, CO: Sounds True Audio, 1996.

Naparstek, Belleruth. *Your Sixth Sense: Unlocking the Power of Your Intuition.* San Francisco: HarperSanFrancisco, 1997.

Nobel, Vicki. *Motherpeace.* San Francisco: Harper & Row, 1991

Norretranders, Tor. *The User Illusion: Cutting Consciousness Down to Size.* Trans. Jonathan Sydenham. New York: Viking, 1998.

Northrup, Christiane, M.D. *Women's Bodies, Women's Wisdom.* New York: Bantam Books, 1994.

Olsen, Andrea. *BodyStories: A Guide to Experiential Anatomy.* Barrytown, NY: Station Hill Press, 1991.

Orlock, Carol. *The Goddess Letters: The Myth of Demeter and Persephone Retold.* New York: St. Martin's Press, 1987.

Orloff, Judith, M.D. *Second Sight.* New York: Warner Books, 1996.

Page, Christine, M.D. *Frontiers of Health: From Healing to Wholeness.* Essex, England: Saffron Walden, The C. W. Daniel Co. Ltd., 1992.

Pearce, Joseph Chilton. *Magical Child*. New York: Bantam New Age Books, 1977.

Perera, Sylvia Brinton. *Descent to the Goddess A Way of Initiation for Women*. Toronto: Inner City Books, 1988.

Pert, Candace, Ph.D. *Molecules of Emotion*. New York: Scribner, 1997

Pesso, Al. *Experience in Action*. New York: New York University Press, 1973.

Pinkola-Estés, Clarissa, Ph.D. *Women Who Run with the Wolves*. New York: Ballantine Books, 1992.

Ponder, Catherine. *The Dynamic Laws of Healing*. Marina del Rey, CA: DeVorss and Co., 1966.

Reeves, Paula, Ph.D. "The Archetype of the Parentified Child: A Psychosomatic Presence," in *Parentified Children: Theory, Research and Treatment*. Ed. Nancy Chase. Thousand Oaks, CA: Sage Publications, Inc., 1999.
_____. "Spontaneous Movement as Healer," in *The International Conference on The Psychology of Health, Immunity and Disease*, Mansfield, CT: *NICABM*, Vol. A, 1994, pp. 479–97.
_____. *Midwifing the Soul at the Thresholds and Borders Where Destiny and Fate Collide*. Balsam Grove, NC: Journey into Wholeness Audio, 1997.
_____. "Inanna's Myth." *The Descent: Naively Going to Meet the Dark Sister*. Balsam Grove, NC: Journey into Wholeness Audio, 1997.
_____. *The Ascent: Sweet Taste of Salty Tears*. Balsam Grove, NC: Journey into Wholeness Audio, 1993.

Rich, Adrienne. *Of Woman Born*. New York: W. W. Norton, 1986.

Rogers, Linda. "Music for Surgery," *Advances: The Journal of Mind-Body Health* 11:3 (Summer 1995), p. 54.

Rossi, Ernest L., M.D., and David B. Cheek. *Mind-Body Therapy*. New York: W. W. Norton, 1988.

Russek, Linda and Gary E. Schwartz. "The Heart, Dynamic Energy and Integrated Medicine," in *Advances: The Journal of Mind-Body Health* 12:4 (Fall 1996), pp. 36–45.

Schindler, Karon. "The Mitochondria Connection," in *Emory Medicine* (Autumn 1991), pp. 11–17.

Schulz, Mona Lisa, M.D., Ph.D. *Awakening Intuition.* New York: Harmony Books, 1998.

Sheldrake, Rupert. *The Presence of the Past: Morphic Resonance and the Habits of Nature.* London, Collins: 1988.

Sontag, Susan. *Illness as Metaphor and AIDS and Its Metaphors.* New York: Doubleday, 1995.

Steadman, Alice. *Who's the Matter With Me?* Marina del Rey, CA: DeVorss & Co., 1966.

Taylor, Jeremy. *Where People Fly and Water Runs Uphill.* New York: Warner Books, 1992.

Todd, M. E. *The Thinking Body.* New York: Dance Horizons, 1968.

Vaughn, Frances E. *Awakening Intuition.* New York: Anchor Books, 1979.

Verny, Thomas, M.D., and John Kelley. *The Secret Life of the Unborn Child.* New York: Dell Publishing Co., 1981.

Walker, Barbara. *The Woman's Encyclopedia of Myths and Secrets.* San Francisco: Harper & Row, 1983.

Wallace, Douglas, M.D. "Migration Patterns and Linguistic Origins of American Indians Traced Using Mitochrondial DNA," in *Genetics* (January 1995).

Weil, Andrew, M.D. *Health and Healing.* Boston: Houghton Mifflin Co., 1995.

Wickes, Frances. *The Inner World of Choice.* Englewood Cliffs, NJ: Prentice-Hall, Inc., 1976.

Wolf, Fred Alan. *The Eagle's Quest.* New York: Simon & Schuster, 1991.

_____. *The Body Quantum: The New Physics of Body, Mind, and Health.* New York: Macmillan Publishing Co., 1986.

Woodman, Marion. *Addiction to Perfection.* Toronto: Inner City Books, 1982.

Woodman, Marion, and Elinor Dickson. *Dancing in the Flames.* New York: Colophon Books, 1996

Woodman, Marion, with Jill Mellick. *Coming Home to Myself: Reflections for Nurturing a Woman's Body and Soul.* Berkeley, CA: Conari Press, 1998.

Conari Press, established in 1987, publishes books on topics ranging from psychology, spirituality, and women's history to sexuality, parenting, and personal growth. Our main goal is to publish quality books that will make a difference in people's lives—both how we feel about ourselves and how we relate to one another.

Our readers are our most important resource, and we value your input, suggestions, and ideas. We'd love to hear from you—after all, we are publishing books for you!

To request our latest book catalog, or to be added to our mailing list, please contact:

CONARI PRESS

2550 Ninth Street, Suite 101
Berkeley, California 94710-2551
800-685-9595   510-649-7175

FAX: 510-649-7190
E-MAIL: Conari@conari.com
http://www.conari.com